THE FIGURE IN THE LANDSCAPE

Also by John Dixon Hunt

The Pre-Raphaelite Imagination: 1848–1900

A Critical Commentary on Shakespeare's
The Tempest

Edited by John Dixon Hunt

The Genius of the Place: The English
Landscape Garden, 1620–1820
(with Peter Willis)

The Country Wife, *by William Wycherley*

Encounters: Essays on Literature
and the Visual Arts

In Memoriam: A Selection of Critical Essays

The Rape of the Lock: A Selection
of Critical Essays

The Figure in the Landscape:

Poetry, Painting, and Gardening during the Eighteenth Century

JOHN DIXON HUNT

The Johns Hopkins University Press
Baltimore and London

Pl. 21, reproduced by Gracious Permission of Her Majesty the Queen; pl. 62,
courtesy of Sir George Beaumont, photograph courtesy of Michael R. Dudley;
pl. 71, by permission of the Birmingham Museum and Art Gallery; pls. 3, 17, 73,
courtesy of the Bodleian Library; pls. 1, 2, 4, 5, 6, 7, 9, 13, 16, 18, 26, 34, 35, 40, 43,
44, 48, 56, 57, courtesy of the British Library Board; pl. 33, courtesy of Bryn
Mawr College; pl. 54, photograph courtesy of R. & H. Chapman; pl. 68, courtesy
of Sir John Colville; pls. 30, 74, photographs courtesy of Country Life; pls. 22, 63,
68, photographs courtesy of the Courtauld Institute of Art, London University;
pl. 66, courtesy of the Derby Museum and Art Gallery; pl. 75, courtesy of the
Edinburgh University Library; pl. 52, courtesy of Brinsley Ford, photograph
courtesy of the Greater London Council as Trustees of the Iveagh Bequest,
Kenwood; pl. 74, courtesy of Heveningham Hall; pls. 38, 60, courtesy of the
Henry E. Huntington Library and Art Gallery; pl. 19, courtesy of the Leeds City
Libraries; pls. 49, 50, 53, courtesy of the Lewis Walpole Library; pl. 37,
photograph courtesy of Maynard Mack; pl. 32, by kind permission of The
Master and Fellows of Pembroke College, Cambridge; pl. 72, courtesy of the
Musée des Beaux Arts, Strasbourg, photograph courtesy of the Greater London
Council as Trustees of the Iveagh Bequest, Kenwood; pl. 22, courtesy of the
Musée du Louvre; pl. 8, courtesy of the Museo Storico di Firenze; pl. 11,
courtesy of the National Galleries of Scotland; pl. 27, courtesy of the National
Gallery of Art, Washington, D.C., Rosenwald Collection, photograph courtesy
of Alverthorpe Gallery, Jenkintown, Pennsylvania; pls. 51, 61, courtesy of the
National Museum of Wales; pl. 59, courtesy of the Earl of Pembroke; pl. 64,
courtesy of the Collection of the Royal Albert Memorial Museum, Exeter; pl.
58, courtesy of Nicholas Sanderson; pl. 39, courtesy of Edwin Smith; pls. 28, 65,
courtesy of the Tate Gallery, London; pls. 25, 69, 70, courtesy of the Trustees of
the British Museum; pls. 31, 41, 42, reproduced by permission of the Trustees
of the Chatsworth Settlement, pls. 31, 41, photographs courtesy of Peter Willis;
pl. 20, reproduced by courtesy of the Trustees, the National Gallery, London;
pls. 12, 14, 15, Christ Church, Oxford, courtesy of the Trustees of the Will of
the late J. H. C. Evelyn; pl. 67, courtesy of the Walker Art Gallery, Liverpool; pl.
47, courtesy of Dr. and Mrs. Peter Willis; pl. 29, courtesy of York Minster
Library, photograph courtesy of York University Library; pls. 45, 46, courtesy
of York University Library; pls. 23, 24, photographs courtesy of York University Library.

The Johns Hopkins University Press, Baltimore, Maryland 21218
The Johns Hopkins Press Ltd., London

Library of Congress Catalog Card Number 76-17227
ISBN 0-8018-1795-1

Library of Congress Cataloging in Publication data will be found on the last
printed page of this book.

For DEAN TOLLE MACE

si quis erit raros inter numerandus amicos
quales prisca fides famaque novit annus

Poetry, Painting, and Gardening, or the Science
of Landscape, will forever by men of taste be deemed
Three Sisters, or the *The Three New Graces* who dress
and adorn nature. —*Horace Walpole*

segnesque nodum solvere Gratiae —*Horace*

Contents

Plates

Preface

'If the Italians were the first improvers of gardens, and plantations', wrote John Shebbeare in 1756, 'the French have excelled [them], and the English carried the taste of that embellishment much higher'. Indeed, many in the eighteenth century would have claimed that, like Liberty, with which it was often compared, the landscape garden was an English invention. Its story has been sufficiently and well told—by Frank Clark, Christopher Hussey, Miles Hadfield—and another narrative of how the collaboration of poetry, painting, and philosophy established a new style of gardening is not needed. But what is rarely discussed are the human consequences of the new designs—the effects upon their users and visitors, the psychological extensions of landscape space. For this there is ample literary evidence; and a consideration of it will further illuminate the extent, far too little realized by either garden or literary historians, to which poetry itself learnt fresh procedures and ideas from the new art to which it had contributed. So the double aim of *The Figure in the Landscape* is to explore how landscape gardening promoted and answered imaginative experience and how poetry emerged from the alliance among what Walpole called the 'three new Graces'. But to do so involves a study of the process and results of their collaboration. An intricate federation it turns out to have been, so that Horace's sense of the 'knot' tied by the Graces' dance has proved an aptly astringent qualification of Walpole's accounts of their endeavors.

On the principle of *reculer pour mieux sauter* the first chapter is devoted to some seventeenth-century, mainly Restoration, figures in their landscapes. They display a variety of attitudes towards natural scenery, whether painted, described in poetry, organized into gardens, or just encountered in areas outside man's control. Some long-established, 'hieroglyphick' habits of mind found themselves increasingly uncomfortable in the contemporary Dutch and French styles of garden or among the empirical attitudes of the horticultural members of the Royal Society. But alongside a taste for geometrically ordered gardens there began to flourish an interest in landscape paintings where nature was not so rigorously marshalled and for poems that seemed to announce a similar delight in 'natural' scenery. Out of these crosscurrents and uncertainties developed fresh relationships between the figure of the solitary contemplator, the hermit, and landscapes, hermitages, appropriate to his new meditations.

The second and third chapters focus upon two poets and their attitudes towards landscape: first, Alexander Pope, a self-styled hermit and his 'hermitage' at Twickenham; second, James Thomson, author of *The Seasons* and celebrant of connections between 'The Varied God' of a seasonal cycle and 'Man's continual changes'. The chapter on Pope discusses his career as a 'gardenist' (this useful coinage by Walpole is borrowed throughout) and the place which gardening occupied in his life and work, especially as this is revealed in his letters and the *Epistles to Several Persons*. For early garden theorists and practitioners, among whom Pope was a prime mover, a landscape garden was designed to stimulate the minds of its visitors by presenting them with a various assortment of statues, busts, inscriptions, and temples; alongside these emblematic devices more scope came to be given to the expressive potential of scenery itself and to less explicit manipulations of visitors' feelings and imagination. Since visitors brought to the experience theories of psychology recently elaborated by John Locke, the landscape garden became an exciting, new territory for meditation and introspection. For poets it sustained new visions of a more personal poetics. And, as the chapter on Thomson will argue, once poets had acquired certain habits of looking and thinking *inside* a garden they found them equally serviceable *beyond* the ha-ha.

The fourth chapter takes as its central image the figure of Gray's bard and the landscapes he inhabited. Gray, too, had learnt to 'read' the meanings of landscape gardens, but, like many of his contemporaries, refused to submit himself to their 'artificial' structures. For those who found the garden too confined and too contrived there were alternative landscapes in sublime mountain scenery, which not only offered more resonant imagery but were traditionally linked with a specifically 'British' imagination. Gray's Welsh bard and Macpherson's Ossian were types of poet who, long before landscape gardens were thought of, had inhabited the wild territory of Snowdonia and the Highlands of Scotland, making the mountains an expressive vocabulary for their bardic visions. They provided a precedent for modern British poetry to seek its meditative landscapes beyond the garden, though without losing imaginative habits acquired there.

In the final chapter the literary treatment of landscape, both as object of meditation and as an expressive language of introspection, is seen struggling to achieve its own distinctive ways of proceeding, independent of the directions in which gardening and landscape painting were moving. This development is traced through various prospect poems—a genre of writing specially dedicated to finding connections between sight and insight—and, more briefly, in the work of Goldsmith and Cowper. Their poetry is increasingly fascinated, not by the painterly modes of description which had pleased earlier poets, but by recording the process of the imagination's dialogue with the natural world. This stress upon *how* the mind reads the 'pleasing scenes the landscape wide displays' and how it makes those images its own was a particularly eighteenth-century concern. This book offers to show that this concern could not have been possible without the new art of landscape gardening.

Because I have occasionally quoted romantic writers and compared some of their landscape poetry with that of late eighteenth-century writers, it must not be thought that I propose only a teleological view of the 'Age of Sensibility', a view of the period that finds it interesting insofar as it successfully struggles to approximate the poetry and ideas of Wordsworth, Coleridge, or Keats. Attitudes to landscape underwent much change and revision during the last third of the eighteenth century. I am concerned to show how they originated in the Augustan age, shaped by its distinctive habits of mind, how they were reworked and developed to suit more extensive ideas of man's response to the natural world in the years after Pope and Thomson died, and how they continued to be revised in the years before Wordsworth or Blake were evolving their own versions of landscape poetry. Rather than being a merely teleological emphasis, my attention to that continuum of literary history should reaffirm how crucial to the Romantics was the work of their predecessors. It is no accident that in 1794 Wordsworth offered to provide essays 'upon Poetry, and upon the arts of Painting and Gardening' for a new review; for his linking of the same arts that Horace Walpole had celebrated testifies to Wordsworth's own education in looking at natural scenery. The Romantic poet's confidence that 'Laying out grounds, as it is called, may be considered as a liberal art, in some sort like Poetry and Painting; and its object, like that of all the liberal arts, is, or ought to be, to move the affections under the controul of good sense' was also an eighteenth-century conviction. It is the theme of these chapters.

My main debts incurred in writing this book have been to the staffs of the Morrell Library and the library of the Institute of Advanced Architectural Studies at the University of York, of the Milton S. Eisenhower Library at the Johns Hopkins University, and of the British Library. For much patient, precise, and understanding criticism of these pages, not to mention her dedicated proof-reading, I am grateful to Phyllis, my wife. Many friends and colleagues have either read and commented upon sections of the typescript or much assisted me in discussions: Ronald Paulson of Yale University; Sandy Cunningham of

Leicester University; Michel Baridon of the Université de Dijon; Arnold Stein at Hopkins; Dinos Patrides at the University of York; Brian Morris at Sheffield University. Claire Pace, of the Department of Fine Art at Glasgow University, and Martin Battestin, of the University of Virginia, have both read and commented extensively upon a final draft of the book. To John Ingamells, Curator of the York City Art Gallery, I owe a special obligation, for many of the ideas here were worked out when we gave a joint lecture course at the University of York some years ago; he has helped me since with many matters in the history of art. The dedication of the book records a longstanding friendship as well as many shared enthusiasms for poems, pictures, and gardens.

I am obliged to the Leverhulme Trust and to the British Academy for a fellowship and a grant respectively to study Italian gardens: though I hope to publish the results of that research in a separate study, my explorations of the literary and architectural history of gardens during the later Italian Renaissance have made an important contribution to the final stages of rewriting this one. For help in collecting the illustrations I am grateful, not only to those individuals and institutions acknowledged elsewhere in this book, but to Professor Maynard Mack, Mr W. S. Lewis, Mr John Sunderland, Mr H. J. R. Wing, and (last but not least) Messrs David Whitely and Gordon Smith of the Photographic Studio in York University Library.

Nunnington, York
Summer 1975

J. D. H.

THE FIGURE IN THE LANDSCAPE

Green Thoughts and Shades

Hermits in Their Landscapes

No landscape garden of the eighteenth century was complete without its hermitage [plate 1] or even its hermit. They were evidently designed to announce, albeit in rather general terms, the idea of solitary meditation, to invoke without excessive realism the austere regimen of the hermit fathers. Augustan gardens realized this idea of the meditative seclusions of early Christian anchorites very differently from such Tuscan versions of the Thebaid as Gherardo Starnina's in the Uffizi or the more visually sophisticated *St Jerome* by Patinir in the National Gallery, London. But hermitages at Richmond, Kensington, or Stowe still provided visual images of solitary meditation among natural scenery. The imagery seemed to appeal to eighteenth-century writers as a readily available language for the idea of philosophical retreat, even when the realities bore little resem-

PLATE 1   The Hermitage, Kensington Gardens. Drawing (date unknown).

1   GREEN THOUGHTS AND SHADES

blance to either the physical or the metaphysical rigours of the early fathers.

Thomas Parnell's *The Hermit*, published in 1722, was a particularly popular poem of the century. It offered all the conventional machinery:

The Moss his bed, the Cave his humble Cell
His Food the fruits, his Drink the Crystal well.

Parnell's hermit is distinguished among his contemporary colleagues by his vision of the mysterious workings of God's providence. The poet also displays an unusual interest in relating the hermit's mental life to the surrounding landscape: his unease is mirrored by the reflections on pools shattered by a stone; his very peregrinations announce the alarm of his mind in such phrases as 'all the travel of uncertain thought'. Similarly the standards of 'improvement' of the houses that the hermit visits are allowed to suggest the spiritual qualities of their owners. But the very fact that he journeys through landscapes that might have been illustrated by Joannes Kip and Leonard Knyff in their *Britannia Illustrata* [plate 2] makes Parnell's use of the machinery of moss and cell particularly empty.

Yet this imagery was continually invoked, not only in poetry, but in practice. A hermitage for certain individuals may have been apt enough. The eccentric antiquary, William Stukeley,

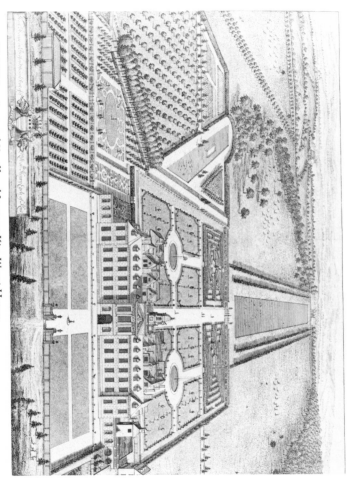

PLATE 2   Leonard Knyff and Joannes Kip, Wrest House.
Engraving from *Britannia Illustrata*, vol. 1 (1720).

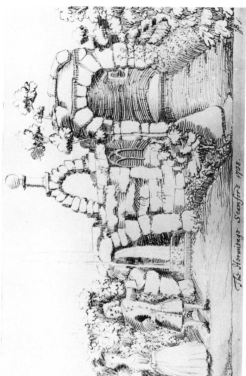

PLATE 3

William Stukeley, Hermitage, Stamford. Drawing (1738).

constructed a rocky hermitage in his garden at Stamford [plate 3], no doubt to recall his curious discoveries at Dale Abbey and Blackstone Hill, where he drew prospects and ground plans of cells and oratories cut in the rock. So that his own garden could sometimes remind him of that time in the Peak District when he took

pains to clamber on hands and knees to the top, and entered another hermit's cell, who had a mind if possible to get quite out of the world; 'tis hewn in the rock, with a most dreary prospect before it. On one end is a crucifix and a little niche, where I suppose the mistaken zeal of the starved anchorite placed his saint, or such trinket.

But Stukeley's fascination struggles with a patronizing scepticism, an ambivalent attitude that he cannot have entirely suppressed in his own hermitage. In *Rasselas*, Samuel Johnson is perhaps more confident of the absurdities of such a retreat:

it was a cavern in the side of the mountain, over-shadowed with palm-trees; at such a distance from the cataract, that nothing more was heard than a gentle uniform murmur, such as composed the mind to pensive meditation, especially when it was assisted by the wind whistling among the branches. The first rude essay of nature had been so much improved by human labour, that the cave contained several apartments, appropriated to different uses, and often afforded lodging to travellers, whom darkness or tempests happened to overtake.

But what is perhaps just as important as Johnson's ironic sense of the impropriety of such a hermitage as a context and source of human felicity is the fact that he included one at all among the objects of Rasselas's quest. For this suggests how accepted it was in the mid-eighteenth century to invoke hermits and their hermitages as tokens of the contemplative life.

PLATE 4   Merlin's Cave, Richmond Gardens.
Vignette from John Rocque's engraved *Plan of Richmond Garden* (1748).

If the accommodation that Johnson's hermit devised seems to convert his cave into a rude approximation of a Palladian villa ('several apartments, appropriated to different uses'), there were attempts at more suitable architectural styles. At Richmond a Hermitage and a Merlin's Cave were erected for Queen Caroline: the former, though symmetrical and domed, had apt decorations of rough-hewn rocks; the latter, where Stephen Duck, the 'thresher poet', was employed as the Queen's hermit in residence, had ogival arches, gothic buttresses, and curiously thatched roofs that were perhaps reminiscent of Druids' conical huts [plate 4]. At Stowe the hermitage was built as a ruin—the left turret is missing—and decorated, according to Gilbert West, with scenes from Spenser: 'sad Malbecco in the secret cell / Hears each rude monster ring his matins bell'. William Kent, who was responsible for the hermitages at both Stowe and Richmond, acknowledged the inspiration for them that he derived from Spenser by picturing them in his illustrations to *The Faerie Queene*; Archimago's cell is the hermitage at Stowe [plate 5].

If the building at Richmond was the object of some merriment, that at Stowe earned the approbation of William Gilpin:

Yon old Hermitage, situated in the midst of this delightful Wilderness, has an exceeding good effect: it is of the romantick Kind; and Beauties of this sort, where a probable Nature is not exceeded, are generally pleasing.

The pleasures of a 'probable Nature' were perhaps also to be found at Stourhead's hermitage of rocks and tree trunks or at the one at Burley-on-the-Hill with its floor of pebbles and knuckle bones and its decor of elm-disease knobs. By contrast, classical hermitages, like that designed for Richmond by Edward Stevens in 1740, not to mention those in an oriental style, complete with Arabic inscriptions and thatch 'in the Chinese taste', must have appeared merely improbable, if their owners or visitors had considered them as traditional images of the contemplative life. But they served, of course, rather as visual ingredients in picturesque scenery: Gilpin evidently found the hermitage at Stowe appealing to his already alert sense of the picturesque; Kent, who designed it, obviously found such a building an apt, poetical image for 'horridness'; even Chinese buildings were part of a more desperate bid for picturesque *frissons*.

There had been, in the previous century, an opportunity for invoking the metaphorical force of the words 'hermit' and

PLATE 5   William Kent, 'Redcross Knight and Una Invited by Subtle Archimago to His Cell'. Detail of engraving from *The Faerie Queene* (1751).

'hermitage': thus, Aubrey's praise of the house of the Hon. Charles Howard of Norfolk which

was not made for grandeur, but retirement—a noble Hermitage—neat, elegant, and suitable to the modesty and solitude of the proprietor, a Christian philosopher, who in this iron age, lives up to that of the primitive times.

Although this metaphorical invocation of hermitage is never entirely lost in the eighteenth century and, as we shall see, is revived by Wordsworth at its end, much minor poetry, like John Cunningham's *The Contemplatist*, manipulates shady haunts and moss-grown cells rather as picturesque decor than as an imagery of responsible contemplation.

If the traditional idea of anchorites in some outlandish Thebaid survives into the eighteenth-century, it is more often than not given a weakly emblematic expression. Poets, like landowners, announce their commitment to philosophical retreat by displaying the emblems of hermit and hermitage instead of thinking for themselves. And they would have found the necessary image and commentary among Tolson's *Hermathenae or Moral Emblems* [plate 6]:

Within this lonely melancholy cell
Should no vain thoughts, no Pride, no Envy Dwell;
The soul within herself serene, should here
Like Nature's golden infancy appear
....
Retired and free from the world's humming Noise,
Sweet is her peaceful State, sincere her joys.

The words invoke well-established traditions—the hermit fathers, myths of Arcadia and Paradise, the *beatus ille* theme, the melancholy syndrome—but without any real significance. Tolson's emblem, dull if it were not so whimsical, is exactly what is deployed by later poets; like Mrs. Hampden Pye, they proclaim their need to live with melancholy by haunting 'the hermit contemplation's cell'.

There is little more strenuousness in Thomas Warton's *Pleasures of Melancholy*, where the poet dedicates himself to 'Mother of Musings, Contemplation sage'. The emblematic hermits appear first only by implication in the 'twilight cells' or ruined abbeys 'where stray'd of old / The cloistered brothers'. But Melancholy is soon encouraged to

wrap me then in shades of darksome pine,
Bear me to caves by desolation brown,
To dusky vales, and hermit-haunted rocks.

It is left ambiguous whether he is to join a fraternity of recluses or merely inhabit a landscape touched by the imaginative possibilities of their presence. The 'musing Hermit' is firmly

PLATE 6   Francis Tolson, Hermit.
Emblem XLVII from *Hermathenae* (?1740).

associated by Warton not with sunny landscapes, but with what another, anonymous, contemplator described as 'solemn scenes':

Thro' silent church-yards, where the sable yews
Spread kindred gloom, and holy musings raise.

The hermit, in short, becomes just another element of church-yard scenery. He may occasionally perform the function of inert spectator (eyepiece, so to say, rather than mouthpiece) of a poet's more theatrical visions, like Warton's hermit:

from the cliff that o'er his cavern hangs
He views the piles of fall'n Persepolis
In deep arrangement hide the darksome plain.

The role that these allusions to hermits and their traditional landscapes are intended to play in this kind of poetry is indicated by the frequent, sometimes clumsy, substitution of some ab-straction where the context has led us to expect a hermit's presence: thus Dyer apostrophizes Grongar in 'whose Mossie Cells / Sweetly-musing Quiet dwells'; Thomas Warton asks summer to 'guide my pilgrim feet / Contemplation hoar to meet'; Mrs. Pye's 'contemplation' is specifically described as a 'hermit'.

As with the poets, so with the landowners. If a hermitage in a garden announced a suitable location for private meditation, it was rarely so used:

A place—for holy meditation,
For solitude, and contemplation;
Yet what himself will rarely use,
Unless to conn his weekly news;
Or with some jovial friends, to sit in,
To take his glass, and smoke, and spit in.

Indeed we know that landowners sought to employ others to do their meditation for them. Charles Hamilton advertised for a hermit at Paine's Hill in Surrey and built him a hermitage where his contract required him to remain for seven years—

with a Bible, optical glasses, a mat for his feet, a hassock for his pillow, an hourglass for his timepiece, water for his beverage, and food from the house. He must wear a camel robe, and never, under any circumstances, must he cut his hair, beard, or nails, stray beyond the limits of Mr. Hamilton's grounds, or exchange one word with the servants.

Another sat in a cave 'with an hourglass in his hand, and a beard belonging to a goat . . . with orders to accept no half-crowns from visitors, but to behave like Giordano Bruno'. This last survived apparently for fourteen years; the first fled after three weeks. Most vacancies had to be filled with stuffed dummies that gave the right emblematic effect at twenty yards.

The persistence of these visual or verbal emblems in gardens or poems throughout the century is strong; they obviously offered themselves to Wordsworth, for example, as a still familiar vocabulary for meditative poetry. His approach to Tintern Abbey and its visions of 'something far more deeply interfused' are heralded by the smoke rising among the trees from 'some hermit's cave, where by his fire / The hermit sits alone'. The opening of *The Prelude*, instinct with 'Trances of thought and mountings of the mind', concerns the poet's choice of his 'hermitage' where his life would have commerce with

the endless store of things
Rare, or at least so seeming, every day
Found all about me in one neighbourhood.

If we feel that Wordsworth has revitalized the imagery of hermit and hermitage, it is perhaps because he could draw upon some fresh experience of the connections between a landscape and a solitary meditator within it. Yet this new treaty with the exterior world is not just a result of Wordsworth's own personal temperament and situation. His poetry relies upon habits of seeing and describing a figure in the landscape that were an outcome of the eighteenth-century landscape garden. Even those gardens which continued to boast an emblematic hermitage also encouraged and shaped a wholly different mode of relating a solitary contemplator to his surroundings. It is the development of this new dialogue and of appropriate territories for it that is the main subject of this study, which must start by exploring their origins in the late seventeenth century.

The Old Hieroglyphic Landscape

If many eighteenth-century poets and landowners found the spiritual rigours of proper rural solitude and meditation uncongenial, their predecessors during the Commonwealth and Restoration had fared no better. There were many 'modern cloistered coxcombs'—in the savage announcement of the Earl of Rochester—who 'retire to think, cause they have naught to do'. Abraham Cowley could not find much evidence that his contemporaries were able to 'learn the art and get the habit of thinking'. For to become a 'husbandman is but a retreat from the city; to be a philosopher, from the world; or rather, a retreat from the world, as it is man's, into the world, as it is God's'. Cowley's formulation is instructive, because it omits any sense of the connections between philosopher and husbandman, between the ideas of one and the landscapes of the other. Although the Restoration discovered new kinds of gardens and fresh attitudes towards reading God's presence in natural phenomena, it was not obvious what structures they shared. The established congruities between the old *hortus conclusus* and religious meditation no longer seemed very engaging.

Some hermits of the later seventeenth century did still cling to prospects of God's world that the *hortus conclusus* had endorsed:

I walke the garden, and there see
Ideas of his Agonie.

Henry Vaughan invokes the ideas of hermit and hermitage frequently in his writings, but they seem to honour traditional meditation more than most contemporary usage. He told Aubrey that he believed 'All things are artificial, for Nature is the Art of God'; accordingly we do not find in his work any direct discoveries of the natural world. He shared with contemporaries like Sir Thomas Browne a determination to marry experimental ('speculations') and devotional ('attendance upon Nature') inquiries. But he also viewed this vocation in the light of his own respect for Jonsonian poetics and for 'true, unfeigned verse'. Hence he can mock a friend's apparent solitude, which is linked to some overenthusiastic and fanciful surrender to a hermit's life:

for who can tell
But that thou may'st prove devout and love a cell,
And (like a badger) with attentive looks

In the dark hole sit rooting up of books,
Quick Hermit! what a peaceful change hast thou
Without the noise of hair-cloth, whip or vow.

[p. 49]

His own 'hermitage', though retired and private, has some physical and spiritual closeness to a *consensus gentium* that he obviously approves: the dedicatee of *Flores Solitudinis . . . collected in his sickness and retirement* is told that

you will find them to lead you from the sun into the shade, from the open terrace into a private grove, and from the noise and pomp of this world into a silent and solitary hermitage.

[p. 158]

The reader is similarly warned:

if the title shall offend thee, because it was found in the woods and the wildernesse, give mee leave to tell thee, that Deserts and Mountaines were the Schooles of the Prophets. . . . It may be thy spirit is such a popular, phantastick flye, as loves to gad in the shine of this world; if so, this light I live by in the shade, is too great for thee. I send it abroad to be a companion of those wise Hermits, who have withdrawn from the present generation, to confirm them in their solitude, and to make that rigid necessity their pleasant choice.

[p. 161]

Vaughan's choice was certainly for 'rural shades' which are 'the sweet sense of piety and innocence' (p. 437), yet we look in vain for any direct observation of his rural surroundings between the Brecon Beacons and the Black Mountains. His eyes are chiefly 'accustomed to the skies' (p. 96). As a man for whom 'mornings are mysteries' (p. 268) his contemplation of 'green field and Bowres' is neither for their own sakes nor for some insight into his own psyche, but for glimpses, through 'veils' and 'shades', of 'the back parts of the Deitye' (p. 96).

There is much, fleeting, suggestion of the hermit's rural surroundings in Vaughan's poetry:

at the door of his low cell
Under some shade, or near some well
Where the Coole Poplar grows

[p. 96]

but the hills he seeks are 'eternal' (p. 249). Elsewhere he deliberates whether he might not write a prospect poem, where actual topography would promote his speculations:

Cotswold and Coopers both have met
With learned swains, and Echo yet
Their pipes, and wit;

but he chooses characteristically the Mount of Olives, the proper hill and the true fountain for poets (pp. 244-45). On one occasion Vaughan alludes rather generally to landscapes apt for meditation, when—in a passage already quoted—he purpose-fully moves from the broad terrace of a country house into a 'private grove'. But, once there, he is wrapped in 'Imaginary flights' (p. 260) that mostly neglect all allusions to the locale of his meditation. In "The Water-Fall" there is an impressively keen description of flowing water that becomes (it is a familiar comparison) a metaphor for human life; but such direct correspondence is rare. More usually when on 'some gilded Cloud or flower / My gazing soul would dwell an hour', it is only so that 'in those weaker glories' he may 'spy / Some shadows of eternity' (pp. 249–50). The shades of Vaughan's retreat are those cast by the divine verities and not by trees in actual landscapes. When he leaves his 'Cell' and goes, like any pastoral figure, to lie beside a 'shrill spring', he summons nature only to pierce through all her store (p. 248) and not even, Narcissus-like, to contemplate himself. His celebration of the wilderness for its schooling of the desert fathers is the apotheosis of a traditional and literary Thebaid. There is nothing yet of James Thomson's loving attention to real landscapes in *The Seasons*, where the same 'vast Lyceum of Nature' is discussed. Rural shades for Vaughan are

the Meek's calm region, where
Angels descend, and rule the sphere:
Where Heaven lies Leiguer, and the Dove
Duely as Dew, comes from above.
If Eden be on Earth at all,
'Tis there, which we the country call.

[p. 437]

Vaughan's study, as that of many contemporaries, was still Nature's 'Hyergliphicks' (p. 249). When he walked a garden, it was to be confronted with 'Ideas' of our saviour's agony. This kind of imagination, then, is properly heralded by an emblem on the title page of his *Silex Scintillans* (1650).

Yet his marvellous freshness of vision comes in part from his refusal to work slavishly in the traditions of emblem, especially the emblems of the *hortus conclusus*. Although we can never demonstrate the extent of his first-hand knowledge of nature, Vaughan's celebration of Eden on earth is unquestionably based upon his attention to the countryside. His meditative landscapes, for example, allude much more to the actual than those which, just twenty years before *Flores Solitudinis*, were offered to the faithful by the Jesuit, Henry Hawkins, in *Partheneia Sacra*. This work is concerned deliberately and explicitly with the closed garden of religious emblem and it rejects an interestingly wide range of actual landscapes and gardens in the process:

I speake not heer of the Covent-Garden, the garden of the Temple, nor that of the Charter-House, or of Grayes-Inne Walkes, to be had and enjoyed at home; nor of the Garden of Padua, or of Mountpellier, so illustrious for simples. I speake not of the Garden of Hesperides, where grew the golden apples, nor yet of Tempe, or the Elizian fields. I speake not of Eden, the Earthlie Paradise, nor of the Garden of Gethsemany,

PLATE 7
Henry Hawkins, The Violet. Emblem from *Partheneia Sacra* (1633).

watered with Blood flowing from our Saviour's precious body: But I speake of thee, that Garden so known by the name of HORTUS CONCLUSUS; wherein are al things mysteriously and spiritually to be found, which even beautifies the fairest gardens; being a place . . . wherein is no season to be seen, but a perpetual Spring . . . where are Arbours to shadow . . . from the heats of concupiscence; flowerie beds to repose in, with heavenly contemplations; Mounts to ascend to, with the study of Perfections; where are . . . the flowers of all vertues.

That this was essentially a mental rather than literal topography is clear from Hawkins's next injunction: that in 'this garden enclosed are certain risings to be seen of Hills in elevation of mind, and Valleys againe in depressions and demissions of the same minde'. The sections entitled "The Contemplation" that follow the emblem [plate 7] and its verses attend to the devotional meanings of the various garden items and rarely touch upon contemporary horticulture or design. For this ardent propagandist of the Counter-Reformation the syntax of his religious thought has outlasted the gardens most appropriate to it. The faithful would have perused his book in gardens of a 'new model'.

As will be seen in a later section, the actual landscapes of the late seventeenth century were unlike the closed garden of either Hawkins's image or Vaughan's mind. Yet their habits of reading natural phenomena as cyphers or analogues of divine wisdom lingered on to coexist with new tastes in landscape. There must have been a most uneasy correspondence, if any, between the inner vision or habit of reading the natural world in a man like Vaughan and the gardens and landscape pictures with which he would increasingly be surrounded: gardens in Dutch or Franco-Italian styles, gardens promoted by the horticulturalist members of the Royal Society, and the rapidly expanding collections of topographical and imaginary landscape paintings hung in the rooms of a house adjacent to such gardens.

As early as 1642 Sir John Denham makes some real attempt to order the natural features of Cooper's Hill to accord with his exploration of its larger meanings: perhaps as a consequence, his poem was to enjoy a long vogue. But, as he himself admits, the prospects are 'more boundless in my Fancy than my eie' and the poem treats the scenery accordingly: Windsor Castle is 'Thy mighty Masters Embleme', St Paul's is emblematic of an harmonious attempt to unify earth and heaven; even the fecundity of topographical and natural incidents in the landscape 'before him' only provides Denham with another opportunity to abstract: 'in the mixture of all these appears / Variety'.

Other writers made no such adjustments between a seen landscape and their affirmation that the 'Heavens, the Earth, nay every Creature . . . [are] Hieroglphicks and Emblems of his Glory'. Sir Thomas Browne was enthusiastic for Nature's 'Universall and publick Manuscript', upon whose 'common hieroglyphicks' he felt Christians cast too careless an eye. His own eyes delighted in the 'quincuncial lozenge' of garden trees, which the subtitle of The Garden of Cyrus promised to consider 'Artificially, Naturally, and Mystically'. In the history of gardens he delights to trace the 'mystical mathematicks of the city of Heaven'. Yet elsewhere he is as vigorous a naturalist in science as his friend, John Evelyn, with whom he corresponded about gardens (though 'never master of any considerable garden' himself).

These curious tensions between hieroglyphic vision and practical horticultural concerns may be seen more sharply in Abraham Cowley. His withdrawal in 1663 'from all tumult and business' is a paradigm for many hermits in the late seventeenth and early eighteenth centuries: flights from court or Parliament, from religious or political faction, from frustrations of advancement or preferment. First at Barn Elms, later at Chertsey, Cowley could indulge himself as gardenist ('husbandman' is his term) and philosopher—thus exemplifying his retreat from the city and from the world. Though Sprat says it was in this 'obscure part of his life' that he laboured with natural science, he had already published the poetic Plantarum in 1661, where his imagination is stimulated to discover perpetual concurrence between phenomenal and spiritual worlds. Unlike Henry Vaughan, whose eye or mind does not seem to have yearned for scientific description, Cowley's poem is determined to combine botanical with divine attributes. This is done not only with such obvious material as the Passion Flower (Maracet or Virginian Climber), where he can 'unfold the Emblems of this mystick Flow'r' through a detailed attention to its morphology, but with such items as the Imperial Crown:

> a flowery Crown
> My Royal Temples to adorn,
> Whose buds a sort of Honey liquor bear,
> Which round the Crown, like Stars or Pearls appear;
> Silver threads around it twine,
> Saffron, like Gold, with them does join
> And over All
> My verdant Hair does neatly fall.

It is sad, of course, that God dealt less justly with Cowley than Cowley felt God had done with Virgil: 'He made him one of the best Philosophers, and best Husbandman, and to adorn and communicate both those faculties, the best Poet' (p. 400). But Cowley's own blend of philosophy, husbandry, and poetry is at least significant for its studied attempt to focus meditation upon and through the quiddities of the natural world. Cowley acknowledges, with Vaughan, the divine ambassadors or 'leiguers' to our sublunary world:

> Hail, the poor Muses richest Mannor Seat!
> Ye Countrey Houses and Retreat
> Which all the Happy Gods so Love,
> That for you oft they quit their Bright and Great
> Metropolis above.
> [p. 395]

But he locates the visitation in some retreat like his own at Chertsey, a natural world that is reverenced as much for its accessibility to the scientist as to the Happy Gods. At Chertsey in the next century Stukeley still found a 'large garden' beside a brook and local memories of a summer-house and seat by the water. Many of the connections between botanical fact and cosmic plan are forced in Plantarum; or rather, the poetry is able to sustain neither the devotion's confederation with science nor the imaginative movement that could 'espy / Ev'n in a Bush the radiant Deitie' (p. 426). But Cowley's significance is that he moved meditative verse out into a garden of real things.

Cowley's dedication to a precisely seen and registered world had its contemporary counterpart in Evelyn's botanical studies and its predecessor in Bacon, the father of empirical science, who had explained in his essay "Of Gardens" how the myth of Ver perpetuum might be realized in terms of horticultural skills and knowledge. Art and science can order larger significances, as a gardener designs his garden's pattern:

Although no part of mighty Nature be
More stor'd with Beauty, Power, and Mysterie;
Yet to encourage human Industrie,
God has so ordered, that no other part
Such space, and such Dominion leaves for Art.

[p. 427]

But the mind now moves among phenomena, where, as Cowley says, 'our senses are . . . feasted with the clear and genuine taste of their Objects' (p. 403). The ambiguity of his sentence, allowing both a scientific and a hieroglyphic meaning, is maintained in his own work. He can pray for a 'mind's purged eye' to view 'Those wonders which to sense the Gods deny' (p. 410); yet he praises the satisfaction of 'seeing nothing but the effects and improvements of [man's] own Art and Diligence' in the countryside (p. 403): and he argues that Oxford should appoint Professors of Gardening not for their 'Ostentation of Critical Literature, but for solid and experimental knowledge' (p. 405).

The example of Cowley reminds us forcibly of the notion, made axiomatic in art history by Sir Ernst Gombrich, that the mind can give expression, other than in exceptional circumstances, only to what is within the limits of its current vocabulary. Thus Cowley tells how when he first went to live in the country he thought it would be full of Sidney's Arcadian shepherds (p. 446); elsewhere, having urged Oxford to appoint professors less for their critical skills than for their scientific knowledge of gardening, he himself continues by saying that 'What I have further to say of the Country Life, shall be borrowed from the Poets' (p. 405). His understanding of various garden and rural landscapes is mediated by the idea of them already available to him.

Marvell's Gardens

It has become a commonplace of recent criticism to stress Marvell's alertness to literary and philosophical traditions within which to write. This sophistication with literary genre and style allows Marvell opportunities of making more radical conjunctions between mind and landscape than writers like Cowley and of invoking a more extensive and subtle syntax to write of their encounters.

He is as capable as Vaughan of emblematic, hieroglyphic readings of nature, as "On a Drop of Dew". But his attention to the observed world—the dewdrop 'scarce touching where it lyes' (p. 12)—which functions as such a vital part of the poem is as fine as anything in Cowley's *Plantarum*, with the added suppleness of Marvell's vision of the analogic world of soul. Further, if we may rely upon Legouis' observation that the fruits in the fifth stanza of "The Garden" are those which were grown in England only with careful horticultural skill, we can see Marvell's garden vision alert equally to the characteristic achievements of contemporary *scientia* and to the larger spiritual prospects of *sapientia*. The fountain and the fruit tree are thus essential to both Christian landscapes and contemporary gardens. We are aware that he manipulates various traditions of garden and retirement poetry within a context that includes Hendrick Danckerts's *Pineapple Picture*, where Charles II is presented with the first such fruit to be grown in England, the presentation made upon the terrace of an English house with its rectangular parterre beyond.

It is not just that Marvell keeps his eyes upon real gardens even as he manoeuvres in what Walter Montague called the 'holy Garden of Speculation'. His skills ensure a more subtle exchange of outside and inside; they sustain a metamorphosis both of mind into matter and of natural into psychological realities: we have only to compare "Upon the Hill and Grove at Billbrough" with "Cooper's Hill" to realize Marvell's preeminence in this.

Yet with perhaps one crucial exception that will be discussed Marvell's vision comes from an intelligent and lively versatility with the available languages. He relies, for example, upon the *topos* which D.C. Allen has stated succinctly as 'the garden is a classical equivalent of the mind' and upon similar pastoral devices that serve as metaphoric vocabulary to describe the mind. Whatever the play of his wit and scepticism upon these received traditions contrives, he still functions within a basically analogic attitude to the world. On some occasions he suggests than man can no longer be reconciled with the world of nature:

My Mind was once the true survey
Of all these Meadows fresh and gay;
And in the greenness of the Grass
Did see its Hopes as in a Glass;

[p. 48]

so that man's only consolation is to invoke natural creation as an emblematic vocabulary of his despair:

And thus, ye Meadows, which have been
Companions of my thoughts more green,
Shall now the Heraldry become
With which I shall adorn my Tomb.

[p. 49]

On other occasions he amuses himself with neglecting the symbolic possibilities of the natural world, as in the first stanza of "The Garden" or, later in the same poem, when the abstractions of 'Quiet' and 'Innocence' are said to be actually growing as plants; but he then returns to arguing that the mind is happiest when contemplating creations of its own faculties.

Should this suggest—and the sundial reference lends some support—that Marvell shares with Cowley a delight in 'the effects and improvements of . . . Art and Diligence' (p. 403), the poem finally allows more metaphysical than gardenist perspectives. Then again, while his celebration of mental control should consort with praise for the English seventeenth-century garden, in both the verses on Billbrough and the Mower's attack on gardens it is the natural world that is praised at the expense of human ingenuity:

> He first enclos'd within the Garden's square
> A dead and standing pool of Air:
> And a more luscious Earth for them did knead,
> Which stupifi'd them while it fed.
> The Pink grew then as double as his Mind;
> The nutriment did change the kind.
> With strange perfumes he did the Roses taint:
> And Flow'rs themselves were taught to paint.   [p. 43]

Yet the curiously prophetic insight that man might find in 'meadows' a more congenial landscape of meditation is not offered as charting fresh directions for either poetry or gardening. The 'sweet fields' are part of Marvell's delighted play with the variables of his inherited ideas. He manoeuvres marvellously and athletically but always *within* analogic modes:

> What but a Soul could have the wit
> To build me (the body) up for Sin so fit?
> So Architects do square and hew
> Green Trees that in the Forest grew.   [p. 23]

Yet part of Marvell's versatility within his received traditions is his very sceptical delight in teasing the accepted habits of thought and poetry; this in its turn contrives the impression that Marvell is alert to fresh possibilities of syntax that would allow more than analogic significances to be discovered in landscape.

He admits in "The Garden" that his mind 'Does straight its own resemblance find', but then allows that it also

> creates, transcending these,
> Far other Worlds, and other Seas;
> Annihilating all that's made
> To a green Thought in a green Shade.   [p. 52]

This certainly means that there is nothing comparable to what the retired contemplatist may imagine; yet its ambiguity also entails a glimpse of the imagination exerting itself beyond merely analogic meaning to recover anew a different rapport with landscape. "The Garden" does not do more than hint at these possible conjunctions, though the dominant presence of metamorphosis controlling the movements of the poem sug-

gests alternatives to the analogic mode; yet even here, I think, the received structures of metamorphosis limit its scope. Only in the long meditation "Upon Appleton House," where metamorphosis seems to learn a new gardening vocabulary, are the possibilities pursued.

"Upon Appleton House", Rosalie Colie tells us, 'deliberately stretches the limits of the country-house poem'. I want to suggest that it does so by recognizing how the landscape of

PLATE 8 Giusto Utens, *Pratolino* (1599). Painted lunette.

country estates was itself changing and how, as a consequence as yet indefinitely plotted, psychological modes of responding to landscape were replacing earlier visions of a 'perfect microcosmic order of an ideal moral ecology'. Marvell had already announced in his Mower poems an important element in these changing landscapes: for "The Mower Against Gardens" argues that the fauns and fairies who 'till' the meadows enter gardens by proxy through iconographical representations—'Their

Statues polish'd by some ancient hand,/May to adorn the Gardens stand' (p. 44)—just as they did in Italian gardens that Marvell might have seen while abroad in 1642. The gardens, meadows, and woods of Appleton House, like those of the Medici villa at Pratolino [plate 8], were interspersed with iconographical images, either real or envisaged by the poet. And these involved the mind of the visitor wandering among them in an exciting drama of ideas and associations, sometimes teased out of the context, sometimes forcing itself irresistibly upon the spectator. Fairfax's flower garden, formed like a fortress to recall his military career, is an obvious example of this at Appleton:

> when retired here to Peace,
> His warlike Studies could not cease;
> But laid these Gardens out in sport
> In the just Figure of a Fort.

[p. 71]

What seems less obvious to critics who invoke Hawkins's *Parthenia Sacra* at such a moment is that whereas Hawkins, or Vaughan, would impose such figures upon or draw them invisibly from a landscape, Fairfax's garden actually contains those images. True, there are some self-conscious examples of the archaic hieroglyphic mode during Marvell's progress around the estate:

> For he did, with his utmost Skill,
> *Ambition* weed, but *Conscience* till—
> *Conscience*, that Heaven-nursed plant,
> Which most our Earthly Gardens want.

[p. 73]

But just as crucial a presence in both garden and poem is the garden's own announced iconography ('all things are composed here', p. 63): an apparatus of garden statue, inscription, and image that direct the mind to read the garden's meaning. Such features of a Renaissance garden share, of course, some iconography with the emblematic traditions of the *hortus conclusus*. What is different is that for the meditator among seventeenth-century gardens the arrangement of images provided him with a natural setting that contained messages visibly announced in the gardens' design. So not only Fairfax's flower garden, but the ruined nunnery (like some later gothic folly), becomes part of a composition that shapes the mind that expatiates within it.

Difficulties with this reading of the poem might well seem to occur when the poet deserts the contrived gardens and area round the house for the water-meadows and woods of the estate. Yet some of this astonishing poem's perplexities—at this point, for example, its apparent disjointedness—are eased if we recall several other features of Italian Renaissance garden art. The masque imagery which Marvell invokes as a syntax for his

PLATE 9   Georg Andreas Boeckler, Boboli Gardens.
Engraving from *Architectura Curiosa* (1664).

visions in the meadows and woods is historically connected with Italian gardens where such entertainments were frequently presented: thus the word 'scene' combines the pictorial languages of masque, of poetic description, and of visual prospects in gardens—Pope's garden at Twickenham was to be celebrated later for *its* 'multiplied scenes'.

Second, Italian gardens had always extended their iconographical design beyond the formal area of the house to areas of wood and field where statues and fountains would be found to entertain more energetic wanderers. Marvell even seems to hint at this second point himself:

Art would more neatly have defac'd
What she had laid so sweetly wast;
In fragrant Gardens, shaddy Woods,
Deep Meadows, and transparent Floods.

                                                              [p. 65]

The 'neatness' of the woods dividing to make a lane—which John Wallace says we 'cannot actually believe'—is not inconsistent with those sections of Italian gardens that lie further from the parterre and the house—the high alleys of the 'wilderness' at the Villa Medici in Rome or the statue-lined Viottolone of the Boboli Gardens in Florence [plate 9]:

PLATE 10 Statue in gardens of Castello, near Florence.

[p. 82]

the two Woods have made a Lane;
While, like a *Guard* on either side,
The Trees before their *Lord* divide;
This, like a long and equal Thread,
Betwixt two *Labyrinths* does lead.

This is not to suggest that Marvell actually sees some image like that of the Boboli; but his language implies that part of his imaginative encounter with the landscape still involves habits and expectations learnt in Italian gardens. Thus the advent of Maria Fairfax, the 'Blest nymph' who presides over the final 'scenes' of the poem, is presented both as some goddess from an *intermezzo* and as a tutelary statue which surveys, orders, and defines a garden's meaning [plate 10]:

See how loose Nature, in respect
To her, it self doth recollect

· ·

'Tis *She* that to these Gardens gave
That wondrous Beauty which they have;
She streightness on the Woods bestows;
To *Her* the Meadow sweetness owes;
Nothing could make the River be
So Chrystal-pure but only *She*;

PLATE 11   Claude Lorrain, *Landscape with Apollo and the Muses.*
Oil painting (1650's).

She yet more Pure, Sweet, Streight, and Fair,
Than Gardens, Woods, Meads, Rivers are.   [p. 83–84]

The language is as consistent with gardenist traditions as with
those literary ones of pastoral hyperbole that J. B. Leishman
explores; indeed, the influence of some lady upon a landscape is
rendered 'real' in Italian garden design. So that Maria might be a
statue,

And for a Glass, the limpid Brook,
Where *She* may all *her* Beautyes look;
But, since *She* would not have them seen,
The Wood about *her* draws a Skreen—   [p. 84]

just as earlier the poet had presented himself in a way that
suggests a reclining river-god, familiar in sculpture and picture
[plate 11]:

Oh what a Pleasure 'tis to hedge
My Temples here with heavy sedge;
Abandoning my lazy Side,
Stretcht as a Bank into the Tide.   [p. 82]

It is also entirely consistent with Marvell's metamorphic
dexterity in the woods and meadows ('all things gaze themselves, and doubt / If they be in it or without, p. 82) to recall the

23   GREEN THOUGHTS AND SHADES

manipulation of our responses in Italian gardens, whereby we are tempted to mistake sculpture for water, water for baroque stonework, and trees for sculpture, each aspiring to the other's condition: so at Appleton House the wood

> in as loose an order grows
> As the *Corinthian Porticoes*.
> The arching Boughs unite between
> The Columnes of the Temple green.

And as the swift transmutations in the poet's mind transfer their speed to the natural setting we may find in the rapidity and wonder of such exchanges the same mental play that was a noted product of Italian gardens. It is presumably to such a one that Henry Wotton refers as early as 1624:

[p. 78]

For as Fabriques should be regular, so gardens should be irregular, or at least cast into a very wild regularity. To exemplify my conceit; I have seen a garden (for the maner perchance incomparable) into which the first access was a high walke like a terrace, from whence might be taken a general view of the whole plot below; but rather in a delightful confusion, than with any plain distinction of the pieces. From this the beholder descending many steps, was afterwards conveyed again, by several mountings and valings, to various entertainments of his sense and sight: which I shall not need to describe (for that were poetical) let me only note this, that everyone of these diversities, was as if he had been magically transported into a new garden.

Such contrived dramas in a garden fascinated seventeenth-century gardenists, some of them, like Evelyn, designing sec-

PLATE 12

THE FIGURE IN THE LANDSCAPE

John Evelyn, garden design. Drawing in manuscript of *Elysium Britannicum* (after 1659).

tions of otherwise straightforward garden plots to accommodate the 'mountings and valings' [plates 12 and 14] that Wotton inferred, quite rightly, are among the delights of exploring Italian gardens.

It is, in short, through all these elements of garden syntax as well as through other traditional vocabularies that Marvell organizes his poetic vision in "Upon Appleton House". Perhaps the most important of these for later developments is the play of associationism within a garden—what is perhaps identified by Wotton's magical and poetical entertainments of a garden visitor. The process by which the mind's activities are released by the succession of images that pass before it— 'this *Scene* again withdrawing brings / A new and empty Face of things' (p. 76)—is a new dimension of metamorphosis. It is a kind of deception, already known in the masque, but just as endemic to garden architecture (witness Wotton's account) as to landscape painting (this we have on the authority of Edward Norgate's *Miniatura*, which was extensively used by another of Maria Fairfax's tutors to prepare her art treatise). The deceptions that Marvell's landscapes encourage are—above all in Fairfax's flower garden—an early form of associationism. As a language for man's relationships with nature, associationism would find support in Locke's new psychology as well as in gardens more directly suited to this associative play.

Gardens of a New Model

It must now be seen what places of retreat, what varieties of garden design and theory, were available to 'hermits' like Fairfax when they withdrew to their estates. Those who avoided, on the one hand, the rigours and enthusiasm of the Puritan Pilgrim and had, on the other, little taste for the unstrenuous diversions of an idle country life found one interest in scientific, especially horticultural, experiment and needed gardens designed accordingly. John Evelyn, writing to Sir Thomas Browne in the late 1650's, contrasted the 'brutish and ambitious persons [who] seek themselves in the ruines of our miserable yet dearest country' with those retired persons, like Browne, whose integrity was dedicated to redeeming 'the time that has bin lost, in pursuing vulgar errors'. To seek oneself through experimental endeavours became a crucial and important alternative to religious introspection and to what Evelyn called 'the land of spectres ... vacuum, occult qualities and other inadequate notions'.

Horticulture and agriculture offered the ideal antidote to both religious enthusiasm and emblematic readings of nature. As Cowley and Evelyn among others insisted, what England needed after the Civil Wars was the re-establishment of horticulture and agriculture rather than any excessive attention to religious enthusiasm. The proper use of a garden, John Lawrence argues in his preface to *The Clergy-Man's Recreation shewing the Pleasure and Profit of the Art of Gardening* (London, 1714), was to keep clergymen fit, and not, presumably, to allow them opportunities for cultivating disruptive theological ideas. Thus the title page of Ralph Austen's *A Treatise of Fruit Trees* of 1653 (to which is added *The Spiritual Use of an Orchard*) provides both an emblem in which Solomon's praise of his bride as a *hortus conclusus* encircles a square garden and a plan of an area geometrically planted with elaborate patterned *broderies*, the whole surrounded with tools used in grafting, pruning, and ordering nature [plate 13]. Austen argues that 'Work is profitable to the Minds, by storing it with variety of objects, and profitable notions, [note the order] both Natural, Moral and Spiritual' (p. 32).

With such moral and mental habits inevitably came suitable locations for them. Gardens became places of horticultural research and, even when only decorative, still proclaimed human control. An obviously ordered garden is an outward and visible sign of man's scientific understanding of nature's processes. In such places the hieroglyphic or analogic reading of nature has surrendered to empirical study. Thus Timothy Nourse is eager to proclaim in *Campania Foelix* (London, 1700)

PLATE 13 Ralph Austen, *A Treatise of Fruit Trees* (1653). Title page.

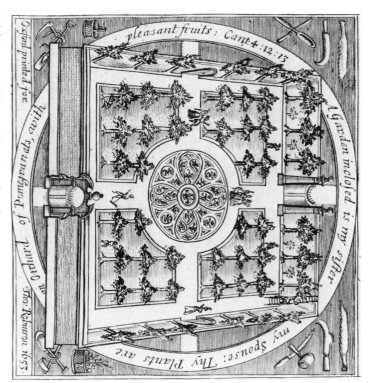

that he has written out of his own experience, his own 'Private and Country Life' (p. 25).

In John Rea's *Flora*, published first in 1665, the scientific spirit manifests itself in his descriptive catalogue of flowers and his instructions for laying out and maintaining gardens. Designs at the end of the volume declare the fascination with geometric ingenuity in flower gardens, a taste for obvious signs of control exercised by man against nature's abundance and apparent anarchy. Similarly, John Woolridge in his *Systema Horti-culturae or the Art of Gardening* (London 1677) advises that even circular flower beds should be divided into quadrants and those into further subdivisions (p. 15). Whatever extravagant cadenzas these rectangular spaces contain, they also restrain them and ultimately they teach fancy to submit to geometry. Even a wilderness conformed to such control, as in Christopher Wren's design for the one at Hampton Court or in that described by Charles Evelyn:

and that I might be properly retired, in the middle of each square of the wilderness, or of two of them at least, there should be a large elm or fir, with a small seat enclosing the body thereof, and the ground open in a grass-walk, for about the space of six, seven or eight foot, etc. round . . . having a very narrow and almost conceal'd entrance from the walks; and for more public use, there might be large trees planted in the centre of the wilderness, with small seats erected round them likewise; these seats, with one or two small moveable ones, of a size to contain one person only.

Despite these private seats and despite the almost concealed entrance to that wilderness from the more public area of the garden, opportunities for solitary meditation found a less than enthusiastic response after the Restoration—Charles Evelyn again:

from those entertainments [i.e. grass plots and square flower beds], you advance to a fountain of the best architecture: from thence you come to other grass-plots of various forms, fine greens and beautiful flower-hedges; with the addition of an excellent contriv'd statue presenting *Flora*; from whence you enter a well-form'd flourishing wilderness; and being no longer pleas'd with a solitary amusement, you come out into a large road, where you have the diversion of seeing travellers pass by.

Though the wilderness is 'well-form'd', it yet detains the visitor for only a short time. The preference seems to be for those vistas which endorse either man's supremacy or his shared humanity. The importance of human authorship is announced in the frontispiece to Nourse's *Campania Foelix* by the squared pleasure gardens separated by a high wall from the land outside, which is shown in its turn under human cultivation. Such gardens encourage man's social disposition, endorsing his preference for landscapes where he can identify with other human beings and where, according to Charles Evelyn, he need not be alone for long. It is such social considerations that control and render harmless John Rea's only poetical and meditational flights in *Flora*. His dedicatory verses are merely graced with rather empty allusions to the emblematic virtues of flowers:

In your garden you can walk
And with each plant and flower talk,
View all their glories, from each one
Raise some rare meditation.

Yet in "Flora to the Ladies" the octosyllabics concentrate upon and obviously enjoy the catalogue of botanical specimens more than the decoration of this theme with mythological allusions or the identification of Daphne in the myrtle grove. In the volume by his namesake, John Ray, *Observations, Topographical, Moral and Physiological Made in a Journey, etc.* (1673) the Boboli Gardens in Florence evoke mainly horticultural excitement, with, otherwise, some passing references to their fitness for social pastimes.

This direction of man's physical and metaphysical energies into an empirical study of nature, which thus submitted to the scientific spirit, seemed to John Evelyn a new direction for modern hermits. In his mind, too, a corollary of these new attitudes was gardens of a new order. He wrote to Browne in 1657 of his

abhorrency of those painted and formal projections of our cockney gardens and plots, which appear like gardens of paste-board and march-pain, and smell more of paint than of flowers and verdure: our drift is a noble, princely, and universal Elysium, capable of all the amenities that can naturally be introduced into gardens of pleasure. We will endeavour to show how the air and genius of gardens operate upon human spirits towards virtue and sanctity, I mean in a remote, preparatory and instrumental working. How caves, grots, mounts, and irregular ornaments of gardens do contribute to contemplative and philosophical enthusiasm; how *elysium*, *antrum*, *nemus*, *paradysus*, *hortus*, *lucus*, etc., signify all of them *rem sacram et divinam*; for these expedients do influence the soul and spirits of man, and prepare them for converse with good angels; besides which, they contribute to the less abstracted pleasures . . . and I would have . . . a society of the *paradisi cultores*, persons of ancient simplicity, Paradisean and Hortulan saints.

How the garden becomes the focus of 'less abstracted pleasures' and recovers some acceptable role as a place for solitary meditation in a less strenuously religious age can be seen from Evelyn's own career.

As a young man Evelyn fled from the 'furious and zealous people' in London to 'possess myself in some quiet' at the family home at Wotton. Here, with his brother's permission, he made 'a fishpond, an island, and some other solitudes and retire-

PLATE 14   John Evelyn, Wotton House. Drawing (1653).

ments'. According to some ms. notes on another drawing of Wotton House by John Evelyn, his brother also created a 'mount of trees', a fountain, and a summerhouse [plate 14]. The garden elements at Wotton, like those in the later letter of 1657 to Browne, are therefore a mixture of old and more advanced features: if the mount is a mediaeval survival, there are more up-to-date forms which announce French and Italian taste, as well as the Renaissance debt via literary sources to Roman gardens. And in Evelyn's handling of these modern elements we may see something prophetic of the 'English garden' of the following century.

This prophetic aspect of Evelyn's gardenist interests is registered best in his own gardens, created at Sayes Court, Deptford, after his marriage. A field of one hundred acres became a unique, radical venture in garden design, the full significance of which has hitherto been ignored. It drew upon his thorough knowledge of gardens in England, Italy, and France but seems to have been tied to none of their traditions. Its significance lies in two related features: first, that the garden obviously mirrored Evelyn's own personal delights and interests—in the phrase that Maynard Mack has used of Pope and his garden seventy years later, it became 'a rallying point for his personal values and a focus for his conception of himself'; secondly, that Evelyn's garden was designed 'to agree with the nature of the place' rather than being one where the plot had been 'enforce[d] to any particular fancy', this also anticipating Pope's recommendation to 'consult the genius of the Place in all'.

As the manuscript plan of Sayes Court reveals [plate 15], Evelyn invoked various contemporary features—axial avenues, geometric lines of walks and meanders in the Grove, the

PLATE 15   John Evelyn, Sayes Court.
Drawn plan (1653).

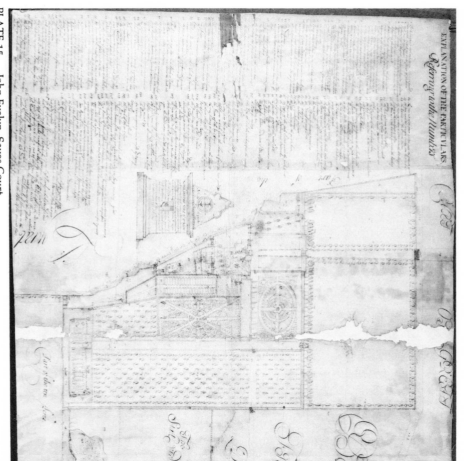

parterre of the Oval Garden, the quincuncial ordering of the
Great Orchard. Yet the overall effect is of great variety (a term
Evelyn uses many years before it becomes a byword of the
landscape gardeners) and of great intimacy. This quality of
autobiographical expression ('As is the Gardener, so is the
Garden') derives both from the garden's provision of various
privacies—what he called 'solitudes and retirements' at Wotton
House—and from its thorough dedication to Evelyn's horticultural enthusiasms. On the one hand, there were 'private walks,
shades, and cabinetts', a miniature banqueting house for the use
of his children, and (properly situated 526 yards away from the
children at the opposite end of a promenade) an island retreat
with fruit trees and summerhouse reached by a drawbridge
across a carp and duck pond which Evelyn maybe modelled upon
the so-called Maritime Theatre in Hadrian's Villa at Tivoli.

On the other hand, the whole disposition of the various
compartments was eloquent testimony to his scientific pursuits:

there were nursery gardens, kitchen and flower gardens, an 'elaboratorie' where he practised chemistry, an aviary and a transparent beehive (where Marvell's 'sentinels' might be subjected to a more empirical regard); plantations where his ambitious and pioneering arboriculture was prosecuted; a walled, private garden of choice flowers and simples (an apt *giardino segreto* for a member of the Royal Society); a Milking Close with walnut trees beside a carp pond. Even the properly allotted formal area of bowling green and cypress walk in front of the house was annexed to Evelyn's interest in fruit trees, which were trained around the encircling walls. And though these extraordinarily varied sections of Sayes Court were ordered into compartments, it was a novel feature of Evelyn's scheme that they should be separated not by walls but by *contr'espaliers* and hedges of shrubs and evergreens. Walls would have declared too severe and rigid lines, whereas divisions formed of natural growth, as in Italian gardens, allowed the mind to play with the metamorphic properties of the garden world. Finally, lest this green world was not sufficient, there was elsewhere a terrace 'of some pretty height to look abroad into the fields'.

These designs and ideas make Evelyn a fascinatingly prophetic gardenist, unique especially in his evident ability to combine what Stephen Switzer was later to call 'private and natural turns' with what would usually be termed a formal design. No wonder Cowley knew of 'nobody that possess more private happiness than you do in your Garden' (p. 421). Evelyn seems a precursor of Pope's generation, too, in his insistence on the need for variety in gardens and in his attention to the 'genius of the place'; he urges 'sweet and gracious varieties . . . which may be effected with a great deal more facility where the site is uneven by Nature or easily made so by Art'. The artificial aids that were available to assist natural topography are listed by Evelyn in his *Plan of a Royal Garden*, offered in abstract form in his volume, *Acetaria* (1699). He provides what is in effect an exhaustive catalogue of garden features—terraces and walks, knots and compartments, groves and labyrinths, cascades and grottoes, artificial echoes and 'hydraulic musick' —all the elements that he had admired in French and, above all, Italian gardens. As we shall see in the following chapters, it is less the formality of such devices that is crucial than the spirit in which and the purpose for which they were deployed.

The spirit and purpose of Evelyn's gardens make them a significant stage in the history of hermit's landscapes, that is to say in the development of a correspondence between garden design and moral idea. When, in the Preface to *Acetaria*, he mocks authors who publish with titles such as the *Complete . . . Gardner*, it is because he realized himself how immense a task it is to comprehend that Great and Universal Plantation, Epitomized in our gardens, highly worth the contemplation of the most Profound Divine, and Deepest Philosopher.

Though the second edition of his *Sylva or a Discourse of Forest Trees* (1670) contained a curiously old-fashioned account, in the manner of Browne, of 'the sacredness and use of standing Groves', Evelyn's usual attention to the 'great and Universal Plantation' is less to its analogic or emblematic scope than to its horticultural needs. About the time Marvell was in Yorkshire, wittily manipulating the various meanings of Fairfax's garden and park, Evelyn was compiling his *Kalendarium Hortense*, to be published in 1664 as an appendix to *Sylva*. This gardener's almanac appears to be his 'deepest philosophy'; as he told the President of the Royal Society, dedicating to him *Acetaria: A Discourse of Sallets*, a 'learned Pleasure' exists in 'Gardens and Rural Employments'; not only 'that of the most refined Part of Agriculture (the Philosophy of the *Garden and Parterre* only) but of Herbs, and wholesome sallets'.

Evelyn's scientific interests were shared by many of his contemporaries. Even Austen, whose *Spiritual Use of an Orchard* declared that a garden of fruit-trees is a volume of good Notions, could temper this hieroglyphic vision with some empirical advice: the Preface to his *Treatise of Fruit Trees* discusses how

When Speculation and practice, Art and Nature, are matched, they are pregnant and fruitful, but the one alone, wanting a mere helper, what fruits can it bring forth: Experience (as a Philosopher sais) is the Root of Art.

In the years of the Royal Society which were soon to follow this dialogue was firmly based on experience and practice. By 1700 Timothy Nourse can link the scientific examination of nature with new kinds of introspection that were not apparently tainted by Puritan enthusiasm: 'When a Man attentively considers the Annual Progress of Nature through all its stages and alterations, it cannot but remind him of his own continual changes' (p. 4.). A traditional equation between micro- and macro-cosm is there refurbished with scientific thinking and looks ahead to Thomson's *The Seasons*. It is no coincidence that Locke's psychological as well as Evelyn's horticultural studies were products of the philosophical climate that the Royal Society established or endorsed.

The garden, then, could be among the new locales of empirical philosophy. Cowley 'cannot recommend solitude to a man totally illiterate' (p. 394); for without 'Science'—which includes 'Chymistry, or History, or Gardening'—a man would live that empty and inane existence that John Rawlet celebrates: 'In a

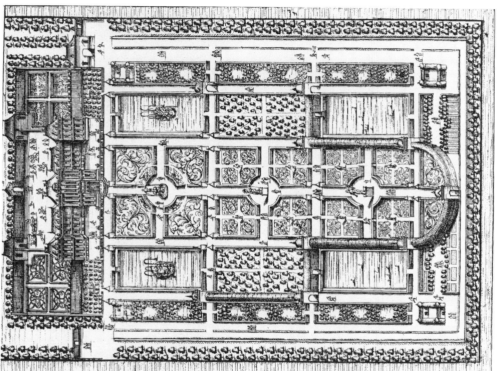

PLATE 16   Jan van der Groen, garden at Ryswyck.
Engraving from *Den Nederlandtsen Hovemer* (1670).

retired hermitage I dwell / Where no disturbance can approach my cell'.

But the gardens of the late seventeenth century were not only created by and for members of the Royal Society, though theirs will promise, as we shall see, more for the future landscape garden. There were also gardens created in the fashionable French and Dutch tastes: the restored Stuarts naturally favoured the first, the House of Orange, the second. French gardens contributed a sense of grandeur and vast scale to their English imitators, while Dutch gardens [plate 16] provided more intricate ideas on how to embroider flower beds and embellish shrubs and trees. In practice, however, these legacies were not very distinct, and the dominant, mediating taste in England by the end of the seventeenth century was French. Some of the great showpieces—Hampton Court, Chatsworth, and Badminton—are exhibited in the 1720 volume of *Britannia Illustrata*: long axial avenues, water caught in basins and canals, all exposed in the engraver's bird's-eye view to an instantaneous and public appreciation of their grandiloquent designs; by the second volume of 1740 these styles have spread to less grandiose sites: at Boughton or Seavenhampton strict avenues stretch out to colonize the park, like sketches for a Versailles. (And by 1740 the rival style of the landscape garden was also established, though obviously not much at the expense of a still flourishing French style). The English exercises in French or Dutch design seem rather to boast a proprietor's means and continental habits than to provide apt or congenial places of retirement. And it was doubtless in the face of so much rather sterile imitations of continental taste that John Evelyn's *Plan of a Royal Garden* urged more variety and subtlety.

There was a more explicit dismay with these ambitious projects. John Lawrence notices with some sarcasm that 'Gardening being of late Years become the general Delight and Entertainment of the Nobility and Gentry', he would make suggestions for more modest gardens, suitable for 'a grave and contemplative Genius'. Similarly John Woolridge in his *Systema Horti-culturae*, which reached its third edition by 1688, advised readers that he catered for modest villas as well as seats of nobility:

not only to excite or animate such that have fair Estates, and Pleasant Seats in the Country, to adorn and beautify them; but to encourage the honest and plain countryman in the improvement of his Ville, by enlarging the bounds and limits of his Gardens, as well as his Orchards.

The horticultural emphasis marks Woolridge of Evelyn's party, as does his insistence on the influence over 'the Passions of the Mind' that a garden's variety must have; 'infinite variety of never dying Objects of Delight . . . all his Senses are satisfied with the great variety of objects'. It comes as no surprise that Woolridge admired Italian gardens, which always impressed visiting Englishmen during the seventeenth century with their variousness as well as with their presence at even the most modest villa. By contrast, the French taste, though derived from the Italian, seemed to lack variety—at least as it was practised in England. Nourse's 'Essay of a Country-House' in *Campania Foelix* objects to the 'dead plains' beyond the palace at Versailles itself as well as to the monotony of its design (p. 299).

These distinctions which lurk in the gardenist writings of the later seventeenth century are crucial: for to the unsympathetic eye, and indeed even to the eye of some garden historians, there is little to differentiate the gardens of the period. 'Formal',

PLATE 17   John Aubrey, Easton Pierse.
Watercolour (1669).

'geometric', the mirror of man's 'logical, scientific, and ordered mind'—these are the terms of analysis and description that are applied equally to the gardens of the *Britannia Illustrata* and to John Aubrey's Easton Pierse. Yet the temper of Aubrey's garden is quite distinct, even allowing for the difference in scale, from the pomp and circumstance which invade so many of the estates that Kip and Knyff illustrate. Some watercolours by Aubrey of Easton Pierse in 1669 show a simple, restrained manipulation of descending rectangles of terrace (rather in the Italian style), formal patterning of trees, fountains and a statue, and what appears to be an embroidered parterre [plate 17]. These features might be explained by the fact that some gardens responded, as did certain contemporary poetry, to the efforts of the Royal Society to purge extravagence and conceit. But a more solid and probable reason lies in the informed advocacy by some gardenists of *variety and irregularity*. For, if the scientific exploration of the natural world exposed its laws, its marvellous logic and fixed principles, it equally and optimistically made apparent its diversities. Hence Aubrey's praise of the 'irregularities, both natural and artificial' at Sir John Danvers's seat at Lavington: hence Lawrence's schemes for an 'irregular piece of Ground, which may be made to have its Beauties as well as the most regular'. Lawrence's prescriptions (pp. 20–25) involve both 'strait Lines' and 'many uncommon Prettinessess wholly owing to the Irregularity or Unevenness of the Ground'.

What is especially significant, as we shall see, is that his designs are offered in such a way as 'Every one may easily please himself in a Form that strikes most his own Fancy'.

It is customary to argue that the taste in gardening of the late seventeenth and early eighteenth centuries lagged behind that in landscape poetry and painting. That is undoubtedly true, and this and the following sections will suggest the radical range of pictorial and literary example that offered itself to the seventeenth-century advocates of irregularity and variety, as, later, to the exponents of the English landscape garden. But it is also worth emphasising, not only that in gardenist matters theory was strangely ahead of practice, but that the same design elements, even the identical garden syntax, could be deployed with very different spirit and aims by followers of French gardens (like the royal gardeners, George London and Henry Wise) and by those who objected to their stiffness and monotony.

Among these latter, radical gardenists there was a tendency to match a garden's leanings to naturalism, variety, and psychological involvement with nearby wall decorations. These might initiate the delightful perplexities of a garden's metamorphic world by providing *trompe-l'œil* glimpses of the outside world for spectator who was still inside the house or in a garden pavilion; or, more simply, they provided images of landscape (both were popular Italian devices.) Wotton, whose advocacy of 'irregular' gardens after the Italian manner has already been cited, also urged that the walls of open terraces, summer-houses, and galleries overlooking gardens should be decorated with 'land-schips', and *Boscage* and such *wilde* workes'. Similarly, John Rea recommends 'landskips' for summer-houses, and Nourse, 'all sorts of landskip' for galleries and crosswalks. It is therefore no surprise that not far from that marvellously intricate and varied garden at Wilton House, engraved in 1645 by Isaac de Caus [plate 18], the Hunting Room was decorated by Edward Pearce with curious georgic scenes of hunting, shooting, and fishing that evince some real and prominent attention to landscape.

Those gardenists who urged variety and irregularity would also have found support in William Sanderson's *Graphice* (London, 1658). Its stress upon sight as the most excellent of the senses is traditional; yet he often seems to anticipate Locke's insistence that our physical vision is the agent of our ideas, especially when he praises the varieties of landscape. Of the three sorts of painting, that of landscape offers a 'wonderful freedom, and liberty, to draw, even, what you list; so various is Nature in that' (p. 32). He links his encomium upon the power of sight with our ideas of the variousness of nature by rehearsing the repertoire of visual objects:

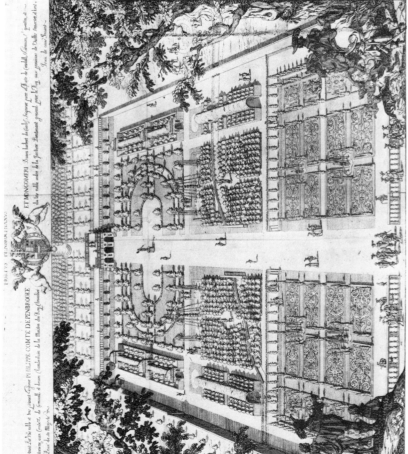

PLATE 18 Isaac de Caus, gardens at Wilton House. Engraving (1645).

To view the towering tops of Mountains, unaccessible Rocks, with ridgie extents, or sudden fractions, by some steepy abruptnesse: Here a vally, so large, that at the end of the plain, it seems to meet Heaven; there a Grove, and here a Green pleasant arbour; rows of trees, spreading their clasping arms, like gentle lovers embracing each other, with intricate weavings; gently swelling hillocks; high delightful plains; flowry meddows; pleasant streams; natural fountains, gushing waters down rocks.

[p. 5]

It is virtually a catalogue of landscapes painted and collected during the seventeenth and early eighteenth centuries; there are also some close parallels between its list and the various configurations of garden scenery that Evelyn itemized in his letter to Browne.

Towards the end of the seventeenth century there was a widespread appreciation of an increasingly varied range of landscape paintings. Not everybody was as unequivocally metropolitan a spirit as Harriet Woodvill in George Etherege's play, *The Man of Mode*: she could not tolerate landscapes even in tapestries. Yet it is equally apparent that much landscape painting collected or admired after the Restoration had little in

PLATE 19 William Lodge, prospect of Nun Appleton House. Drawing (?1670's).

common with most contemporary gardens. The most admired paintings were topographical. This sort of subject echoed the philosophical and scientific temper of the time: an *Essay towards an English School* (1706) noted that a Dutch artist, Gérard de Edema, painted cliffs, cascades, and 'views (as the learned Dr Burnet in his *Theory* calls it) of a broken world'. Artists like Francis Place sought to record large topographical panoramas as well as more intricate features of geology and geography. William Lodge drew prospects like that of 'ye Ld. Fairfax House at Nun Appleton' [plate 19], carefully noting that the scene was drawn 'from the foot way to Cawood'; though he shows the 'Abbyss' of riverside meadows where Marvell's entertainments were set, Lodge is more concerned to provide an objective record of the ingredients of the country scene. Many of the artists providing topographical subjects were Dutch—Danckerts, Jan Griffier, Jan Siberechts—and some of their English drawings in the British Museum are among the most remarkable of this genre. A taste for topographical pictures coincided with the expression of reservations about French gardening, if Evelyn's case is typical: he pleaded in *Sculptura* (1662) for more topographical painting, and he interested himself in Dutch genre painting, which mediates between the stricter recording motive of topography and an idealizing vision of landscape.

Rubens's *Castle of Steen* [plate 20] combines all these recipes: there is the topographical motive, for the painter describes his own country seat; the genre elements are there in the man stalking game, the cattle in the fields beyond the stream, the market cart and the gentry airing themselves beside the castle; suffusing the whole landscape is a keen sensibility to the lights and rhythms of the land, to the expressive features of the countryside, yet this attention to phenomena rather sustains than works against an insistent sense of the ideal quality of the pastoral scene—as Richard Blome explained in his section on painting in *The Gentleman's Recreation* (1686), borrowing in his turn from Peacham's *Graphice* (1612), a 'landskip is the expressing the perfect vision of the Earth'. And, presumably for reasons similar to Blome's, Addison in the *Spectator* 417 describes the perfect visions of Virgil's *Georgics* as 'a collection of the most delightful Landskips that can be made out of Fields and woods, Herds of Cattle, and Swarms of Bees'.

It has been suggested that the history of landscape painting might be written in terms of the process by which a distinction between topographical and ideal landscape disappeared: 'the esthetic values created by artists in their ideal landscapes were transferred to their topographical pictures. From there it was an easy step to transfer the same values to natural scenery itself, to find the same kinds of enjoyment in actual views as in ideal prospects, and to associate with external nature the moods imparted by landscapists to their canvases'. Although it is suggested that this process may be traced between Patinir and Turner, it is also a movement visible within the late seventeenth century itself. Rubens allows his topographical account of the *Castle of Steen* to be suffused with the elegaic mood of his less specific, pastoral pictures (*The Castle of Steen* itself is properly an autumn piece and so partly an ideal subject). Similarly he offers a combination of topography, contemporary conversation piece, and ideal mythological landscape in *St George and the Dragon* [plate 21].

Besides Dutch art there were also paintings from Italy that were beginning to make some impact in England by 1700. The work of Claude Lorrain [see plate 11], Nicolas Poussin [plate 22], Gaspard Dughet, and Salvator Rosa would have been known to travellers long before they were copied by artists like John Wootton in the 1720's or circulated later in engravings [plates 23 and 24]. These landscapes from Italy were mainly idealized scenes, compositions dedicated both to moods, whether the pastoral landscapes of Claude or the wilder scenes with banditti for which Rosa was known, and to mythological subjects, ideal histories appropriately located in redolent and heroic territory. Travellers who visited the Roman Campagna or the Naples area might have recognized the inspiration that Claude or Rosa derived from real scenery, but the force of their pictures was undoubtedly and primarily that marvellously *imagined* visions of landscape were offered.

This ideal art was particularly attractive to those who advocated a new style in gardening, for it provided apt visual images

PLATE 20   Peter Paul Rubens, *The Castle of Steen*.
Oil painting (after 1635).

for the ideas of paradise and the golden age, with which gardens
were associated. It also provided, if not actual blueprints of
design, at least suggestions for the arrangement of temples and
statues among wooded and watered landscapes. It was this art,
as well as Dutch paintings, that was invoked both by Addison,
when he talked of a man making 'a pretty Landskip of his

possessions' (Spectator 414) or of composing a garden into a 'picture of the greatest variety' (Spectator 477), and by Vanbrugh, when in a famous episode he advised the Duchess of Marlborough to 'send for a landscape painter', considering that the Old Woodstock Manor provided a vista as good as 'the best Landskip Painters can invent'. The debt of the early landscape

PLATE 21   Peter Paul Rubens, *St George and the Dragon*.
Oil painting (after 1629).

PLATE 22   Nicolas Poussin, *Diogenes*.
Oil painting (1648).

THE FIGURE IN THE LANDSCAPE

gardeners to foreign scenes and foreign pictures was summarised in the 1770's, when William Mason came to write the history of *The English Garden* in indifferent verses:

    your eyes entranc'd
Shall catch those glowing scenes, that taught a Claude
To grace his canvas with Hesperean hues:
And Scenes like these, on Memory's tablet drawn
Bring back to Britain; these give local form
To each idea; and, if Nature lend
Materials fit of torrent, rock and shade,
Produce new Tivolis.

Mason records another, crucial element in this early taste for landscape paintings when he writes of localizing an 'idea'. For later landscape gardens, designed as a (more or less complex) series of exercises in associationism, owed their basic assumptions about how minds react to scenery as much to a taste for seventeenth-century pictures as to the epistemological theories of John Locke and his followers. Paintings related some incident or story to the expressive scenery in which it was depicted. An idea or event was felt to have some distinct correlation to where it took place—treatments of the story of Echo and Narcissus were the most obvious opportunity on which to explore the connections. But in a work like Claude's *Landscape with Psyche at the Palace of Cupid*, known also as *The Enchanted Castle*, the poignant figure of Psyche is placed in a scene of intensely elegiac colouring that evidently mirrors her grief. This was one of the earliest pictures to reach London from Italy, bought by a Mr. D'Avenant in the 1720's. In a different mood Rosa's landscapes suggested connections between 'horrid' and rocky scenery and incidents of solitary exile. Rosa's own professed wish for solitude and hermit simplicity could easily be melodramatized (see, for example, his self-portrait in the National Gallery, London); but in some potent landscapes, like that with *St John the Baptist pointing out Christ or Empedocles leaping into Etna*, he provides ideas of the central dramatis persona with a suitably expressive visual imagery.

One image of melancholy seclusion, especially famous in the seventeenth century through engraved reproductions, was Rosa's *Democritus in Meditation* [plate 25]. Democritus was virtually synonymous with the idea of solitary meditation: he enjoyed a double reputation, being both a mocker of the vanities of life seen from the vantage point of retirement, which appealed to English satirists, and a lonely master of great knowledge, notably a student of anatomy, which attracted the scientific spirits. Rosa shows his character meditating in a large landscape, surrounded with an academic apparatus of emblematic props. Though the painting was executed at a stage in his career (1650) when Rosa was stimulated to move away from land-

PLATE 23   Gaspard Dughet, *Landscape*.
Engraving published by Pond (1744).

scapes towards more important themes, he can still call upon
his expertise with expressive scenery to augment the more
learned machinery.

Painted landscapes articulate and localize ideas both by
iconographical images and by expressive manipulation of the
colouring and 'mood' of scenery. Our reading of these two-
dimensional forms and our conversion of them in the imagina-

PLATE 24 Salvator Rosa, *Landscape*.
Engraving published by Pond (1744).

tion into 'real' scenes was discussed in the seventeenth century by Norgate in his *Miniatura*:

The greatest conning is to beguile and cossen your own eyes, which yet you cannot do without their own consent and assistance by an apt accommodation of variety of colours in their due places, in such manner that many times in a table [i.e., picture] of not a spanne long a man's imagination may be quite carried out of the country over seas and cities by a surprise of his owne making.

Such imaginative activity is still rather mistrusted and is identified by Norgate in the published version with 'Deceptive visions'. But the process by which a pictured landscape incites the mind was easily transferred to real ones or those described in words. If the one early eighteenth-century commentator, already quoted, was provoked by Edema's pictures to think of the theories of Thomas Burnet, the author of *The Sacred Theory of the Earth* had himself already connected quite explicitly the actual sight of confused and irregular mountains with our mental ideas: 'There is nothing doth more awaken our thoughts or excite our minds to enquire into the causes of such things, then the actual view of them'. Similarly Shaftesbury, undoubtedly influenced by Burnet's *Theory*, found that 'the apparent spoil and

PLATE 25 Salvator Rosa, *Democritus in Meditation.*
Etching with drypoint (1662).

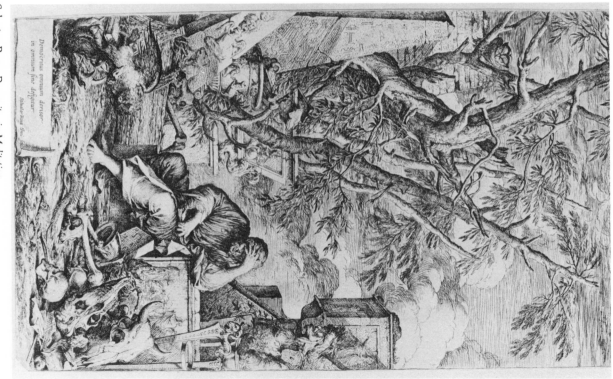

irreparable breaches of the wasted mountain' were productive
of ideas that worked with 'an unknown force . . . on the mind'.

By the end of the seventeenth century these mental exchanges between figures and painted or real landscapes had
been given a proper vocabulary and thus considerable status by
the writings on the human mind first of Hobbes and then, more
importantly as far as the eighteenth century was concerned, of

Locke. In his *Essay Concerning Human Understanding* (1690) Locke explains how sense stimuli—notably what we see—provide the mind with simple ideas, which are afterwards compared and combined into more complex ones. His chapter "Of the Association of Ideas" was added to the fourth edition of the *Essay* in 1700. Though it emphasized association as an unusual activity of the mind, which 'hinders man from seeing and examining' and which is prejudicial to the understanding, Locke's perjorative emphasis did not prevent much favourable application of the theory; later writers like Hume provided a less prejudiced interpretation. All of this psychological theory was of particular consequence to those, like gardenists and painters, who set themselves to construct various relationships between a figure and a landscape. By providing a spectator with certain stimuli, such as images or inscriptions in a garden, one might revive in his mind a whole range of ideas, combining them with ideas already deposited there from previous encounters. Thus in 1719 Jonathan Richardson describes one of the chief ends of painting in *Two Discourses* as 'to Communicate Ideas' (p. 12), a phrase that draws upon the language of Lockean epistemology. Addison, as will be seen in the next chapter, discusses garden art in a similar fashion.

The associative potential of painted landscapes, then, and the connections contrived within a picture between figures and scenery powerfully influenced the new thinking about gardens. Rosa's Democritus inhabits a large and varied landscape of meditation; by contrast, the figure of Democritus who appears on the title page of Burton's *Anatomy of Melancholy* [plate 26] is confined within a walled and neatly ordered garden. Burton

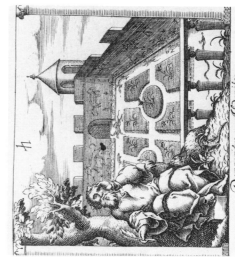

PLATE 26   Christian Le Blon, *Democritus*. Engraved vignette from title page of Burton's *Anatomy of Melancholy* (1628).

Borrowed from
the Poets

certainly recommended gardens and landscapes for the melancholic man; maybe it is therefore apt that the figure has turned
his back upon that simple and unvarious garden and has retired
to the shade of a tree, which seems—if we can trust the
perspective—almost outside its walls. Perhaps the placing of the
figure in Le Blon's engraving is a subtle reference to the tale
L. B. Alberti tells of Democritus condemning 'the inclosing a
Garden with any Sort of Wall'. But, in comparison with the
vignette and its old-fashioned image of a walled garden,
whether rejected or not, the type of landscape in which Rosa
places his Democritus has obviously more potential for stimulating ideas. Even the garden of Wilton House, let alone those at
Hampton Court, cannot match the flexible and various scenery
of paintings by Dughet, Rosa, Claude, or Poussin. There were
no gardens that could provide, as Edema did, both a scenery that
recalled Burnet *and* the calmer prospect that he painted from
Richmond Hill (at Hampton Court).

The variety of landscapes and variety in landscapes to which
such paintings introduced the late seventeenth-century gardenist—Evelyn is particularly eloquent on this topic in his *Essay
on . . . Lucretius* (London, 1656)—matched the sense of change
and variety in the human passions and soul. From Montaigne to
Pope, connections between the two were made constantly and
became a basic equation, as will be seen, in the philosophy of the
English landscape garden. Their identity and congruence were
undoubtedly helped by the growing attention to landscape
paintings in the seventeenth century, especially those where
some sympathetic connections between scenery and figures
seemed to be established. For example, Paul Brill's engraving of
'The Hermitage' contrasts the rigours of the hermit's section of
the landscape—broken branches, twisted roots—with the
gentler prospects of georgic activity in the valley below. Many
landscapes engraved by Aegidius and Raphael Sadeler, popular
engravers, contrive some relationship between figures and their
surroundings: either an artist sketching rocks and a bridge
[plate 27] or two travellers pausing in the foreground of a
mountainous landscape, the pointing arm of the seated figure
gesturing to the refreshing valley seen from the rocky, dark
path.

The taste for landscape which painting declared was supported,
if somewhat tendentiously, by literature. When Switzer issued
his enlarged volume of *Ichnographia Rustica* (1718), he collected
for it an anthology of writings that endorsed the new spirit in
garden design. Or rather, they were passages which were
susceptible to radical interpretation.

Cowley invoked literature for his vision of the countryside:
'what I have further to say of the Country Life, shall be

PLATE 27   Aegidius Sadeler, *The Draughtsman at the Foot of the Rocks Facing the Bridge.*
Engraving after Roelandt Savery (date unknown).

borrowed from the Poets' (p. 405). Yet it is unclear whether he
found their descriptions answered his own experience or he
preferred to surrender autobiographical accuracy to the delights
of conventional allusion. Sometimes we can believe that Cowley's 'country-houses and retreat' were not a conspicuously
artificial world:

Here, Nature does a house for me erect:
Nature, the wisest architect,
Who those fond artists does despise
That can the fair and living trees neglect;
Yet the dead timber prize.

[p. 395]

But the possible allusion to Marvell's "Dialogue Between the
Soul and the Body" should make us wary of reading this
literally. As a boy, Cowley tells us, he would steal 'into the
fields, either alone with a book, or with some one companion, if
I could find any of the same temper' (p. 456). Yet we should
avoid imagining him as Joseph Wright of Derby was later to
paint Brooke Boothby, reclining at ease in the forest with his
copy of Rousseau [plate 28]. Among the books Cowley took
with him were Spenser, Virgil, or Horace: and these were
susceptible to various readings.

The *Georgics*, as Cowley explained, seemed consistent with the Royal Society's own horticultural and agricultural ambitions. His essay "Of Agriculture" concludes with a translation of Virgil's famous vision of the husbandman:

Mean while, the prudent Husbandman is found,
In mutual duties striving with his ground,
And half the year he care of that does take,
That half the year grateful returns does make.
Each fertil month does some new gifts present,
And with new work his industry content.
This, the young Lamb, that the soft Fleece doth yield,
This, loads with Hay, and that, with Corn the Field:
All sorts of Fruit crown the rich *Autumns Pride*:
And on a swelling Hill's warm stony side,
The powerful Princely Purple of the Vine,
Twice dy'd with the redoubled Sun, does Shine.

[p. 411]

Such an agricultural paradise seemed to combine the intimations of Arcadia or Eden that were an essential tradition of gardens with the urge for experimental science that persons like Evelyn found a place for in their gardens. It was a combination that Francis Bacon had also contrived in his provision of an 'eternal spring' through horticultural experiment. Cowley's

version of Horace made that poet, too, speak of these endeavours:

Sometimes the beateous, Marriageable Vine
He to the lusty Bridegroom Elm does joyn;
Sometimes he lops the barren Trees around,
And grafts new Life into the fruitful wound;
Sometimes he shears his Flock, and sometimes he
Stores up the Golden Treasure of the Bee.
He sees his lowing Herds walk o'er the Plain,
Whilst neighbouring Hills low back to them again.   [p. 412]

These rural activities seemed to provide a fresh and appropriate theology for what might be called the 'hermits of a new model'. Dryden's translation of Virgil gave exactly this meaning to the *beatus ille* theme: 'Happy the man, who studying nature's laws, / Through known effects can trace the sacred cause'.

If Virgil and Horace appeared to support the philosophical enquiries of the Royal Society they also provided a suitable vocabulary for solitude and gardens—from Cowley's essays on those topics, which invoke the Roman poets, through Pope whose Twickenham villa became (at least in his Horatian imitations) some English equivalent of the Roman's Sabine Farm and solitudes, to Akenside's *Odes* that seem to speak in Horace's and Virgil's phrase:

How oft shall I survey
This humble roof, the lawn, the greenwood shade,
    The vale with sheaves o'erspread,
The glassy brook, the flocks which round thee stray?

Simply because Horace's Sabine farm was not fully delineated ('si vacuum tepido cepisset villula tecto') nor its exact location then known, there was ample scope for reading the Latin in contemporary English ways. Thus Horace's prayer,

Hoc erat in votis: modus agri non ita magnus,
hortus ubi et tecto vicinus iugis aquae fons
et paulum silvae super his foret

becomes Pope's

I've often wish'd that I had clear
For life, six hundred pounds a year,
A handsome house to lodge a friend,
A River at my garden's end,
A Terras-walk, and half a Rood
Of land, set out to plant a Wood.

The basic Latin ingredients could be interpreted to endorse anything from Pope's grotto to Queen Caroline's Hermitage. And similarly Horace's lines on the gladiator who retired deep into the country—'Vejanius armis / Herculis ad postem fixis latet abditus agro'—were rendered both by Poussin's arcadian scenery, with a figure of Vejanus set far back into its rich serenity, and by Pope's lines that discover for Horace a particularly English flavour again:

Our generals now, retir'd to their Estates,
Hang their old Trophies o'er the Garden gates,
In Life's cool evening satiate of applause,
Nor fond of bleeding, ev'n in Brunswick's cause.

The very appeal of the Latin writings was perhaps the vagueness of their prescriptions for a country retreat:

        at mihi cura
non mediocris inest, fontis ut adire remotos
atque haurire queam vitae praecepta beatae.

But where they received, by the nature of the medium, some definition was the illustrated editions. Since many of the artists employed on these texts were Dutch, the tastes in landscape painting that we have already noticed came to be associated with the Roman poets. In the *Emblemata Horatiana* (Antwerp, 1607) Otto van Veen provided a series of natural, rural images—a man reading in the countryside, away from a walled town; a scene where buildings are being constructed beside a stream, a team is led off to plough, and a man rests on his shovel; a visual version of the *beatus ille* theme, with ploughing and the culture of vines. Such images must have directed the readers of the text towards visualizing Horace's poetry in various contemporary modes. This is equally true of Cleyn's pictures for Virgil, used in 1633, 1654 and, most magnificently, in the folio of Dryden's *Virgil* of 1697: here is the same range of landscape imagery, which again draws upon Dutch painting, and which runs from descriptive rural scenes, through horticultural activities that proceed at the edge of some formal garden [plate 29], to pastoral visions where gentlemen in contemporary full-bottomed wigs inhabit a Claudian landscape. If Cleyn seems to have rephrased Virgil in the various visual idioms of his age, Dryden's translation similarly keeps its options open with a mixture of pastoral language, the vocabulary of English country estates and ambiguous suggestions of parks and gardens:

The country king his peaceful realm enjoys —
Cool grots, and living lakes, the flow'ry pride
Of meads, and streams that through the valley glide,
And shady groves

Dryden is probably recalling Cowley's translation of the same passage in *Georgis* II, where 'artless grots' (p. 409), rivers, and forest already suggest an English landscape garden. But it is doubtful whether, when Cowley left his 'Hired house and

Garden, among *Weeds and Rubbish*' (p. 421), he found many gardens that owed as little to human contrivance and artificiality as his verses suggest. When, on another occasion, he wishes to imitate Scipio's 'voluntary exile . . . at a private house in the middle of a wood', we can be fairly sure that the wood, as

To Sʳ William Bowyer Baronet
of Denham Court in the County of Bucks.

R. Cleyn inv.
W. Hollar fec.

Geor. I. li.

PLATE 29   Franz Cleyn, engraved by Hollar.
Design for John Dryden's *The Works of Virgil* (1697).

53   GREEN THOUGHTS AND SHADES

Timothy Nourse advises, would be kept at the same height as the house and lightened by various approach roads and walks radiating from the semicircle in front of the building. In short, if the illustrations and texts of Horace and Virgil suggest a taste for less controlled landscapes, contemporary topographical paintings of Siberechts and Robert Streater show estates ordered without much respect for variety let alone irregularity.

The Latin poets provided Dryden (and, it would generally appear, Cowley) with models of what he called 'the First innocence, and Simplicity'; yet the golden age imaged in their poetry is, for the moderns, only 'fabulous, and impracticable' and therefore aptly represented by landscapes with no signs of mankind's acquired technologies. We are contending here with an intricate matrix of cultural ideas. For the followers of what Arthur O. Lovejoy called the school of 'hard primitivism', man had evolved from a bestial state, and gardens of the French model declare the technical and intellectual supremacy that man has finally achieved over the beasts. For the theorists of 'soft primitivism', the original state of ideal perfection from which man relapsed was approximated in modern times by landscapes innocent of human skill and artistry. Dryden declares himself of the 'hard primitivist' persuasion, then, when his stage direction for the Garden of Eden in *The State of Innocence* requires a normal Restoration garden as best representing an ordered and rational innocence. Contrarily, when James Shirley rejects gardens that display the 'art of man' and requires a more natural plot of land where he may meditate alone he is writing within the tradition ('soft primitivism') that equates the fabulous golden age with natural landscapes.

These intellectual debates were registered also in discussions of garden design. The pomp and circumstance of French gardening, that mirrored man's supreme control over his environment, were unpopular with those gardenists in England who wished for less controlled spaces and more intricate and subtle, because more natural, manipulations of garden scenery. For these latter, contemporary landscape paintings from Holland and Italy and their reading of Virgil and Horace offered images of the golden age that gardens could imitate. But poems and pictures were still visions of art. It was a rare spirit who actually preferred the Derbyshire Peak to representations of it, or its moors to the marvellous ingenuities of Chatsworth, that appear, in Siberechts' famous painting, as an oasis among horrid wastes [plate 30]. Even Charles Cotton, whose poem on *The Wonders of the Peake* takes a perverse delight in its wild prospects, a kind of hard primitivist's *nostalgie de la boue*, still finds the garden of Chatsworth a 'Paradise' in the 'midst of Deserts, and of barren Sands'.

PLATE 30   Jan Sieberechts, *Chatsworth*.
Oil painting (c. 1710).

There were some literary precedents for natural landscapes
that declared themselves without ambiguity. Shaftesbury's
view of the innate goodness of natural man was inevitably
towards 'things of a natural kind; where neither Art, nor the
Conceit or Caprice of Man has spoil'd their genuine order'. He
links his philosophical love for 'rude Rocks, the mossy Caverns,
the irregular unwrought Grotto's . . . all the horrid Graces of
the Wilderness itself' with an aversion to contemporary styles
of garden that he sardonically categorizes in a footnote to
Miscellaneous Reflections. His objection to the latter is that their
contrived 'harmony' and 'symmetries' are a presposterous mirror of the usual minds of their 'princely' possessors.

Perhaps the most famous literary declaration in favour of
'natural' gardens came in Milton's description of Eden, in
distinct contrast to the topography of one of his sources.
Illustrations to Andreini's *L'Adamo* (Milan, 1613) show the

55   GREEN THOUGHTS AND SHADES

Earthly Paradise as a strictly planned garden, with the animals dutifully honouring the geometry by placing themselves along the axes; it is only for the scenes of Adam's temptation and of life after the expulsion that the humans are shown in a hostile landscape of rocks, woods, and even broken trees in the manner that was to become Salvator Rosa's signature. By contrast, Milton chooses to present his prelapsarian world as miraculously free from the contrivances of art. The passage in the fourth book of *Paradise Lost* became almost a sacred text for those, from Switzer onwards, who championed the 'landscape garden'. From it they derived authority for serpentine lines, natural treatment of water, rural mounds, wooded theatres, and for the rejection of 'nice Art / In Beds and curious Knots' in favour of 'Nature boon / Powrd forth profuse on Hill and Dale and Plaine'. Admirers of Milton's prototype landscape garden were content to ignore the ambiguities of the passage: its invocation of the art term, 'Lantskip', for what is supposed to be a scene freed from art; Milton's linking of his Eden with 'Hesperian Fables', as if to suggest the ultimate unreality or, in Dryden's terms, impracticality of such a scene. Nevertheless, upon Milton's picture of the garden inhabited by our first parents were to be based many rural seats of various view during the century that followed *Paradise Lost*.

Not only in his account of Eden but in the exercises of *L'Allegro* and *Il Penseroso* did Milton provide fresh visions of landscapes, and landscapes, too, which established some real connections with their human occupants. Two types of mind are provided with their expressive scenery: the mirthful —'Straight mine eye hath caught new pleasures, / Whilst the landscape round it measures'—and the melancholic—the 'uncouth cell, . . . under ebon shades and low-browed rocks'. The conventional pastoral scenery of *L'Allegro* is transformed into a fresh landscape of the spirit. *Il Penseroso*, destined to appeal more forcibly to eighteenth-century taste, offers more exact parallels and forms of identification. The hints of Orphic mysteries or Hermetic skills, announced by the motifs of lonely towers and 'peaceful hermitage', could be ignored to concentrate upon ideal retreats for the pensive man—'trim gardens' certainly, but also the 'arched walks of twilight groves . . . in close covert by some brook'; or the solitary could

> walk the studious cloister's pale,
> And love the high embowed roof,
> With antique pillars massy proof,
> And storied windows richly dight
> Casting a dim religious light.

Il Penseroso is invoked by the author of *Spectator* 425 (possibly Pope), as he says, 'naturally', while walking in his garden. That is just one of many testimonies during the eighteenth-century to the inspiration that gardenists derived from the poets.

Tomorrow to Fresh Fields

The *hortus conclusus*, its religious emblems, and the ways of thinking it had once appropriately imaged were gradually abandoned in the years of the Restoration. Something of the new temper may be guessed from Walter Montague's remarks on melancholy:

We are to be found truly no where but in our selves, everywhere else we meet but with our fantasme or our shadow. And therefore many have reason to say, that Meditation is harder than Extasie, as it is easier to go out of our selves, than to re-enter in to them, without the use of this noble thoughtfulness, to which the temper of Melancholy is disposed.

The ecstasy of religious fervour gives way to the noble thoughtfulness of empirical meditation. And this new role for the 'hermit' meant new landscapes and 'hermitages' that would be suitable for him: as Thomas Gray was to say much later, 'I had an Idea, but did not know where to put it, for an Idea must have a place *per campeggiar bene'*. Among those who had seen where the modern temper of melancholy could well pitch camp was Robert Burton, who listed the ingredients of its proper landscape—

bowers, mounts, and arbours, artificial wildernesses, green thickets, arches, groves, lawns, rivulets, fountains . . . some pleasant plain, park . . . a steep hill . . . a shady seat.

His and others' prophetic vision was realized in the parks of the landscape garden. Yet what we today identify as the 'English landscape garden'—the open spaces, the lakes and woods and streams that seem but more carefully maintained segments of the English landscape itself—these came only very gradually into being. There were many stages in the long progress between what Edmund Waller celebrated in *A Poem on St James's Park As Lately Improved by His Majesty* of 1661 and what Gainsborough shows of *St James Park* in 1783.

Among those who contributed most to this slow revolution in design were Addison and Alexander Pope, of whom Bolingbroke said that he 'had contributed very much . . . to the making of a hermit of me'. The vocabulary of hermit still persists. But it was Pope and his friends who managed fresh revisions of an old idea as well as fresh landscapes for it to occupy. We must now turn to the villa in Twickenham where Pope

Enjoys his Garden and his Book in quiet
And then—a perfect Hermit in his diet.

TWO

Gardening, and Poetry, and Pope

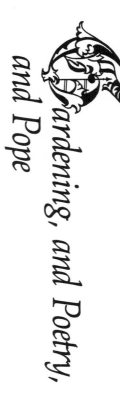

*Scenes for
Contemplation*

An Essay on Man begins with a various landscape employed as a metaphor of human territory:

Let us (since Life can little more supply
Than just to look about us and to die)
Expatiate free o'er all this scene of Man;
A mighty maze! but not without a plan;
A Wild, where weeds and flow'rs promiscuous shoot,
Or Garden, tempting with forbidden fruit.
Together let us beat this ample field,
Try what the open, what the covert yield;
The latent tracts, the giddy heights explore
Of all who blindly creep, or sightless soar

[*Poems*, 3/i: 11–12]

The word 'expatiäte' (i.e., talk freely *and literally* wander about) establishes an implicit equation between the mind's activity and the different features of an English park that the conversationalists visit during their philosophical stroll. The poem borrows much from Pope's friend, Bolingbroke, whose advice that 'Every man's reason is every man's oracle; this oracle is best consulted in the silence of retirement' was also Pope's conviction. The retirement that Pope organized for himself—that is to say, both his consultations with the oracle and the landscape in which they take place—is the initial subject of this chapter.

We possess two striking images of Pope in this role of hermit—those sketches by the Countess of Burlington (or maybe by William Kent) that show him at work in his grotto [plate 31]. So strong, indeed, was the contemporary identification of the poet with this part of his Twickenham landscape that after his death the titlepage of William Mason's monody, *Musaeus*, carried Hayman's engraving of Pope as a patrician Roman dying in the grotto among his friends [plate 32]; the design is feeble and, of course, circumstantially inaccurate, but its iconography is significant. Another item of visual evidence —an oil painting possibly by Pope and certainly based on his own design for *An Essay on Man*—completes our initial orientation [plate 33]: it recalls, as perhaps it was meant to, Rosa's *Democritus in Meditation* [plate 25] and shows a passable self portrait in an emblematic and expressive landscape.

PLATE 31   Dorothy, Countess of Burlington (?), Pope in his grotto.

This dedication to solitary reflection in a suitably chosen landscape was announced as early as 1717, when Pope told Atterbury that the 'Contemplative life is not only my *scene*, but it is my habit too'. For the 'Hurry, noise, and the observances of the world', he told another correspondent eight years later, 'take away the power of just thinking or natural acting. A man that lives so much in the world does but translate other men; he is nothing of his own'; and he adds Seneca's apophthegm, 'Qui notus nimis omnibus / Ignotus moritur sibi'. The self-knowledge that he himself acquired during his career is closely linked to his activities as a gardenist. The contemplative habit he spoke of to Atterbury found its ideal mirror in his garden: 'my Garden like my Life, seems every *Year* to want Correction and require alteration'. Near the end of his life he devoted enormous energies to completing his grotto: he explained that this was both because 'I should be more sorry to leave it unfinished, than any other *Work*' and because it provided an ideal 'study for Virtuosi, and a Scene for Contemplation'.

PLATE 32   Francis Hayman, engraving from title page of William Mason's *Musaeus: A Monody* (1747).

Artful Wildness to Perplex

In *Spectator* essay 406 (1712) Pope distinguished between two human inclinations by invoking two kinds of waterworks:

Some men, like pictures, are fitter for a corner than a full light; and I believe such as have a natural bent to solitude, are like waters which may be forced into fountains, and exalted to a great height, may make a much nobler figure and a much louder noise; but after all run more smoothly, equally, and plentifully, in their own natural course upon the ground.

Pope's dismay at forcing water into what W. H. Auden calls 'conspicuous fountains' is closely related to his satire on topiary the following year in *The Guardian* (No. 173). 'Monstrous attempts beyond the reach of art' distort the natural and regular shapes of garden trees and bushes into the 'most awkward figures of men and animals': among others—

Adam and Even in yew: Adam a little shattered by the fall of the tree of knowledge in the great storm: Eve and the serpent very flourishing.

St. George in box: his arm scarce long enough, but will be in condition to stick the dragon by next April.

A topping Ben Jonson in laurel.

A quickset hog, shot up into a porcupine, by its being forgot a week in rainy weather.

Noah's ark in holly, standing on the mount: the ribs a little damaged for want of water.

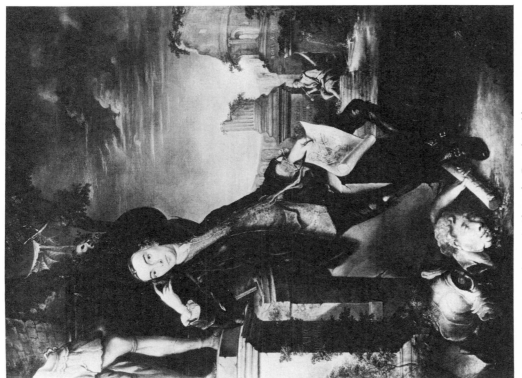

PLATE 33 Anonymous (once attrib. Pope), Alexander Pope (1730's).
Oil painting after Pope's own design for *An Essay on Man*.

The thrust of Pope's wit should not be interpreted as a plea for uncompromising naturalism. Though he begins by regretting any recession from nature 'in the various tonsure of greens into the most regular and formal shapes', his main theme in fact is that difficult and proper balance between art and nature: 'those who are most capable of Art, are always most fond of Nature; as such are chiefly sensible, that all Art consists in the imitation and study of Nature'. Such an attitude has been nicely glossed by Maynard Mack as '"nature" . . . discovered in (and also brought to) her perfection only by means of art'. We have already seen one example of this in Gilpin's praise of Stowe's hermitage for not exceeding a probable nature. Another would be Pope's explanation that his grotto was designed to 'resemble Nature in all her workings'.

Modern adjudications of these continuous Renaissance debates over art and nature can be peculiarly ineffective. At the point when we think to understand the exact drift and emphasis of an argument, it is illustrated in ways that compromise our sense of perspective. Nowhere is this demonstrated better than in Addison's *Spectator* 477. It takes the form of a letter from a garden enthusiast whose self-declared taste is for 'confusion' and 'the greatest Variety' in his garden, which would seem to a foreigner 'a natural Wilderness and one of the uncultivated parts of our Country'; his 'little wandering rill', like that of Pope's *Spectator* piece, flows 'as it would do in an open Field'. Yet his letter continues by praising the conversion by London and Wise of the gravel-pit in Kensington Gardens, of which we have independent visual evidence. Certainly it is, in the terms of his argument, an example of the 'heroic' style in gardening, which he distinguishes from his own 'Pindarick' preference; but it is described in ways that make it seem consistent with his own garden: there are 'several little Plantations' on one side, and on the other a 'seeming Mount, made up of trees rising one higher than another in proportion as they approach the Centre'. But it is impossible to square surviving designs for this gravel-pit with the writer's sense that it answers his own taste for the natural. Even Addison's contemporaries could see it in a different light, as Thomas Tickell's lines reveal:

That hollow space where now, in living *rows*
Line above line the yew's sad verdure grows,
Was, ere the planter's hand its beauty gave,
A common pit, a rude unfinished cave.

Unless we are just to abandon the debate, we must find—in the absence of any absolute scale of ratios between art and nature—some other considerations. These may be discovered, I suggest, in the *reasons* given or implied for some natural or artificial taste. In other words we should ask *why* Pope, or Addison (who shares with Pope the early promotion of the English landscape garden), urged upon his contemporaries gardens where art studies to imitate nature. Addison, more explicitly than Pope, champions them because they satisfy fresh visions of the human mind, because they answer to new habits of thought. To adapt Pope's phrase used as a title for the next section, gardens grew according to the structures discovered in the human psyche.

Pope's attack on topiary—Addison joins him in scorning the 'Marks of the Scissors' in *Spectator* 414—focuses upon its absurd associations, which his humorous obscenities in the catalogue are perhaps, like the pun ('Adam and Eve in yew'), meant to imply. Faced in some garden with 'A pair of maidenheads in fir, in great forwardness', the mind is not at liberty to contemplate anything but the suggestions of the shaped trees. Confronted with such a pair of evergreen maidenheads the mind is not free to function as Addison had explained it in *Spectator* 417: the train of its thoughts, the 'whole Scene of Imagery . . . and Ideas', is unpleasantly, not to say weirdly, frustrated.

Now this liberty of association that both Addison and Pope champion is neither much emphasized nor at all connected by historians with the design of the English landscape garden. Yet it is as important as, and obviously connected with, another idea of liberty that *is* generally linked with the ideologies of the English garden. James Thomson formulated an already established notion when in his poem entitled *Liberty* (Book 5) he equated France's tyrannical government with her gardens:

Those parks and gardens, where, his haunts betrimmed,
And Nature by presumptuous art oppressed,
The woodland genius mourns

. . . .

Detested forms! that, on the mind imposed,
Corrupt, confound, and barbarize an age

By contrast, as Pope put it, 'brave Britons, Foreign Laws despis'd' and let their new landscape garden proclaim their freedom from tyranny, oppression, and autocracy. Addison's vision in *Tatler* 161 of the province of Liberty presents a landscape of 'greater variety' and 'a wonderful profusion of flowers'

that, without being disposed into regular borders and parterres, grew promiscuously; and had a greater beauty in their natural luxuriancy and disorder, than they could have received from the checks and restraints of art. There was a river . . . that by an infinite number of turnings and windings seemed to visit every plant, and cherish the several beauties of the spring.

But as Addison's dream and its associative structure proclaim, there is a further liberty that the garden may mirror—the 'fantastical phenomenon' that Locke discusses in his *Conduct* whereby the mind is filled by a rapid succession of fleeting images. So behind Pope's and Addison's advocacy of 'natural' forms in landscape lay their determination to provide contexts in which the mind in its many manifestations could 'expatiate' freely.

Addison is quite explicit in making this connection. On Sir Roger de Coverly's estate is an old abbey with an 'Eccho among the old Ruins and Vaults' that occasions some remarks on Locke's theory of associationism. These epistemological ideas are further explained in one of the famous *Spectator* papers on the Imagination by invoking the example of gardens and prospects:

a particular Smell or Colour is able to fill the Mind, on a sudden, with the Picture of the Fields or Gardens, where we first met with it, and to bring up into View all the Variety of Images that once attended it. Our Imagination takes the Hint, and leads us unexpectedly into Cities or Theatres, Plains or Meadows.

The role of a varied landscape in stimulating this sequence of mental ideas is a constant theme of Addison's; the 'perpetually shifting' movement of water particularly occupies the mind and for this reason

there is nothing that more enlivens a Prospect than Rivers, Jetteaus, or Falls of Water, where the Scene is perpetually shifting, and entertaining the Sight every Moment with something that is new. We are quickly tired with looking upon Hills and Valleys, where every thing continues fixt and settled in the same Place and Posture, but find our Thoughts a little agitated and relieved at the sight of such Objects as are ever in Motion.

It is the movement, too, of the landscapes projected through a camera obscura that attracts Addison, as it did Pope, to this device: 'the chief Reason is its near Resemblance to Nature, as it does not only, like other Pictures, give the Colour and Figure, but the Motion of the Thing it represents'.

If landscapes themselves do not include such motion to preoccupy the eye and mind, a diversity of their elements has the same psychological effect. The imagination, says Addison, is more fully and excitingly involved among the 'rough and careless Strokes of Nature' than in the 'nice Touches and Embellishments of Art':

The Beauties of the most stately Garden or Palace lie in a narrow Compass, the Imagination immediately runs them over, and requires something else to gratifie her; but, in the wide Fields of Nature, the Sight wanders up and down without Confinement, and is fed with an infinite variety of Images.

It is therefore this 'variety of Images' that Pope and Addison celebrate. Since the Dutch gardens of the Restoration years or the large set pieces in the French taste did not often seem to yield such diversity, it was to other scenery that they looked. If Pope thought that 'All Gardening is landscape-painting' it was in part because in the landscapes of a Claude or Dughet or Rosa there was a variety to answer the mind's own multiplicity. When this varied scenery was joined to the physical movement of a visitor through a garden, the variety was augmented. In *Spectator* 425, possibly by Pope, the writer visits his own garden by moonlight and the experience suggests to him a passage of Milton's "Il Penseroso" which 'exquisitely suited . . . my present *Wanderings of Thought*'. The phrase is eloquent of the new attitudes towards landscape. Nor should it perplex us that the garden actually explored by moonlight with such a rich associative response seems 'formal':

You descend at first by twelve Stone Steps into a large Square divided into four Grass-plots, in each of which is a Statue of white Marble. This is separated from a large Parterre by a low Wall, and from thence, thro' a Pair of Iron Gates, you are led into a long broad Walk of the finest Turf, set on each side with tall Yews, and on either Hand finest Turf, set on each side with tall Yews, and on either Hand a Canal, which on the Right divides the Walk from a Wilderness parted into Variety of Allies and Arbours, and on the Left from a kind of Amphitheatre, which is the Receptacle of a great number of Oranges and Myrtles.

The symmetry and patterns of this garden actually intensify the experience of its variety. The same seems to be true of Addison's rather surprising praise of continental gardening:

We have before observed, that there is generally in Nature something more Grand and August, than what we meet with in the Curiosities of Art. When therefore, we see this imitated in any measure, it gives us a nobler and more exalted kind of Pleasure than what we receive from the nicer and more accurate Productions of Art. On this Account our *English* Gardens are not so entertaining to the Fancy as those in *France* and *Italy*, where we see a large Extent of Ground, covered over with an agreeable mixture of Garden and Forest, which represent every where an artificial Rudeness, much more charming than that Neatness and Elegancy which we meet with in those of our own Country.

It is as much that 'agreeable Mixture' as the forest's 'Rudeness' that attracts Addison. A variety that agrees with 'the Mind of the Beholder' may be either natural and accidental or the result of art: the best variety will have the effects of *both*, since the mind is thereby even more involved in adjudicating the rival elements of Art and Nature, as, for example, at Bramham [plate 34]. This is explained in the same *Spectator* paper:

But tho' there are several of these wild Scenes, that are more delightful than any artificial Shows; yet we find the Works of Nature still more pleasant, the more they resemble those of Art: For in this case our Pleasure rises from a double Principle; from the Agreeableness of the Objects to the Eye, and from their Similitude to other Objects: We are pleased as well with comparing their Beauties as with surveying them, and can represent them to our Minds, either as Copies or Originals. Hence it is that we take Delight in a Prospect which is well laid out, and diversified with Fields and Meadows, Woods and Rivers; in those accidental Landskips of Trees, Clouds and Cities, that are sometimes found in the Veins of Marble; in the curious Fret-work of Rocks and Grottos; and, in a Word, in any thing that hath such a Variety or Regularity as may seem the Effect of Design, in what we call the Works of Chance.

If the Products of Nature rise in Value, according as they more or less resemble those of Art, we may be sure that artificial Works receive a greater Advantage from their Resemblance of such as are natural;

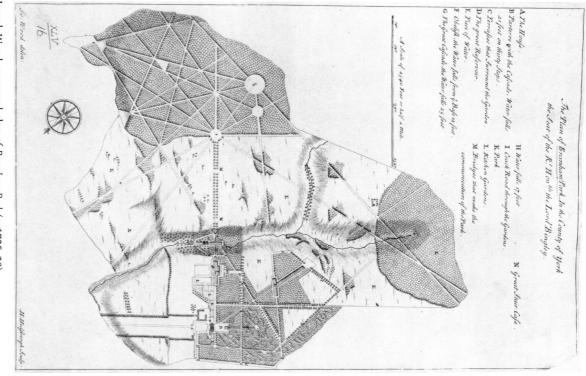

The Plan of Bramham Park. In the County of York
the Seat of the R.t Hon.ble the Lord Bingley.

A The Hous[e]
B Parterre with the Cascade, Water falls
21 feet on thirty Steps.
C Terrass that surmount the Garden.
D The great Reservoir.
E Piece of Water.
F Obelisk, the Water falls from ¾ Mile 12 feet.
G The great Cascade, the Water falls 25 feet

H Water falls 17 feet . . . N Great Stair Case
I Coach Road through the Garden.
K Park
L Kitchen Gardens.
M Bridge that make the
       communication of the Park.

PLATE 34   Joseph Wood, engraved plan of *Bramham Park* (c. 1725–28).

because here the Similitude is not only pleasant, but the Pattern more
perfect.

If the papers on the 'Pleasures of the Imagination' were
Addison's philosophical explanation of the mind's delight in
answering landscapes, there were other occasions on which he
discussed the same ideas less technically. The 'Pindarick' gardener, already quoted on the Kensington gravel-pit, is allowed
his own mode of explication. His whole garden is 'a Picture of the
greatest Variety': its collusion between art and nature especially

intrigues him, for he is 'pleased when I am walking in a Labyrinth of my own raising, not to know whether the next Tree I shall meet with is an Apple or an Oak, an Elm or a Pear-Tree'. (It is the reverse of Timon's Villa where Pope satirizes the groves nodding to predictably matching groves.) But this writer also tells us that he is 'looked upon as an Humorist in Gardening'—and that title's allusion to old-fashioned psychology enforces his boast that he has a garden that satisfies all his various mental needs at all times of the year. This gardener for all seasons has a winter garden of evergreens—rather an unpopular feature at the time, though one that Evelyn had pioneered at Sayes Court—and proves another example of Addison's theory, adumbrated later in *Spectator* 583, that '*you may Trace* [a man] . . . in the Place where he has lived'.

Varieties of garden not only became a means of declaring various psychological traits and habits, they were invoked to describe different kinds of imaginative skills: this concerns us particularly, because the literary history of the eighteenth century could partly be written in terms of the development of precisely those genres that were identified with the landscape garden. This in its turn may serve to show how the garden is an increasingly prominent and crucial feature of the century's aesthetic patterns.

In Addison we may find these ideas clearly set out. He first distinguishes between two kinds of literary talent: the genius of one sort is like 'a whole wilderness of noble Plants rising in a thousand beautiful landskips without any certain Order and Regularity'; the other sort is rather a garden 'laid out in Walks and Parterres, and cut into Shape and Beauty by the skill of the Gardener': too much imitation cramps this second sort's 'own natural parts'. From this it is clear in theory where Addison's tastes lay and that he looked to writers like Homer or Shakespeare for the superior genius as he did to naturally ordered gardens. In his later discussions of the Imagination he offers the classical poets as examples of noble writers who were 'able to receive lively ideas from outward objects, to retain them long, and to range them together' and who took pains to 'gain a due Relish of the Works of Nature, and be thoroughly conversant in the various Scenery of a Country Life'. Since Homer, Virgil, and Ovid stimulate our imaginations correspondingly, Addison's account of their talents is couched in terms of landscape:

The first strikes the Imagination wonderfully with what is Great, the second with what is Beautiful, and the last with what is Strange. Reading the *Iliad* is like travelling through a Country uninhabited, where the Fancy is entertained with a thousand Savage Prospects of vast Desarts, wide uncultivated Marshes, huge Forests, mis-shapen Rocks and Precipices. On the contrary, the *Aeneid* is like a well ordered

Garden, where it is impossible to find out any Part unadorned, or to cast our Eyes upon a single Spot, that does not produce some beautiful Plant or Flower. But when we are in the *Metamorphoses*, we are walking on enchanted Ground, and see nothing but Scenes of Magick lying round us.

Further landscapes and their correspondent literary talents are added in *Spectator* 477:

I think there are as many kinds of Gardening as of Poetry: Your Makers of Parterres and Flower-Gardens, are Epigrammatists and Sonneteers in this Art; Contrivers of Bowers and Grotto's, Treillages and Cascades, are Romance Writers. *Wise* and *London* are our Heroick Poets. . . . As for my self, you will find, by the Account which I have already given you, that my Compositions in Gardening are altogether after the *Pindarick* Manner, and run into the beautiful Wilderness of Nature, without affecting the nicer Elegancies of Art.

These catalogues and analogues suggest several themes that this and succeeding chapters will pursue. Certain long-established genres of literary history are linked rather uneasily to freshly discovered possibilities in gardening. Pope strove, in Addison's phrase, to 'go beyond Pastoral, and the lower kinds of Poetry', and compose poems of more ambitious scope to rival Virgil's; he attempted, in short, *all* the forms. Yet at the same time he came to dislike those gardens which Addison matched with epigram and even epic. Though he certainly championed variety in gardens, this corresponded to human variousness and not to neat schemes of literary versatility. Further, precisely those genres of romance and Pindaric ode that in the early part of the century seemed closest to the new landscape gardening were to gain in prestige by the 1750's at the expense of those tastes that Pope in his public pronouncements seemed to stand for. As will be seen, because romance and Pindaric passion had already found landscapes appropriate to their own visions and because those landscapes were fashionable, they mutually endorsed and promoted each other's interests.

Before Pope had his own garden, his poetry attested his interest in meditative and expressive landscapes. When he was only twelve his "Ode on Solitude" invoked the *beatus ille* theme with an emphasis that we can only see as prophetic:

Happy the man, whose wish and care
A few paternal acres bound,
Content to breathe his native air,
In his own ground.

Four years later his *Pastorals* explore the variety of grounds that match mood and idea: as Strephon says in "Spring":

In spring the fields, in autumn hills I love,
At morn the plains, at noon the shady grove,

[Poems, 6:3; my italics]

But Delia always; absent from her sight,
Nor plains at morn, nor groves at noon delight.   [Poems, 1:68]

The Pastorals make constant play with allusions to Echo and Narcissus—

To you I mourn, nor to the deaf I sing,
The woods shall answer, and their echo ring   [Poems, 1:72–73]

—simply to assert through a commonplace metaphor the responsiveness or lack of responsiveness between introspection and a surrounding scenery.

The dominant idea of the Pastorals—celebration of a golden age and its corollary, the golden kingdom of art—is expressed in landscapes of pastoral perfection and artistry that recall the ideal paintings of Claude and Poussin:

Here where the mountains less'ning as they rise,
Lose the low vales, and steal into the skies.
While labouring oxen, spent with toil and heat,
In their loose traces from the field retreat;
While curling smokes from village-tops are seen,
And the fleet shades glide o'er the dusky green.   [Poems, 1:84]

They are landscapes of mood, emblems of an impossible perfection, that the images of artifice ('And lavish Nature paints the purple year') are designed to recall:

Resound ye hills, resound my mournful strain!
Now bright Arcturus glads the teeming grain,
Now golden fruits on loaded branches shine,
And grateful clusters swell with floods of wine;
Now blushing berries paint the yellow grove   [Poems, 1:85]

These ideal landscapes, simply because of their mythic potency, are the appropriate scenes for gods. Just as Poussin's miraculous painting of Blind Orion Searching for the Rising Sun accommodates legendary visitors in a preternatural setting, so Pope celebrates the 'delights' of sylvan scenes where 'Descending Gods have found Elysium'. It is part of the poet's pastoral play that by the presence of these divinities 'natural' scenes are made a paradise, thus matching the poetic metamorphosis of 'real' into artful elysiums.

In woods bright Venus with Adonis strayed,
And chaste Diana haunts the forest shade.
Come lovely nymph, and bless the silent hours,
When swains from sheering seek their nightly bowers;
When weary reapers quit the sultry field
And crown'd with corn, their thanks to Ceres yield.   [Poems, 1:76–77]

The pastoral vision employs language which allows the possibility of realizing the impossible: most obviously in those terms which apply equally to gardens:

Oh deign to visit our forsaken *seats*,
The mossy *fountains*, and the green retreats!
Where'er you walk, cool gales shall fan the *glade*,
Trees, where you sit, shall crowd into a shade

....
Your praise the birds shall chant in ev'ry *grove*

[*Poems*, 1:77–78]

But gardens, too, are art's manipulation of nature, fashioning, with the introduction of statues of presiding deities, what Evelyn had called 'a place of all terrestriall enjoyments the most resembling Heaven'.

In 1713 *Windsor Forest* continued to play with these visions of sympathetic landscapes. The twin ideas of active and contemplative life find their vehicles in images of contrasting river scenes—the busy and mercantile Thames, and the secluded, private Loddon which reflects an appropriate surrounding ambience:

Oft in her glass the musing shepherd spies
The headlong mountains and the downward skies,
The watry landskip of the pendant woods,
And absent trees that tremble in the floods;
In the clear azure gleam the flocks are seen,
And floating forests paint the waves with green.

The springs and shades of Windsor become the apt haunt of poetry. Its natural landscape, visited by the creative energies of Pope's muse, becomes an artful and mythic world. Yet this dialogue of the real and the contrived—"Where order in variety we see'—is once again prophetic of the prospects of a landscape garden, which shares with the pastoral a characteristic vocabulary:

[*Poems*, 1:169]

Here waving groves a chequer'd scene display,
And part admit, and part exclude the day;

....
There, interspers'd in lawns and op'ning glades,
Thin trees arise that shun each other's shades.
Here in full light the russet plains extend:
There wrapt in clouds the blueish hills ascend.

[*Poems*, 1:150]

Just two years before Pope gave up any idea of building a house for himself in London and rented the villa at Twickenham, he published two poems which canvass more successfully the meditative possibilities of solitude. Though the landscape images of the "Elegy to the Memory of an Unfortunate Lady" are fleeting and unimportant to the poem, the theatrical sublime of the opening lines announces a dominant theme of the mid-eighteenth century: the linking of high passion 'Above the vulgar flight of low desire' with suitable landscapes. But the whole poem is, perhaps, too public a statement, too organized a record of the mind's associative patterns (whether the poet's or the lady's) in the scene's 'congenial place', to be particularly effective. Much more subtle is the attempt of "Eloisa to Abelard" to match a distressed mind with its context. The hermit imagery of the opening is, for once, precisely apt; yet it is marvellously undercut with Eloisa's announcement of her rival and disruptive meditations:

In these deep solitudes and awful cells,
Where heav'nly-pensive contemplation dwells,
And ever-musing melancholy reigns;
What means this tumult in a Vestal's veins?
Why rove my thoughts beyond this last retreat?
Why feels my heart its long-forgotten heat?

[*Poems*, 2:319]

Eloisa's predicament separates her from the machinery of rugged rocks and 'grots and caverns shagg'd with horrid thorn'. The flame of her passion rekindles among scenery where 'stern Religion quench'd th'unwilling flame'; her mind's contrary motions are displayed in the poem's skillful management of her memories and associations.

The first climax of the poem comes with the mind's instinctive colouring of its surrounding landscape:

The darksome pines that o'er yon rocks reclin'd
Wave high, and murmur to the hollow wind,
The wandering streams that shine between the hills,
The grots that echo to the tinkling rills,
The dying gales that pant upon the trees,
The lakes that quiver to the curling breeze;
No more these scenes my meditation aid,
Or lull to rest the visionary maid.
But o'er the twilight groves and dusky caves,
Long-sounding isles, intermingled graves,
Black Melancholy sits, and round her throws
A death-like silence, and a dread repose:
Her gloomy presence saddens all the scene,
Shades ev'ry flow'r, and darkens ev'ry green,
Deepens the murmur of the falling floods,
And breathes a browner horror on the woods.

[*Poems*, 2:332–33]

Two aspects of this crucial passage are relevant: first, the invocation of both an emblematic figure of Melancholy and an equivalent expressive landscape; second, the fashion in which what stirs the mind at any moment influences what the eye sees in the world around it. Every contemporary reader would have recognized the provenance of the 'gloomy presence' of a seated female figure: she would have appeared most recently in the 1709 edition of Cesare Ripa's *Iconologia: or Moral Emblems*, issued in London. This volume contained 'Various Images of Virtues, Vices, Passions, Arts, Humours, Elements and Celestial Bodies'; these, readers were further advised, were 'the representations

PLATE 35 Cesare Ripa, emblem of Pensiveness. Engraving from *Iconologia* (1709).

of our Notions; they properly belong to Painters, who by colours and shadowing, have invented the admirable secret to give body to our thoughts, thereby to render them visible.' But the edition was directed generally at 'Orators, Poets, Painters, Sculptors' in the hope that it would aid their inventions. One emblem [plate 35] showed the conventional figure of a seated woman with her head resting on her hand; it is a pose that Pope adopted, or had suggested to him, in 1722 when he was painted by Godfrey Kneller, so that he would be identified at a glance as an example of the reflective and meditating man, *il penseroso*. Yet these emblems were already losing their prestige as a visual vocabulary of human emotion: Pope significantly sets the Ripa emblem in an expressive scene, reminiscent of Dughet's or Rosa's paintings, that seems far more eloquent of Eloisa's mood than the conventional emblem. It is more fully articulate, of course, simply because it allows more complexity: the tensions and vacillations of her mind are announced in the various readings of surrounding scenery: 'The dear Ideas, where I fly,/pursue,/Rise in the grove, before the altar rise'. What is an aid to meditation becomes an image of horror and dread. Only by the poet's introduction of these contrasted landscapes, comparable—at its most obvious—to a painter's emotional manipulations of light and shade, is something of the actual state of Eloisa's mind displayed. Ripa's emblem could only declare the simple *idea* of her melancholy. Pope's use of emblem and expression becomes a central feature of his own garden at Twickenham. And the history of English gardening in the eighteenth century, for at least one commentator, Thomas Whately, came to be written in terms of the eventual triumph of expressive over emblematic design.

A further link between Pope's early poetry and the later landscape garden is their hospitality to dream and vision. The pastoral dreams, even the elegiac vision of the death of the year in "Winter", spring from and are sustained by their landscape settings. The poet who meets the 'beck'ning ghost, along the moonlight shade' and Eloisa who encounters among the walks and groves apparitions that are 'more than Echoes' and images that steal 'between my God and me' are stimulated to dream by their surroundings. The romance ambience of both poems perhaps recalls Addison's account of Leonora's garden (in *Spectator* 37): 'her Reading has lain very much among *Romances* . . . and discovers itself even in her House, her Gardens': her estate is situated 'in a kind of Wilderness . . . and looks like a little Enchanted Palace':

The Rocks about her are shaped into Artificial Grottoes covered with Wood-bines and Jessamines. The Woods are cut into shady Walks, twisted into Bowers, and filled with Cages of Turtles. The Springs are made to run among Pebbles, and by that means taught to Murmur very agreeably. They are likewise collected into a Beautiful Lake, that is Inhabited by a Couple of Swans, and empties itself by a little Rivulet which runs through a Green Meadow, and is known by the Name of *The Purling Stream*.

Addison rather archly notes that these 'Innocent Entertainments' divert the imagination and do little to enlighten the understanding. But the enchantments are an essential ingredient of Addison's landscape enthusiasms; nor, in fact, does he neglect visions that are addressed to the understanding—for his dream of Liberty (*Tatler* 161) is set in a natural landscape full of devices that his mind must comprehend. These enchanting and masque-like spectacles seem an appropriate extension of a garden's potential. In *Spectator* 425 the author (it is possibly Pope) dreams that the 'Genius of the Garden' presents him with an iconographical pageant of the seasons; the garden had called Milton to the dreamer's mind before he fell asleep, and the masque of the seasons is a realisation of 'some strange mysterious Dream' that the older poet had celebrated in "Il Penseroso".

These connections of dream and garden are not surprising, for the latter was always associated with our nostalgia for perfection: thus Evelyn explained that 'As no man can be very miserable that is master of a garden here; so will no man ever be happy who is not sure of a garden hereafter'. When we would 'frame a type of Heaven', therefore, we describe a garden. The landscape garden not only maintained these associations, but lent them anew their characteristic forms: for since a garden implied paradise and since the theories of at least "soft primitivism" described the golden age as free of conspicuous human art, these images always represent ideally natural landscape compositions. Zacharias Heyns's picture of Tempe in his *Emblemata* of 1625 is such a one [plate 36]. It is therefore the vocabulary of dream and vision that is invoked to praise the best landscape gardens: at Stowe Horace Walpole figured himself 'at Tempe or Daphne' and surrendered himself there to 'all these images [that] crowd upon one's memory, and add visionary personages to the charming scenes, that are so enriched with fanes and temples, that the real prospects are little less than visions themselves'. For Dodsley, after his first visit to William Shenstone's garden at The Leasowes, the many inscriptions there were a direct stimulus of these magic visions:

And see, the spells
The powerful incantations, magic verse
Inscribed on every tree, alcove, or urn.

And so it was with Pope at Twickenham. Whatever other delights and stimuli his gardens produced, dreams and visions were a central feature of his concept of this retreat:

Bear me, some God! oh quickly bear me hence
To wholesome solitude, the nurse of sense:
Where contemplation prunes her ruffled wings,
And the free soul looks down to pity kings.
There sober thought pursu'd th'amusing theme
Till fancy colour'd it, and form'd a dream.
A *vision* Hermits can to hell transport,
And force e'en me to see the damned at court.

[*Poems*, 4:41–43]

He confessed to one correspondent an admiration for fairy tales, 'the more wild and exotic the better, therefore a *Vision*, which is confined to no rules of probability, will take in all the variety and luxuriancy of description you will'. That variety and luxuriancy of fancy were echoed in his garden and grotto, however much their design honoured 'a probable nature'. At Twickenham, he was what he told Robert Digby in 1722 he fancied himself at Lord Bathurst's 'enchanted forest';

I look upon myself as the Magician appropriated to the place, without whom no mortal can penetrate into the recesses of those sacred shades. I could pass whole days, in only describing . . . the future and as yet visionary beauties, that are to rise in those scenes.

Whimsy perhaps, but it nonetheless declares a mood and frame of mind that Pope entertains in gardens. Early in his residence at Twickenham he wrote to tell John Caryll of his vision-filled indolence:

Like a witch, whose carcase lies motionless on the floor, while she keeps her airy sabbaths, and enjoys a thousand imaginary entertainments abroad, in this world, and in others, I seem to sleep in the midst of the hurry, even as you would swear, a top stands still, when 'tis in the whirl of its giddy motion.

Even, I suspect, his imitations of Horace in poetry and landscape are coloured by this delight in dream and fantastic vision.

One critic has talked of the 'romanticism' of Pope's Horace. An essential element in these poems is the fantasy that is involved in emulating the Roman poet. His dreams of making Twickenham his Sabine farm are mediated by his delight, sometimes his annoyance, at the difference between their situations. The traditional rivalry between country and city for which Horace was often a spokesman both sustains and fails to fit Pope's professional predicament. But a large part of his enjoyment of Twickenham was obviously the play it provoked between 'visionary beauties' and the realities of his life. Horace's Sabine retreat, for example, was a present from his patron, Maecenas: since Roman Catholics were not allowed to own property, Pope only rented a villa, paying for its improvements with his income as translator and writer:

All this is mine but till I die;
I can't but think 'twould sound more clever
To me and to my heirs for ever.

[*Poems*, 4:251]

Yet without these obligations to posterity or the anxieties of inheritance that are mooted at the end of his imitation of *Satires* II.ii, Pope may concentrate (not like Horace upon 'vivite fortes') but upon his own 'free soul'—'Let Us be fix'd, and our own masters still'. For the 'clear, still Mirror of Retreat' best shows the nature of human worth.

Independence and privacy are Pope's characteristic claims for his garden, even though they are sometimes violated: 'What walls can guard me, or what shades can hide? / They pierce my thickets, thro' my Grot they glide'. While the role of solitary recluse, indifferent to the lures of court or Grub Street, is played with skill in the satires, some of its success is the partial truth of that fiction. Though London is not the place for poets, as Rome was not for Horace in *Epistles* II.ii, yet escape is no solution: 'Alas! to Grottos and to Groves we run, / To ease and silence, ev'ry Muse's son.' Pope even argues ironically to George II that poets are best rendered harmless by allowing them country retreats, where they can keep up 'nothing but mere metre': an occupation as far from Pope's as from Horace's visions of their careers. But it is, as we saw in the first chapter, part of a traditional role to yearn for mindless rural peace:

Oh, could I see my Country Seat!
There leaning near a gentle Brook,
Sleep, or peruse some ancient Book,
And there in sweet oblivion drown
Those Cares that haunt the Court and Town.

The irony of such attitudes is their pastoral naivety amid the urban 'sea of folly': the grass, as the fable of the town and country mice displays, only *looks* greener. But Pope is not his Sir Job (in *Epistles* I.i) who begins to build a country seat and as quickly reverts to a town life. Twickenham affords genuine advantages to both poet and private person. The play with his horticultural self-sufficiency is a subtle revision of Horace, who tells of *others'* independence in that way:

In Forest planted by a Father's hand,
Than in five acres now of rented land.
Content with little, I can piddle here
On Broccoli and mutton, round the year;
But ancient friends, (tho' poor, or out of play)
That touch my Bell, I cannot turn away.
'Tis true, no Turbots dignify my boards,
But gudgeons, flounders, what my Thames affords:

To Hounslow-heath I point and Bansted-down,
Thence comes your mutton, and these chicks my own:
From yon old walnut-tree a show'r shall fall;
And grapes, long ling'ring on my only wall.

[Poems, 4:65]

Pope translates a defence of the virtues of frugal living into a moral independence couched in the fanciful terms of rural self-sufficiency. The generals, too, who retire to their estates in *Epistles* I.i are distinct from Horace's gladiator, Vejanius, in their independence of political manipulation or patronage: maybe Pope had Sir Richard Temple, later Lord Cobham, in mind, behind the garden gates of Stowe after his dismissal from the army.

But just as his mother, commemorated by the obelisk, surveyed the garden, it was above all the example of his father that guided Pope's retreat:

Stranger to Civil and Religious Rage,
The good Man walk'd innoxious thro' his Age.
No Courts he saw, no Suits would ever try,
Nor dar'd an Oath, nor hazarded a Lye:
Un-learn'd, he knew no Schoolman's subtle Art,
No Language, but the Language of the Heart.

[Poems, 4:126]

The language of the heart finds its proper syntax in rural seclusion. Pope ends that passage some lines later by protesting that he would himself be happier than kings if he could emulate such a life, thereby implying his proximity to the topos of the philosopher-king whose 'kingdom is in his mind or lies all about him in nature'. The grotto at Twickenham was linked with Egeria, wife of a legendary philosopher-king, Numa, to make this connection explicit: for according to both Livy and Plutarch Numa and Egeria 'entertained familiar conversation with the Muses [in their grotto], to whose teaching [Numa] ascribed the greatest part of his revelations'. The genius of a place, its presiding deities, determine the life of the philosopher who lives there. Addison illustrated this same idea, together with its corollary that a man is mirrored in his kingdom or landscape, in an unused manuscript for *Spectator* 414: an Eastern king actually realizes the idea by making 'his Garden Ye map of his Empire; where ye great Roads were represented by ye Spacious walks and allies, ye woods & forests by little thickets & tufts of Bushes' and so on. This 'draught of his Dominions' was, in short, but a portrait of the king.

Pope's kingdom was his garden, 'a setting that expressed him', laid out over the years to serve him as the retirement in which to consult the oracles of his own heart and reason and as a base from which to utter his satires:

Soon as I enter at my Country door,
My Mind resumes the thread it dropt before;

Thoughts, which at Hyde-Park-Corner I forgot,
Meet and rejoin me, in the pensive Grott.
There all alone, and Compliments apart,
I ask these sober questions of my Heart.

[*Poems*, 4:179]

Not only, as Kent's sketches depict it, a scene for solitary contemplation, the grotto, together with the garden beyond, served equally as the locale for friendship that could prosper without deceit or pretence away from the public world:

Know all the distant Din that World can keep,
Rolls o'er my Grotto, and but soothes my Sleep.
There, my Retreat the best Companions grace,
Chiefs out of War, and Statesmen out of Place.
There St John mingles with my friendly Bowl
The Feast of Reason and the Flow of Soul:
And He, whose Lightning pierc'd th'*Iberian* Lines,
Now forms my Quincunx, and now ranks my Vines,
Or tames the Genius of the stubborn Plain,
Almost as quickly as he conquer'd *Spain*.

[*Poems*, 4:17]

The intricacies of communion between friends and equals ('the Flow of Soul') need the sympathetic surroundings of an equally subtle landscape. Significantly, the corresponding passage in Horace (*Satires* II.i, ll. 71ff.) neglects these intimate activities and their conjunction with a garden setting. Horace is englished here with a keen sensitivity to both contemporary and personal culture; the Latin poetry yields to Pope's originality in a way that Virgil, asked to 'sport on Windsor's blissful plains' at the opening of the *Pastorals*, never achieved.

Twickenham provided Pope's personal landscape. When it is the 'chief point of Friendship to comply with a Friends Motions and Inclinations', and so attend to the finest movements of the human mind, Pope considered the context of such encounters all-important. In 1720 he told Robert Digby that the 'best account I can give of what I am building is that it will afford me a few pleasant rooms for such a friend as yourself'. Digby's garden at Sherborne seems to have reciprocated. Even the language of friendship in Pope's circle seems occasionally to borrow its metaphors from gardening, as when Bolingbroke is told that 'Your every word is kind to me, and all the *openings* of your mind amiable'. This in its turn is reciprocated when Bolingbroke writes that his thoughts 'shall be communicated to you [in a letter] just as they pass thro my mind, just as they use to do when we converse together on those, or any other subjects; when we saunter alone, or as we have often done with good Arbuthnot and the joose dean of St Patrick's among the multiplied scenes of your little garden'.

The famous advice which the poet addressed to Lord Burlington in 1731 was wisdom learnt at first-hand since his removal to

Twickenham twelve years before. Though his gardening projects were not executed there without expense, nor without taste, it was 'Sense', as he told Burlington, that guided the whole scheme. As *The Guardian* paper of 1713 had noted, those most capable of art were equally most fond of nature:

> To build, to plant, whatever you intend,
> To rear the Column, or the Arch to bend,
> To swell the Terras, or to sink the Grot;
> In all, let Nature never be forgot.
> But treat the Goddess like a modest fair,
> Nor over-dress, nor leave her wholly bare;
> Let not each beauty ev'ry where be spy'd,
> Where half the skill is decently to hide.
> He gains all points, who pleasingly confounds,
> Surprizes, varies, and conceals the Bounds.
>   Consult the Genius of the Place in all;
> That tells the Waters or to rise, or fall,
> Or helps th'ambitious Hill the Heav'ns to scale,
> Or scoops in circling theatres the Vale;
> Calls in the Country, catches op'ning glades,
> Joins willing woods, and varies shades from shades;
> Now breaks, or now directs, th'intending Lines,
> Paints as you plant, and as you work, designs.

Though Pope's garden and grotto have frequently been discussed, perhaps no one has seen quite how conscientiously he applied his own prescriptions nor the particular reasons for his individual adjudication of the claims of art and nature.

The language itself of the passage declares one adjustment of those claims. The human, artificial activity (build, column, arch, terrace) is controlled always by a natural agency and idiom (plant, rear, bend, swell); yet both work in conjunction to the same end. If half the investment is human skill, it is complemented by what the natural materials contribute; yet these have their own magical ingredient of art, for the Genius of the Place 'paints' and 'designs' even as the human gardener merely plants and works. These subtle variations of the basic contributions to a garden are devised to provide a space for human existence. People encounter the space of a garden psychologically as much as physically: they respond to its invitations—paths that invite, steps that lead up or down, inscriptions that ask to be deciphered—and to its confirmation or ingenious denial of expectation. Pope's language ('pleasingly confounds': 'surprizes') endorses this psychological experience of a garden. Variety in a garden plan, as well as mediating between natural and artificial elements, augments that experience: to call in the country, to conceal the boundaries of a garden, allows the mind even further territory. If the ha-ha was indeed the crucial factor in the development of the landscape garden, by opening the garden to the world beyond the ditch, it still remained just another, if more radical, manipulation of space for the delight of the human mind.

At Twickenham Pope worked energetically at contriving these variations and psychological involvements: the smallness of scale only made the challenge more tempting:

I am as busy in three inches of Gardening, as any man can be in threescore acres. I fancy my self like the fellow that spent his life in cutting the twelve apostles in one cherry-stone. I have a Theatre, an Arcade, a Bowling green, a Grove, & what not? in a bitt of ground that would have been but a plate of Sallet to Nebuchadnezzar.

The country was called in to augment these five acres both by the camera obscura (whereby 'are formed a moving Picture in their visible Radiations') and by the openings upon the Thames ('Sails . . . passing suddenly and vanishing'). One such prospect particularly struck a visitor of 1748: from the Shell Temple there ran a walk in the 'natural Taste, being rather strew'd than pav'd with Flints and Pebbles, inclos'd with Thickets, and over arch'd with wild and interwoven Branches of Trees' and it was down this arcade, 'a sort of continued Tube', that he was aware of a small expanse of the Thames 'beheld as in a Perspective, making a beautiful remote Appearance; where Vessels that pass up and down the River, suddenly glance on the Eye, and again vanish from it in a Moment'.

The garden itself exemplified Pope's reiteration to Spence of his one basic principle of design, namely that variety is achieved mostly 'in the contrasts'. For the straighter lines of its paths and walks, the geometry of the quincunx groves, were surrounded by 'many narrow serpentine walks'; in these 'entangled' sections were placed statues, urns, and inscriptions to entertain the energetic and curious visitor. The one who was there in 1748, maybe recalling Pope's own lines about 'willing woods', described how 'Trees unite themselves more closely'. And we know from Pope himself that shades were varied from shades, since he explained to Spence that 'You may distance things by darkening them and by narrowing the plantations more and more toward the end, in the same manner as they do in painting, and as 'tis executed in the little cypress walk to that obelisk'. Thus, he painted even as he planted.

A tiny 'vale' with its shell temple was scooped into a theatre. Hills and mounts were helped to rise—some only into small 'Hillocks . . . entirely cover'd with Thickets of Lawrel, Bay, Holly, and many other Evergreens and Shrubs, rising one above another in beautiful Slopes and Intermixtures, where Nature freely lays forth the Branches, and disports uncontrol'd'. One mount, much higher than the other two, was 'covered with Bushes and Trees of a wilder Growth, and more confused Order, rising as it were out of Clefts of Rocks, and Heaps of rugged and mossy Stones; among which a narrow intricate Path leads in an irregular Spiral to the Top; where is plac'd a Forest Seat or Chair'. The excitements of exploring this garden, which today may seem only rather whimsical, are declared by several commentators: the correspondent to the *Newcastle General Magazine*, already quoted; Pope himself, pleased that Lady Mary Wortley Montagu did not stir from his 'great Walk', thereby answering 'the Intention of its Contriver, when it detain'd her there'; Horace Walpole, alert to the psychological drama of Twickenham's calculated picturesque structure—'the passing through the gloom from the grotto to the opening day, the retiring and again assembling shades, the dusky groves, the larger lawn, and the solemnity of the termination at the cypresses'. Atterbury's compliment to Pope, that he hopes Bathurst will 'have as much satisfaction in building the House in the Wood and using it' as Pope in designing it, must have voiced an essential commonplace among this circle of gardenists.

For the Newcastle writer of 1748 the grotto was undoubtedly the tour de force. For Pope, too, as we have seen, it must have been eloquent of his whole endeavour, like that "Grotto of Shells at Cruxeaston, the Work of Nine Young Ladies", about which he had written:

The glittering emblem of each spotless dame,
Clear as her soul and shining as her frame.   [*Poems*, 6:353]

The grotto at Twickenham fully exemplified two gardening maxims of the *Epistle to Burlington*: the telling of waters where to rise or fall, and the starting 'even from Difficulty'. Dr. Johnson explained the second most trenchantly in his observation that 'Pope's excavation was requisite as an entrance to his garden [that in fact lay on the far side of the road from the villa], and . . . he extracted an ornament from an inconvenience, and vanity produced a grotto where necessity enforced a passage'. And as Pope anticipated, time assisted to make it a work to wonder at. But what has rarely been understood about this part of Pope's landscape is the variety of its essentially private iconography and the elaborate fashion in which its elements contributed to psychological excitement.

There was some iconography at Twickenham that was generally available: the Christian emblems, the Crown of Thorns and the Five Wounds, at the river entrance to the grotto; a design for the grass plot at the river's edge, an account of which is given by Spence:

a swan, as flying into the river, on each side of the landing-place, then the statues of two river gods reclined on the bank between them and the corner seats, or temples with

Hic placido fluit amne Meles
on one of their urns, and

Magnis ubi flexibus errat Mincius

on the other. Then two terms in the first niches in the grove-work on the sides with the busts of Homer and Virgil, and higher, two others with those of Marcus Aurelius and Cicero.

This elaborate contrivance, properly decyphered, would lead the spectator to recall the birth of Homer from Politian and the poetic conquest of Greece from Virgil and so to identify Pope's own role in rededicating this classical literary heritage to his own age.

But there were other items with only private resonance. The whole grotto, in fact, was contrived with geological specimens designed to stimulate geographical associations and personal recollections. Pope's gardener, Serle, published a full account of them after the poet's death and he had presumably a unique opportunity to understand this collection of materials. But really only Pope himself could have appreciated the rich associations with friend and topographical location that were offered by each specimen embedded into the grotto walls: in the first room, according to Serle's lists, were 'Several fine Fossils and Snake-stones', with petrified Wood, and Moss in various shapes, from the petrifying Spring at Nasborough in Yorkshire' alongside 'Fine Verd Antique from Egypt; in the third room are pieces from Kent, Bath, Plymouth, Cornwall; and in the fourth

Fine sparry Marble from Lord Edgcumb's Quarry, with different sorts of Moss. Several fine Pieces of the Eruptions from Mount Vesuvius, and a fine piece of Marble from the Grotto of Egeria near Rome, from the Reverend Mr. Spence; with several fine Petrifications and Plymouth Marble, from Mr. Cooper; Gold Clift from Mr. Cambridge in Gloucestershire; and several fine Brain-stones from Mr. Miller of Chelsea.

Emblems, all of them, which were tangible reminders to the one man capable of appreciating them of much correspondence and much 'flow of soul'.

The private scene of the grotto extends much further. Its variety of rooms, each with an anthology of reminiscence, was augmented by Pope's manipulation of the natural spring he was lucky enough to discover there. Some of his own notes preserved on a sketch [plate 37] suggest the attempt to imbue each room of the grotto with its own character, as the waters were taught to rise in 'a spring of water', 'the small waterfall', an underground stream or finally a 'bagnio'. Elsewhere he speaks of 'three falls of water' and of the additional image of water afforded by glimpses of the Thames.

The visitor to the grotto in 1748 was especially impressed with the variety of water effects:

Here it gurgles in a gushing Rill thro' fractur'd Ores and Flints; there it drips from depending Moss and Shells; here again, washing Beds of

Sand and Pebbles, it rolls in Silver Streamlets; and there it rushes out in jets and Fountains; while the Caverns of the Grot incessantly echo with a soothing Murmur of acquatick Sounds.

Yet the resourcefulness of Pope's grotto did not end there. For the same writer goes on to describe a contraption that enlarged this aquatic imagery into the one kind that the small grotto could not otherwise have achieved—namely, a Salvator Rosa-like torrent, savage and terrifying, which is how it was visualized in a sketch by another visitor[plate 38]:

This is effected by disposing Plates of Looking glass in the obscure Parts of the Roof and Sides of the Cave, where sufficient Force of Light is wanting to discover the Deception, while the other parts, the Rills, Fountains, Flints, Pebbles, etc. being duly illuminated, are so reflected by the various posited Mirrors, as, without exposing the Cause, every Object is multiplied, and its Position represented in a surprising Diversity. Cast your Eyes upward, and you half shudder to see Cataracts of Water precipitating over your Head, from impending

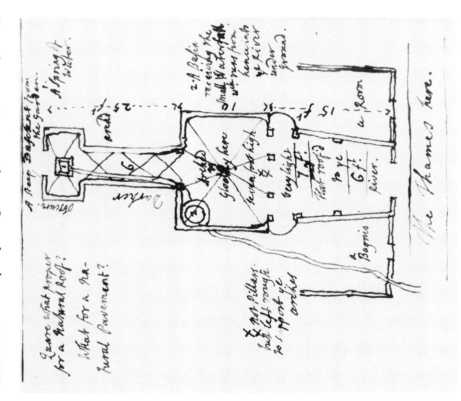

PLATE 37   Alexander Pope, plan of his grotto. Drawing (January 1740).

PLATE 38   Anonymous, Pope's grotto.
Drawing (date unknown).

Stones and Rocks, while salient Spouts rise in rapid Streams at your Feet: Around, you are equally surprised with flowing Rivulets and rolling Waters, that rush over airey Precipices, and break amongst Heaps of ideal Flints and Spar. Thus, by a fine taste and happy Management of Nature, you are presented with an undistinguishable Mixture of Realities and Imagery.

What the writer identifies very clearly is the cooperation of art and nature to achieve the various 'characters which water can assume' and which are described later in the century by Thomas Whately:

So various are the characters which water can assume, that there is scarcely an idea in which it may not concur, or *an impression which it cannot enforce*: a deep stagnated pool, dank and dark with shades which it dimly reflects, befits the seat of melancholy . . . A gently murmuring rill, clear and shallow, just gurgling, just dimpling, imposes silence, suits with solitude, and leads to meditation; a brisker current, which wantons in little eddies over a bright sandy bottom, or babbles among pebbles, spreads cheerfulness all around; a greater rapidity, and more agitation, to a certain degree are animating; but in excess, instead of wakening, they alarm the senses; the roar and the rage of a torrent, its force, its violence, its impetuosity, tend to inspire terror.

The aquatic effects in Pope's grotto are virtually as varied a psychological programme as those in Whately's catalogue. Their significance has never been clearly recognized; they provide a machinery of meditation, various landscapes where the expressive character of water determines mental activity. Yet, as with Eloisa, this influence works both ways: the poet is master of his thoughts and can colour the surrounding landscape according to his mood. Pope himself acknowledges this crucial element of personal control over the links between scenery and meditation: in a famous, often quoted, description of his grotto he explains that the varieties of image which the camera obscura recreates for him are invoked precisely *'when you have a mind to light it up'*.

The artificiality of Pope's grotto, as of parts of the garden beyond, is not disputed. Like Stephen Switzer, he saw little to object to in 'a little regularity' near the house or in what Walpole called the 'specific garden', as long as the 'extended garden' beyond was 'laid out in a more Natural and Rural Manner'. But what is always in question for Pope and these early gardenists is a garden's adequate provision of a sufficient variety to occupy the mind. In an early letter of 1719 to Lord Bathurst he recounts an overheard discussion on the improvements to the Royal Garden at Richmond: what he mocks is the failure to attend to variety of effects in a garden because of some narrow, a priori theory of garden design:

One declar'd he would not have too much Art in it; for my notion (said he) of gardening is, that it is only sweeping nature: Another told them that Gravel walks were not of a good taste, for all of the finest abroad were of loose sand: A third advis'd peremptorily there should be one Lyme-tree in the whole plantation; a fourth made the same exclusive clause extend to Horse-chestnuts, which he affirm'd not to be Trees, but Weeds; Dutch Elms were condemned by a fifth; and thus about half the Trees were proscrib'd, contrary to the Paradise of God's own planting, which is expressly said to be planted with *all trees*. There were some who cou'd not bear Ever-greens, and call'd them Never-greens; some, who were angry at them only when cut into shapes, and gave the modern Gard'ners the name of Ever-green Taylors; some who had no dislike to Cones and Cubes, but wou'd have 'em cut in Forest-trees; and some who were in a passion against any thing in shape, even against clipt hedges, which they call'd green walls.

The greater the variety, whether of natural or artificial features, the more pleasures and entertainment were provided for the mind. Hence the satire of Timon's Villa:

His Gardens next your admiration call,
On every side you look, behold the Wall!
No pleasing Intricacies intervene,
No artful wildness to perplex the scene;
Grove nods at grove, each Alley has a brother,
And half the platform just reflects the other.

What might delight the visitor in the artificial management of natural effects only offends by its abrupt or nonsensical attempts:

The suff'ring eye inverted Nature sees,
Trees cut to Statues, Statues thick as trees;
With here a Fountain, never to be played;
And there a Summer-house, that knows no shade;
Here Amphitrite sails through myrtle bowers;
There Gladiators fight, or die in flowers;
Un-watered see the drooping sea-horse mourn,
And swallows roost in Nilus' dusty Urn.

[*Poems*, 3/ii:148–49]

The fullest account Pope has left of his experience of a good garden other than his own is the long description he wrote for Martha Blount of his visit to Lord Digby's estate at Sherbourne in 1724:

The Gardens are so Irregular, that tis very hard to give an exact idea of 'em but by a Plan. Their beauty rises from Irregularity, for not only the Several parts of the Garden itself make the better Contraste by these sudden Rises, Falls, and Turns of Ground; but the Views about it are lett in, & hang over the Walls, in very different figures and aspects.

Yet his appeal for a plan is, I believe, misleading. For his verbal account that follows is enormously more eloquent about the actual experience of being in the gardens at Sherbourne; marvellously communicated to Martha Blount, this experience consists above all in the skilfully managed progress through the site:

You come first out of the house into a green walk of Standard Lymes with a hedge behind them that makes a Colonnade, thence into a little triangular wilderness, from whose Centre you can see the town of Sherborne in a valley, interspersed with trees. From the corner of this you issue at once upon a high green Terras the whole breadth of the Garden, which has five more green Terras's hanging under each other, without hedges, only a few pyramid yews & large round Honisuckles between them.

But even when the extent of the garden is thus discovered and spread out before the eyes, the spectator is still involved in the actual exploration of what has been glimpsed briefly in diagrammatic perspective from the first terrace. It is this surrender to the delightful variety of Sherbourne, where different styles of design are gratuitously mixed, that makes Pope's account such an important item in his pronouncements upon gardening, together with his remarks on Stowe and on his own Twickenham. And what, in fact, is common to all three is the *combination* of what would usually be termed formal and informal elements: at Lord Digby's there is 'a natural River thro green banks of turf' as well as a 'Canall, that runs quite across the Groves and also along one Side, in the form of a T'; 'wild winding walks' as well as a 'semicircular Berceau'. Similarly at Stowe there were both oblong canal or octagonal lake and the meandering waters of the stream that runs through the Elysian fields. While, as we have seen, Twickenham countered the predominantly straight walks down the centre of the garden with the wandering paths toward the edges, and the grotto's 'natural' decoration and unsymmetrical groundplan with one statue in a niche just reflecting the other. These apparent stylistic conflicts are resolved in the actual experience of exploring them. At Sherbourne one

walk winds you up a Hill of venerable Wood overarch'd by nature, & of a vast height, into a circular Grove, on one side of which is a close high Arbour, on the other a sudden open Seat that overlooks the Meadows and river with a large distant prospect. Another walk under this hill winds by the river side quite covered with high Trees on both banks, over hung with Ivy, where falls a natural Cascade. . . . On the opposite hanging of the Bank . . . is plac'd, with a very fine fancy, a Rustick Seat of Stone, flagged and rough, with two Urns in the same rude taste upon pedestals, on each side; from whence you lose your eyes upon the glimmering of the Waters under the wood, and your ears in the constant dashing of the waves. In view of this, is a Bridge that crosses this stream, built in the same ruinous taste: the Wall of the Garden hanging over it, is humoured so as to appear the Ruin of another Arch or two above the Bridge. Hence you mount the Hill over the Hermits Seat (as they call it) . . . & so to the highest Terras, again.

Pope reads the 'psychology' of this landscape design with an expert eye, alert to the effects of what he also praises at Stowe as well as to *properly managed* versions of what he satirizes at Timon's Villa—for Sherbourne had shaped trees, six terraces and 'at the ends of these Terras's . . . two long walks under the side *Walls of the Garden*'. Pope's concern with the nice arbitrations between art and nature was in the interests, not of merely formal stylistics, but of the effects upon a visitor's mind. Such, anyway, seems to be the import of William Cleland's letter to Gay in 1731: he notes that Pope 'respects (as one may say) the *Persons of the Gladiator, Amphitrite, the Nile, and the Triton'* at Timon's Villa, but is 'only sorry to see them . . . ridiculous, by being in the wrong place'.

Elements of a garden in the 'wrong place' betray the owner ('A Man not only shows his Taste but his Virtue, in the Choice of such Ornaments') as well as strike awkwardly upon the perceiving mind: 'E'en in an ornament its place remark, / Nor in an Hermitage set Dr. Clarke.' Pope's quip refers to the absurdity, in his view, of including a bust of that particular theologian among those of Boyle, Locke, Newton, and Wollaston in the Queen's Hermitage in Richmond Park, for the mind would only remark the ineptness of Clarke's presence. In contrast, the

PLATE 39

The Temple of Ancient Virtue from the Temple of British Worthies, Stowe.

busts of Homer and Virgil beside the river at Twickenham, the apt configurations of statuary around the parterre at Stowe or in the temples dedicated to Ancient Virtue and the British Worthies [plate 39], were organized precisely to stimulate a visitor's thoughts and involve him in 'reading' the gardens.

It is worth, finally, considering what connections Pope maybe saw between his gardening enthusiasms and his career as a writer, why he came as early as 1724 to consider that 'Garden-ing is . . . nearer God's own work than Poetry', and what place in Pope's oeuvre should therefore be given to what he called his gardening poem, the *Epistle to Burlington*.

The *Epistle* was published in 1731, the first to appear of the *Epistles to Several Persons*. Yet when the *Moral Essays* appeared in their final form the Burlington poem was placed fourth and last. It is a reorganization, I suggest, that argues for Pope's thinking

Public and Private Virtues

it provided some resolution of the ideas canvassed in the other three. We do not have to deny the looseness of structure that the *Epistles to Several Persons* display in order to argue, nonetheless, for some vital if subtle development of theme throughout them. Their modern editor considers Pope's inclusion of the *Epistle to Burlington* in the scheme of the '*Opus Magnum*' an 'artificiality' and finds 'ominous' Pope's remark to Spence in May 1730 that 'there in particular yr some of ye Gardening Poem will be of Service'. Yet it seems to me that Pope's particular vision of what garden designs must mean to creator and spectator alike has an exact relevance, as the poet himself recognized, to the larger inquiry into human nature.

The *Epistles to Several Persons* were themselves to be one quarter of Pope's 'Opus Magnum' or 'system of Ethics in the Horatian way'. They open with that addressed to Lord Cobham, first published in 1734; it resumes the discussion of human psychology that had been published the previous year in the second epistle of *An Essay on Man*, another quarter of the projected opus. But the resumption is fraught with fresh perplexities and complicated by new perspectives. For Lord Cobham was dismissed from his regiment sometime in the second quarter of 1733 and his removal provoked *The Craftsman* 364 (23rd June) to exclaim how 'strange' it was 'that a Man, who was turned out of one Regiment in the last year of Q. Anne, should be now turned out of another by Persons protesting to act upon opposite Principles', and to speculate upon 'some secret Demerit' that occasioned the second disgrace. A week later *The London Journal* 731 replied that it was a 'villainous' insinuation to suppose Cobham had been dismissed for 'the same way of Thinking and Acting'; the *Journal* continued with speculations that must surely have caught Pope's attention:

Can the same way of Thinking and Acting be the Cause of Dismissing the same Person at this Time? Are the Actions of the Court the same now, as in the Four last Years of Q. Anne? It must be a different Way of Thinking and Acting; and what Wonder? Are Men always the same? Don't they grow peevish with Age and Infirmities? Don't they carry about them strong Passions, which bear them sometimes, like a Torrent against all Principles of Reason? . . . Why should we suppose some Design laid by the Court which an honest Man can't come into? Why not rather suppose, that the same Person who was once for Liberty, is now for Faction?

The same month that these speculations appeared Pope was staying at Stowe with Lord Cobham, to whose defence he springs in the concluding lines of the *Epistle*.

But personal loyalty and obligations to the literary mode of panegyric do not entirely distract the poet from an enthralled consideration of the 'Quick whirls, and shifting eddies, of our minds'. By the time he comes (at line 147) to invoke the 'Ruling

Passion', the clue which supposedly unravels and explains a personality, he has testified, far more eloquently and with more poetic subtlety than he spends upon considering the 'Ruling Passion', to the multitudinous intricacies of our minds:

There's some Peculiar in each leaf and grain,
Some unmark'd fibre, or some varying vein:
Shall only Man be taken in the gross?
Grant but as many sorts of Mind as Moss.

[*Poems*, 3/ii:17]

The inclinations towards 'sedate reflections' (line 33) and the ambitions of 'sage historians' (line 85) are alike frustrated by the perplexity of human psychology:

But these plain Characters we rarely find;
Tho' strong the bent, yet quick the turns of mind:
Or puzzling Contraries confound the whole,
Or affectations quite reverse the soul.
Or Falsehood serves the dull for policy,
And in the Cunning, Truth itself's a lye:
Unthought-of Frailties cheat us in the Wise,
The Fool lies hid in inconsistencies.

[*Poems*, 3/ii:25]

The weight of Montaigne is thrown behind these celebrations of human complexity—and Pope, we know, considered Montaigne's "Of the Inconstancy of Our Actions" the 'best in his whole book'.

The same preoccupation with the ineluctable density of human psychology informs the succeeding *Epistle to a Lady*. Pope moves his discussion now into the field of portrait painting, that art most conspicuously devoted to the representation of a 'likeness':

How many pictures of one Nymph we view,
All how unlike each other, all how true!
Arcadia's Countess, here in ermin'd pride,
Is there, Pastora, by a fountain side:
Here Fannia, leering on her own good man,
Is there, a naked Leda with a Swan.

[*Poems*, 3/ii:48–49]

How, in fact, is the portraitist to register the particular 'romantic' follies of the fair sex, above all to capture the 'Cynthia of *this* minute'? The artistic difficulties are firmly linked to the psychological by an allusion to La Bruyere's 'but how shall I fix this restless, light and inconstant man, who changes himself into a thousand and a thousand figures?' A formal and considered portraiture, committed to *fixed* poses and gestures, fails totally, Pope argues, in registering the various expressive *phases* of the human soul:

Pictures like these, dear Madam, to design,
Asks no firm hand, and no unerring line;
Some wand'ring touch, or some reflected light,

Some flying stroke alone can hit 'em right:
For how should equal Colours do the knack?
Chameleons who can paint in white and black?   [*Poems*, 3/ii:62–63]

'Equal', that is to say simple and unmixed, colours will not serve the need to capture the succeeding and multiplying perspectives of human character.

If we bypass (for the moment) the third epistle *To Bathurst* and come to the 'gardening poem', *To Burlington*, some fascinating links can be suggested. The difficulty of submitting any empirical experience of the workings of a human mind to the hypothesis of a 'prevailing passion' that ultimately accounts for all inconsistencies has proved in the first two epistles too huge for either the systematic philosopher or the formal portraitist. Yet this reluctantly admitted mistrust of excessively formal prescriptions for psychological behaviour is answered in the fourth epistle by a warmly endorsed vision of landscape gardens that are organized by and designed for precisely that flexibility, variety, and surprise in the human mind.

The apparently inchoate structure of *To Burlington* yields, in fact, a subtle theme: the need for art to emanate from and so to satisfy the individual. The epistle begins by registering the vanity of collecting objets d'art, however fine in themselves; the pleasure of such activity is diminished when expert connoisseurs take the decisions and track down necessary items for wealthy clients, when 'Magnificence' is achieved at the expense of personal involvement—and when nothing is exempt from this delegated acquisition and vicarious enjoyment:

Think we all these are for himself? no more
Than his fine Wife, alas! or finer Whore.   [*Poems*, 3/ii:136]

By contrast, the Earl of Burlington, however much he may seek examples for the modern arts in Roman precedence, is dedicated to displaying not only the usefulness of architecture—'You show us, Rome was glorious, not profuse, / And pompous buildings once were things of Use'—but also the need for 'sense' to control 'taste'. And 'sense' is defined, in part at least, as the proper recognition of an inner light, as the honouring of one's personal instincts:

Good Sense, which only is the gift of Heav'n,
And tho' no science, fairly worth the sev'n:
A Light, which in yourself you must perceive;
Jones and Le Notre have it not to give.   [*Poems*,3/ii:140–41]

The syntax of Pope's praise of Burlington—'(my Lord) your just, your noble rules'—insists upon Burlington's proper regulation of architectural principles according to his own judgement. By contrast, the land will soon be full of imitating fools:

Who random drawings from your sheets shall take,
And of one beauty many blunders make;
Load some vain Church with old Theatric state,
Turn Arcs of triumph to a Garden-gate;
Reverse your Ornaments, and hang them all
On some patch'd dog-hole ek'd with ends of wall,
Then clap four slices of Pilaster on't,
That, lac'd with bits of rustic, makes a Front.

[Poems, 3/ii:140]

Such eclectic stupidities are merely an 'act' with no instinct for the relationship of design elements to personal existence:

Or call the winds thro' long Arcades to roar,
Proud to catch cold at a Venetian door;
Conscious they act a true Palladian part,
And if they starve, they starve by rules of art.

[Ibid.]

The rules of art, slavishly followed, do not answer human nature. Nor does an insensitive and programmatic imposition of pattern or artifice upon a garden. The rigidity of either 'vast Parterres' or the excessive naturalism of 'One boundless Green, or flourish'd Carpet' make no appeal to the mind; they are examples of landscape design undirected by the 'sense' of an informing personal idea. At Timon's Villa the scale diminishes and dwarfs the human, and what is not predictable ('Grove nods at grove, each Alley has a brother') is inimical to the demands of human use—as Pope's note to line 130 reminds us, the 'Approaches and Communications of house with garden, or of one part with another, [are] ill judged and inconvenient'.

The admonition, 'let Nature never be forgot', is an appeal to actual topography, to a 'probable nature' and to the humanity of the persons who create and use gardens. The language of design, as we have seen, signals these connections with its 'pleasing', 'Surprises', and 'perplex'. But at the high point of the gardening poem, which comes with the apotheosis of Cobham's Stowe, these psychological aspects of good landscape design are celebrated in conjunction with the very factor which threatened systematic study in the first two epistles: time. For the art of gardening flourishes among those very intractable and messily 'real' aspects of the world that the arts are generally concerned to ignore or reshape. The landscape artist works along with nature rather than imposes patterns upon her and is encouraged to

Start ev'n from Difficulty, strike from Chance;
Nature shall join you; Time shall make it grow
A Work to wonder at—perhaps a STOW.

[Poems, 3/ii:143]

Landscaping thus becomes the only art that, far from seeking to evade time, actually chooses to exist within it and needs the cooperation of growth to accomplish its special kind of perfection. Unlike Pope's claim for the permanence that literature allows ('The Muse shall sing, and what she sings shall last'), unlike the testimony to his friend Charles Jervas's painting —'Beauty, frail flower that every season fears, / Blooms in thy colours for a thousand years'—landscape gardening is an art that grows with the seasons. Furthermore, it is an art of four dimensions, requiring a visitor's experience in time to discover its spaces. The landscape artist who is alert to the challenge of such contingencies holds the mirror up to human nature in subtle, if oblique, fashion. And this English gardening of the early eighteenth century both reflects and effects changes in contemporary habits of explaining the workings of the human mind.

This perhaps accounts for the value that Pope placed upon his gardening activities and made him close part of the 'Opus Magnum' with a 'gardening poem': for 'I am as much a better Gardiner, as I'm a worst Poet, than when you saw me: But Gardening is near a-kin to Philosophy, for Tully says *Agricultura proxima sapientiae*'. It becomes increasingly evident, the more one studies the full range of Pope's gardening career, that—just as much as his public dedication to philosophy and poetry—landscape design allowed him a vehicle for expressing himself, for understanding the complexities of the human being, for achieving *sapientia*. For this self-styled 'Hermit of Twickenham' a garden would, as he said of Stowe, 'set me beyond all Earthly Cogitations'. His frequent allusions to the gardening tasks that Adam was set in Eden are no empty repetitions of a familiar topos or the conventional salutation of moral husbandry. Pope, like Bacon, deemed gardens a 'greater perfection' of the human spirit than 'buildings and palaces'. He discovered in his own garden and grotto and in those of the many friends who sought his help in theirs an art that consorted with his own deepest inquiries into the 'proper study of mankind'.

The choice of Burlington as dedicatee of the conclusion to *Epistles to Several Persons* is no accident. While primarily an architect of buildings, he contributed significantly to the shaping of the English landscape garden as an apt territory for the mind with his own garden at Chiswick, his collaborations with William Kent and his patronage of Colin Campbell and Robert Castell. The former's project, the *Vitruvius Britannicus*, contains garden designs that chart the history of early eighteenth-century gardens as well as provide inspiration for their future. To Robert Castell we may look for a fascinating study of *The Villas of the Ancients Illustrated* (London, 1728), in which a commentary on Pliny's villas together with some speculative reconstructions of them obviously mirror at the same time as they give effect to the landscape theories of Burlington's circle.

The plan of Chiswick by John Rocque [plate 40], published in the third volume of the *Vitruvius Britannicus* of 1739, is a suitable starting point. At first perhaps its geometric elements are the

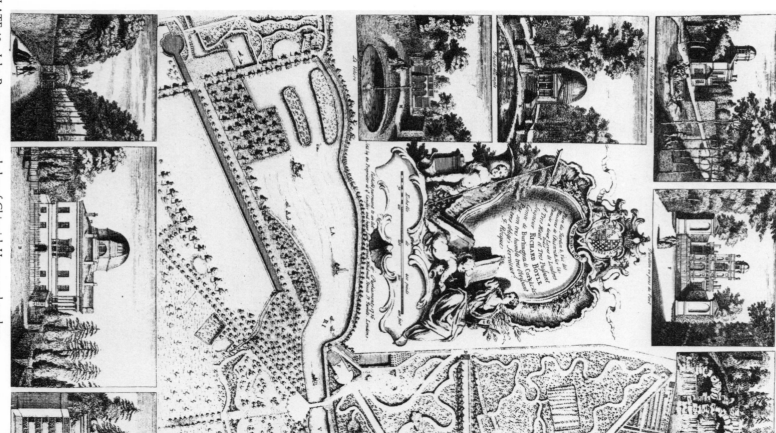

PLATE 40   John Rocque, engraved plan of Chiswick House and gardens.

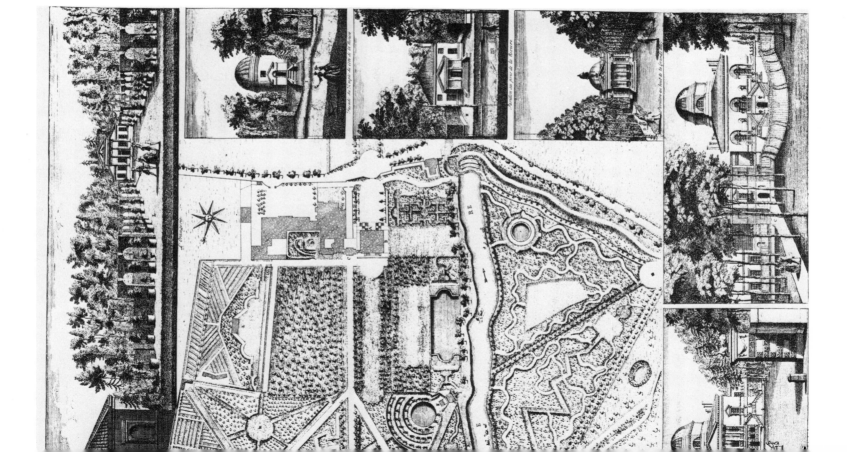

most conspicuous—the axial avenue with its branches on each side towards the Rustic Arch and the Bridge Pavilion; the Tempietto with its circling terraces around a pool; the calculated angles of the Orangery. But, as it is still possible to experience today, the exploration of Chiswick gardens is not so predictable. The main axis did not in fact start from the main stairway on the garden front, but just to one side. Nor, once embarked down its straight path, were there anything but frequent openings that tempted to left and right; once such invitations to divert from the main avenue were accepted the windings and intricacies of the garden were quickly discovered. Above all, Chiswick provided a rich example of certain termination points (Rocque's vignettes illustrate most of them), each of which is designed to be discovered on several occasions, when seen from time to time at the end of different paths. It is a device central to Pope's schemes also, for he tells Bathurst that a building he has designed 'is to answer three walks'; his verb stresses the dialogue between a garden's design and its human spectators.

Many other plans in the volumes of *Vitruvius Britannicus*, if read with what we may call this 'psychology of exploration' in mind, yield similar excitements as Chiswick. On the other hand, it is true that in face of examples like Tring in Hertfordshire, Belton in Lincolnshire or Eastbury in Dorset, we may rightly judge that even the actual experience of those gardens would have added little more sense of variety and surprise than the prospects and plans on the page declare. Equally, it is also clear that the inclusion within the larger scheme of a French-style garden of some small, rather wildly irregular segment, as at Goodwood in Sussex, does not answer the mind's need for a garden of multiplied scenes. The plans and prospects that manage to suggest some suitable answers are those where variety is sustained through the whole garden: this may take the form, as at Wrest, of a carefully modulated pattern of criss-cross walks, interspersed with more modishly meandering paths; or, as at Claremont, of certain formal elements absorbed into the irregularities of a large park. The effects of straight lines and symmetrical features are readily subdued to more absorbing intricacies, either when at Esher they somehow take their cue from one specifically irregular feature (the river), or as at Weybridge deploy their geometric structures in a wide arc around the house and so allow cross-views and cuts into a more subtle pattern.

Scale, too, determines a garden's play upon the mind. When Kent changed his plans for the exedra at Chiswick, it could not have been entirely because Burlington, in Wittkower's words, desired to reserve Kent's 'more picturesque escapades for the further parts of the garden'; the first plan for an architectural feature with a huge central pyramid [plate 41] seems too bulky

PLATE 41   William Kent, design for the Exedra at Chiswick (detail) (c. 1730–35).

PLATE 42   William Kent, view into the Exedra at Chiswick (early 1730's).

for the setting and too insistent an image for the mind to register (it was used more effectively later in the more spacious Elysian Fields at Stowe). In its place at Chiswick were substituted herms, statues, urns, and seats, set among shaped boskets, [plate 42] which contrive a quite different mingling of realities and imagery more in proportion to the scale of the garden and therefore more apt for the psychological experience of the garden.

The patronage of Robert Castell is a facet of Burlington's larger Palladian ambitions; for while they centred upon the architecture they also seem to include attention to the garden design of modern Italy and Roman antecedents. *The Villas of the Ancients* is an important document in the history of the English landscape garden, for it echoes many ideas on gardening that were canvassed by Pope and the Burlington circle. Its importance consists, above all, in the recognition that a villa answers the various social, agricultural, and psychological needs of its inhabitant. Pope's praise of Burlington, to whom Castell's volume is dedicated, that he showed us 'Rome was glorious, not profuse, / And pompous buildings once were things of Use', is echoed by Castell's evident delight that Pliny's villas were so thoughtfully shaped to the various needs of their users. And in Pliny's and Castell's constant attention to the exclusion of winds and draughts we may surely suspect the inspiration for Pope's lines—'Shall call the winds through long arcades to roar, / Proud to catch cold at a Venetian door'.

Castell's frequent emphasis upon the empirical nature of Pliny's garden design jibes with Pope's refusal to be bound by principles. The Roman writer, we are told in the Preface, did not provide 'direct Rules'; instead, the various elements of the villa 'were at once accommodated by the Architect for enjoying the Benefits, and for avoiding the inconveniences of the Several Seasons'. Otherwise the guiding principle seems to be the flexible one of ensuring that buildings and landscape answered a full humanity: 'they endeavoured, while they were pleasing their palates|in the dining-room|, to indulge their sense of seeing, as their Ears were pleased with the Musick which at the same time played' (p. 39). Pliny's delight with his Laurentine home is expressed as Pope's was with Twickenham: 'my villa is large enough to afford a convenient, tho' not sumptuous reception for my friends' (p. 3). The role of art and contrivance in the design of such villas was, according to Castell's commentary, to ensure that even the best sites came to 'contain every thing that was completely agreeable'; for the 'intent of Gardens being within a fixt compass of ground, to enjoy all that Fancy could invent' (p. 116).

In Castell's reconstructed plans we should note how the layout of buildings allows, by the varied interpenetration of the wings of the villa into the garden areas, as many views as possible. Pliny's much praised *diaetae*, or sitting-rooms-cum-summer-houses, often placed at the extreme edges of the villa, increase the spectators' sense of an intermingled house and garden. Pope's principle of 'calling in the country' is clearly anticipated in this interpenetration of rooms and landscapes, with a consequent increase in the number of prospects. Pliny is at one point quite explicit that the spectator must be fully involved in what he has before him: from 'this room, which looking only on a large Body of water, there was something wanting to terminate the view, the eye being never pleased with one that is unbounded'; yet the deficiency is mostly supplied by the various movements of sun and moon upon the waters and the progress of ships at sea (p. 40). Pliny praises the variety of views even on the approach roads to Laurentum; from the villa itself these extend in different directions over the sea ('view as it were of three several seas'), over the woods and mountains (pp. 4–5). Pliny even anticipates a central tenet of the English landscapists in his explanation of our delight in these views over the countryside from his gardens: they are landscapes as in 'an exquisite Painting' (p. 58).

At Tuscum, in Castell's reconstruction, the variety of scenery is accommodated within the villa itself: there is an informal landscape in the manner of a 'beautiful Country, Hills, Rock, Cascades, Rivulets, Woods, Buildings, etc. [which] were possibly thrown into such an agreeable Disorder, as to have pleased the Eye from several views, like so many beautiful landskips' (p. 117); yet there is also ground where 'Rule and Line' have still ensured an artificiality that is pleasing (p. 116).

Another important aspect of Castell's discussion is the role of agriculture in villa architecture. It was a matter of pride to Roman authors that they could live off the resources of their own land: Pliny praises the seafood at Laurentum, just as we have seen Pope imitating a Horatian passage on georgic self-sufficiency. The same ideas concerned the English landscapists: Pope praises Bathurst in those terms in the Fourth Epistle:

His Father's Acres who enjoys in peace,
Or makes his Neighbours glad, if he increase;
Whose cheerful Tenants bless their yearly toil,
Yet to their Lord owe more than to the soil;
Whose ample Lawns are not ashamed to feed
The milky heifer and deserving steed.

[Poems, 3/ii:154–55]

This georgic imagery is a crucial ingredient also in the third Moral Essay, as well as in landscape gardens themselves: not only and most obviously in the ferme ornée, such as Southcote's Woburn Park, but also at Stowe. In the views of Stowe issued by Sarah Bridgeman in 1739 we may observe the enclosures for animals and the interest of the visitors in such georgic features [plate 43]. Even Horace Walpole, too cramped at Strawberry Hill to have these agricultural elements himself, could nevertheless look out across the Thames to watch the haymaking.

PLATE 43

Jacques Rigaud, view from Gibb's building.
Engraving by Bernard Baron from *Stowe Gardens in Buckinghamshire*.
Published by Sarah Bridgeman (1739).

Robert Castell interprets the georgic aspects of ancient villas for the eighteenth century by reconstructing from various Roman authors a landscape that includes agricultural features [plate 44]: the engraved plan concludes the second section of his book. It shows how the necessary buildings are disposed round a largely informal landscape; how some, like the Ornithon (somewhat reminiscent of the Tempietto and pool at Chiswick —seen at the centre of Rocque's plan) are made attractive for human visitors; how the needs of farming do not preclude, rather they enforce, the inclusion in such a landscape of temples to Ceres, Flora, Bacchus, Luna, Sol, Jupiter, and Venus (goddess of gardens). At such points the practical business and the mental suggestions of a garden coincide, and the authority for the disposition of similar structures in gardens at Stowe, Stourhead, Rousham, and Chiswick is advanced.

*Professors
of Gardening*

The *Epistle to Burlington* is chosen to conclude the *Moral Essays* then because it treats of many topics central to Pope's career and to its dedicatee's. For the historian of landscape gardening Pope can make explicit the relationship of purely stylistic matters of design to moral concerns. For the literary critic of Pope's poetry the larger context of architectural history should help in reading the full extent of the poet's exploration of 'a system of ethicks in the Horatian way'.

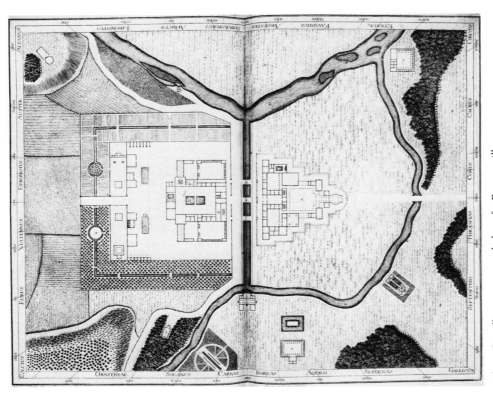

PLATE 44 Robert Castell, reconstructed plan of a Roman villa.
Engraving from *The Villas of the Ancients Illustrated* (1728).

Before Pope started his 'Opus Magnum' he had ridiculed the petty and pointless activities of Grub Street in *The Dunciad* of 1729. The great work of the 1730's was his commitment to a public and philosophical role for the poet. The contribution to it of the *Epistles to Several Persons* was the exploration of 'practical morality' to supplement the treatment of 'Man in the abstract' offered in the *Essay on Man*. But Pope's practical inquiries somehow brought to an end his larger ambitions. Maybe he came to realize more thoroughly than he did when he first wrote it in 1725 that no 'publick Professors of Gardening (any more than any publick Professors of Virtue) are equal to the Private Practisers of it'. For the *Moral Essays* celebrated private worlds of mind and friendship and invoked the personal landscapes of Twickenham, Mapledurham, Stowe, Chiswick, Riskins, and Cirencester Park. The combination of these gardening enthusiasms of the 1730's and the increasing identification of landscape design with his 'internal view' of mankind made him more and more dissatisfied with the bedlam and chaos of the outside world. This chaos is the hideous muse of *The New Dunciad* of 1742, a force so 'inertly strong' that it finally extinguishes all learning and all art:

Nor *public* Flame, nor *private*, dares to shine:
Nor *human* Spark is left, nor Glimpse *divine!*
Lo! thy dread Empire, CHAOS! is restored;
Light dies before thy uncreating word:
Thy hand, Great Anarch, lets the curtain fall;
And universal Darkness buries All.

[*Poems*, 5:409]

Pope's refusal to compete with Grub Street is expressed in the heroic celebrations of the enfolding blankness of the Dunces' *logos*. He has meanwhile withdrawn into the personal elysium of garden and grotto: a base for the satirist, as Maynard Mack has shown, but not to be jeopardised. And Pope makes the position of his private world vis-à-vis the public perfectly clear: the hacks of the literary world/die daily . . . and . . . raise nothing', whereas 'every stick you plant, and every stone you lay is to some purpose'.

In 1736 he was writing to Swift about the progress of his 'Opus Magnum':

But alas! the task is great, and *non sum qualis eram!* My understanding indeed, such as it is, is extended rather than diminish'd: I see things more in the whole, more consistent, and more clearly deduced from, and related to, each other. But what I gain on the side of philosophy, I lose on the side of poetry: the flowers are gone, when the fruits begin to ripen.

But if the flowers were gone, his gardens grew. There is some covert but firm bond between his dedication to gardens and the 'Contemplative habit', which we have already noticed. As he came to value 'just thinking' and 'natural acting' and as his contemplative habits grew in sophistication ('I love to pour out all myself, as plain / As downright Shippen, or as old Montaigne'), so did he cling to the notion that 'Gardening [is] more Antique and nearer God's own work, than Poetry'. The antiquity of gardening was no idle *jeu d'esprit*: for Pope it was an 'innocent employment' simply because it was that which God had 'appointed for his First Man'; it was perhaps the precedent of paradise that urged him to accommodate 'all trees' in a garden and achieve an ideal variety. Yet it was no prelapsarian perfection that Pope sought through his gardening activities or when he spent every available daylight hour in the gardens at Stowe. He had written facetiously once to Lord Bathurst:

THE FIGURE IN THE LANDSCAPE

I believe you are by this time immers'd in your vast *Wood*; and one may address you as to a very abstracted person, like Alexander Selkirk, or the Self-Taught Philosopher.

But the Self-Taught Philosopher, one Hai Ebn Yocktan, had dedicated himself solely to the 'mystic contemplation of Divine Essence', whereas Pope's philosophical ambitions had been more modest and humanistic. When 'Mr Pope himself talks like a Philosopher and one wholly retired', as he did to Swift, his discourse was of human nature.

So we may suspect some undercurrents in Pope's frequent remarks upon the progress of his grotto, upon the skill with which he works to make it 'resemble Nature in all her workings'. When he tells one correspondent that he hopes it 'will be the best imitation of Nature that I ever made' or another of the grotto's 'Extensive View of Nature in her most curious Works', Pope is not innocent of the moral implications of representing the diversities of moss or of nature's geological riches. He had, after all, written in the *Epistle to Cobham*: 'Grant but as many sorts of mind as Moss'. The grotto was as studied an image of the complexities of man's mind as anything in the 'Opus Magnum', and the poet's comparison of it to Plato's cave supports this interpretation.

Pope's two lifelong interests, both of which are treated in the *Moral Essays*, are 'the Nature and State of Man *with respect to Himself*', and gardening ('when you talk of Building and Planting, you touch my string'). His concerns with the one are to determine how to read and explain the human personality; with the other to shape varieties of landscape to those of mind. His use of 'formal' and 'informal' elements in garden design matches both his inclination towards abstract philosophical theories and his Montaigne-like observation of the awkwardness of such rules in face of human variety and unpredictability. The *Epistles* may only be loosely structured, but their framework quite deliberately allows a movement from the philosophical to the horticultural that, in fact, makes connections between them.

Three of the epistles are directed to patrons and creators of famous gardens, where variety and surprise are arranged in both schematic and apparently unstructured modes and so parallel Pope's insights into the 'Nature and State of Man'. Even the third epistle, which at first seems neither a part of the psychological interests in the first two nor related to the gardenist topics of the fourth, contributes to the collective endeavours of the *Moral Essays*. At the centre of its exploration of man's fallen or capitalist nature is the moral exemplum of the Man of Ross: he, like the addressee of Pope's epistle, has dedicated himself to a life that is expressed among other ways in the richest of georgic and landscaping imagery:

Who hung with woods yon mountain's sultry brow?
From the dry rock bade the waters flow?
Not to the skies in useless columns tost,
Or in proud falls magnificently lost,
But clear and artless, pouring thro' the plain
Health to the sick, and solace to the swain.

[*Poems*, 3/ii:114]

That georgic strain, amusingly opposed to gambling and political bribery elsewhere in the *Epistle*, echoes both Pope's *Spectator* essay of 1712 and Castell's investigation of the agricultural aspects of Pliny's villas, which in their turn were echoed in most Augustan gardening. The paradisal point of this golden age imagery in the *Epistle to Bathurst*'s inquiry into man's fallen nature is not only rhetorical: it gestures, more importantly, towards the art of landscaping that Pope and his friends found to be 'nearer God's own work' even than poetry.

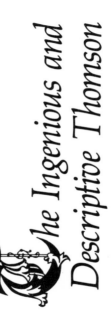

THREE

The Ingenious and Descriptive Thomson

Unlike Pope, James Thomson was himself no gardener. But he came to recognize what landscape gardening meant to his poetry by visiting other people's estates, particularly Lord Lyttelton's Hagley Park. So one of this chapter's themes is the increased role of landscape gardens in *The Seasons* (notably its revised versions), as Thomson realized their usefulness as a means of formulating and shaping his meditations and introspection among natural scenery. More generally, and as a complement to the discussion of Pope's career, this chapter will explore how an early eighteenth-century poet sought to link the internal territory of his mind with the external world; and how, in searching for a vocabulary to articulate these links, he chose to replace traditional emblems and iconographical language with more expressive images. It was in the early English landscape garden, I suggest, that these expressive images were first discovered by Thomson as well as by Pope.

The Seasons may be read in part as Thomson's extended illustration of the remark by Timothy Nourse, already quoted (p. 32): 'When a Man attentively considers the Annual Progress of Nature through all its stages and alterations, it cannot but remind him of his own continual changes'. Such attentive men are frequently singled out for praise by Thomson: in his account of the aurora borealis (*Autumn*, ll. 1108 ff.) the 'superstitious din' of the crowd is contrasted with

> the man of philosophic eye
> And inspect sage: the waving brightness he
> Curious surveys, inquisitive to know
> The causes and materials, yet unfixed,
> Of this appearance beautiful and new.

It is such learned philosophers who will be most sensible of analogies between the 'Annual Progress of Nature' and their own 'continual changes'. Thus Thomson celebrates in *Autumn*

> the man who, from the world escaped,
> In still retreats and flowery solitudes
> To Nature's voice attends from month to month,
> And day to day, through the revolving year—
> Admiring, sees her in her every shape;
> Feels all her sweet emotions at his heart.

[ll. 1304–9]

Thomson, however, has larger ambitions for his poem than Nourse's suggestion contains, and these are also frequently adumbrated: he tells us in *Summer* (ll. 40–41) that beneath the all-alterations and changes of the seasons may be identified 'the all-perfect Hand / That poised, impels, and rules the steady whole'. It is this divine control that the poet also celebrates. Here, too, there will be intimate correspondences between the 'revolving year' and the 'emotions' at man's heart, but they will quickly initiate the process by which

larger prospects of the beauteous whole
Would gradual open on our opening minds;
And each diffusive harmony unite
In full perfection to the astonished eye.

[*Winter*, ll. 579–82]

As with Thomson's human or sentimental interests, these divine meditations are often couched in terms of some exchange between exterior world, attentively surveyed, and the mind —each responding to the other in some simultaneous dialogue: the 'open' landscape of the passage just quoted being answered by and itself compelled by the 'opening' mind three words later.

Thomson will, inevitably, bring these two interests together at various moments in the poem. His address to 'serene Philosophy' in *Summer* (ll. 1730 ff.) first notices how science, the 'Effusive source of evidence and truth', tutors his poetry, teaching it to rise above the 'fluttering crowd'; he then proceeds to explain his dual interest in Nature, which is 'To reason's and to fancy's eye displayed':

The first up-tracing, from the dreary void,
The chain of causes and effects to Him,
The world-producing Essence, who alone
Possesses being; while the last receives
The whole magnificence of heaven and earth,
And every beauty, delicate or bold,
Obvious or more remote, with livelier sense,
Diffusive painted on the rapid mind.

As with many of Thomson's connections, the 'while' that serves to join his two sentences there is required to perform almost impossible tasks. 'While' simply evades an explanation of how the two themes of Thomson's song coexist in the poetry, except as alternating modes of vision. Thomson's divine meditations and his humanist or sentimental ones may each be informed with something of the other's interest and both may be sustained by an active and scientific attention to the physical universe, but they remain uneasily separate. Their separation, announced in Thomson's syntax, pervades the whole poem and has a crucial effect upon our particular interest in the poetry—its debts to painting and to landscape gardening and its efforts to win from those other arts adequate (that is to say, properly verbal) means of structuring and formulating introspection.

The illustrations that William Kent provided for the 1730 edition of *The Seasons* seem to identify in their own way these and other dichotomies in the poem. Kent manages to interpret the verbal world in his own painterly and landscapist terms and so to isolate certain characteristic structures of Thomson's imagination. In each design he divides the visual space into two distinct areas, related almost entirely by mere contiguity, connected at most by some ambiguous lines—the descending rain and wind in *Winter*, the rays of the sun in *Summer*, the rainbow's arc in *Spring* [plate 45] and the aspiring and mounting impulse of the stag's head in *Autumn* [plate 46]. The higher of these pictorial spaces is occupied by a cluster of deities and putti, poised on or descending from the heavens like the figures of some baroque ceiling by G. Lanfranco or G.-B. Gaulli. Above and among these celestial personages appear the relevant zodiacal signs, drawn upon an arc of white page that it is possible to read naturalistically as a shaft of bright sunshine among the massed chiaroscuro clouds that support the figures or, in the illustration for *Spring*, as a fragment of secondary rainbow. The lower half of each design is occupied by an image of some extensive landscape, dotted with buildings, peopled with incidents more or less related to the incidents of Thomson's succeeding verses.

Kent isolates then not only two of the basic strategies in *The Seasons* but also their awkward relationship. For in the verbal spaces of the poetry Thomson employs both emblem and expressive scenery as metaphors for man's relationships with nature. Both are evident in the opening lines of *Winter*, considered by John Constable 'as a beautiful instance of the poet identifying his own feelings with external nature':

See, *Winter* comes to rule the varied year,
Sullen and sad, with all his rising train—
Vapours, and clouds, and storms. Be these my theme;
These, that exalt the soul to solemn thought
And heavenly musing. Welcome, kindred glooms!
Cogenial horrors, hail! With frequent foot,
Pleased have I, in my cheerful morn of life,
When nursed by careless solitude I lived
And sung of Nature with unceasing joy,
Pleased have I wandered through your rough domain;
Trod the pure virgin-snows, myself as pure;
Heard the winds roar, and the big torrent burst;
Or seen the deep-fermenting tempest brewed
In the grim evening-sky. Thus passed the time,
Till through the lucid chambers of the south
Looked out the joyous Spring—looked out and smiled.

PLATE 45
William Kent, *Spring*.
Engraved illustration for *The Seasons* (1730).

Winter starts with verbal reminders of familiar Renaissance iconography, a visual language with which poets were perfectly familiar and, furthermore, which both Kent and later Thomson would have encountered on their visits to Italy: Kent indeed translates Thomson's first three lines exactly simply because the images were pictorial in the first place. We see the allegorical figure of winter accompanied by his train, who dispense —from urn or lungs—vapours, clouds, and storms. They are '*kindred glooms*' and '*congenial* [i.e., congenial] horrors' because they both arouse and also answer the weather in the poet's soul. Yet it is, besides the iconographical, a real weather which Thomson associates with his youth in Scotland, when he was 'nursed by careless solitude', so that he identifies the snow with his own youthful purity; the mature poet can recall how he heard winds roar and the torrent burst and retrospectively see

PLATE 46   William Kent, *Autumn*.
Engraved illustration for *The Seasons* (1730).

the 'grim evening sky' together with the other horrors as somehow prophetic of manhood and life in a more hostile world. But the coming of spring in those early days is treasured also for its (again implied) analogies to the pleasures of approaching manhood; at this point the poetry neglects the fragmentary suggestions of real landscape and weather and resumes the emblematic vocabulary. For the varied gods of Thomson's personifications are readily invoked when some expected human response to the 'revolving year' is needed: Spring 'looked out and smiled'—as she does in the upper space of Kent's first design—because that is how man himself reacts to her advent.

Where Thomson is most easily and mechanically a 'descriptive poet', the usual claim his sympathetic critics generally make for him, is in such iconographical moments. When at the start of

Summer, the poetry presents the season 'In pride of youth . . . attended by the sultry Hours' from whose 'ardent look the turning Spring / Averts her blushful face', Thomson is drawing upon a vast Renaissance iconography, visible in painting and fresco, and its grammar made available in innumerable hand-books. The seasonal change from springtime to summer heat thus becomes an amorous exchange between some baroque ceiling deities. Later (ll. 81 ff.) the sun becomes some monarch on triumphal progress—

> round thy beaming car,
> High-seen, the Seasons lead, in sprightly dance
> Harmonious knit, the rosy-fingered Hours,

—and this conventional visual hint (doesn't 'High-seen' even suggest some ceiling decoration?) is readily absorbed by Kent into his memories of famous baroque artworks. It is usual to cite Guido Reni's *Aurora* alongside such a passage: but for both poet and illustrator there were other famous precedents, like Pietro da Cortona's *Aurora* in the main gallery of Villa II Vascello, near the Porta S Pancrazio in Rome, a gallery that significantly combined a frieze of landscapes and seascapes with allegories of *Midday* by Francesco Allegrini and *Night* by G. F. Grimaldi, as well as Cortona's. In the vault of the loggia at the Villa Turini, also in Rome, was Giovanni da Udine's stucco, *Chariot of Dawn*, while yet another *Aurora*, by Guercino and Agostino Tassi, was in the Casino dell'Aurora, at Villa Ludovisi. Although Thomson had no chance to see any of these for himself before the first edition of *The Seasons* (he reached Rome in November 1731), their fame would have reached him via copies, engravings maybe, and guidebook descriptions. So that Thomson's invocation of these varieties of image, termed by the 1709 edition of Ripa's *Iconologia* the 'various Images of Virtues, Vices, Passions . . . Humours, Elements' that are 'representa-tions of our Notions', is an instinctive device to use in shaping ideas of seasonal phenomena, especially when some human response to climate or geography is also intended. *Summer's* excursion to tropical climes does not necessarily leave such devices behind, and the impressiveness of the sources of the Nile (ll. 805 ff.) is imaged by presenting some river gods, majestically recumbent and at ease, pouring their streams from classical urns into pools where statues of Naiads play [cf. plate 11].

Thomson is equally ready to employ this iconography when psychological states are to be described:

> In these green days,
> Reviving Sickness lifts her languid head;
> Life flows afresh; and young-eyed Health exalts
> The whole creation round. Contentment walks

The sunny glade, and feels an inward bliss
Spring o'er his mind, beyond the power of kings
To purchase. Pure Serenity apace
Induces thought, and contemplation still.
By swift degrees the love of Nature works,
And warms the bosom; till at last, sublimed
To rapture and enthusiastic heat,
We feel the present Deity, and taste
The joy of God to see a happy world.

[*Spring*, ll. 891–903]

As in Pope's *Eloisa to Abelard*, such allegorical imagery can only be of very general force. 'Sickness' and 'Health' are rather mechanical; the 'sunny glade', with its warmth and seclusion, instigates and controls the *idea* of contentment without particularising it. Both scenery and corresponding feelings and notions are distanced by this generalized idiom ('the bosom' or 'a happy world'); the personal pronoun scarcely intrudes any particularity by virtue of its unspecific reference ('We').

Where, by contrast, Thomson attempts 'a new kind of poetry', which is how Dr. Johnson judged *The Seasons*, is when landscapes alone, uncluttered with iconographical 'representations' of 'Passions . . . Humours', are called upon to articulate some particular human involvement with the natural world. Not only is Thomson attempting particularity in these instances but also some more direct annotation—that is to say, avoiding at least one stage in representing human states by omitting the description of iconographical images and working instead at establishing some properly poetic congruence between outside and inside.

One of these passages, too lengthy to quote, concerns the poet's walk with Amanda (*Spring* ll. 480 ff). The lines invoking Elizabeth Young under the name of Amanda (483–88) were added to the edition of 1744, after Thomson's proposal of marriage had been refused the previous year; the personal allusion confirmed the original movement of the passage away from generalizations. It is also perhaps significant that this long account of a walk in the countryside, ending at the 'finished garden', immediately follows the poet's anxiety whether imagination and language can match the 'colours and . . . power' of the natural world. We shall examine later how Thomson's various ideas of the imaginative process affected his poetic meditations among landscapes: here it is necessary only to remark how the challenge of nature's immense variety of distinct items seems to require of the poetry an exceptional specificity.

The landscape is visited briefly at the start by the iconographical glimpse of 'rosy-footed May / [who] Steals Blushing on', but the emphasis is quickly directed to Thomson's own excursion with Amanda:

together let us tread
The morning dews, and gather in their prime
Fresh-blooming flowers to grace thy braided hair
And thy loved bosom.

It is still a generalized, conventional image of lovers in spring-time; but there is something specific now about the first person plural, and this in its turn is confirmed by the first of the two prospects that follow. Unlike other prospects described by Thomson, this of 'winding vale' and 'extended field' neglects any painterly antecedents, those Claudian imitations in verse that we shall discuss in the next section. The address, '*See* where the winding vale', and the other syntactical gestures towards the scenery ('*yon* extended field') are the poet's involvement of himself and Amanda—and thereby of the reader—in the various landscape before them. (Kent echoes this technique—or maybe realizes what Thomson borrowed in the first place from landscape painting—in the gesturing shepherd in the bottom left of his *Spring* landscape, inviting us to survey the scenery that he knows and of which he is already an informed part). But the landscape into which we enter by that invitation to 'see' is like any vision of nature 'undisguised by mimic art'; compounded of both vague impressions of general scope—'the winding vale its lavish stores / Irriguous, spreads'—and the sharply defined, yet random, details of that prospect:

See how the lily drinks
The latent rill, scarce oozing through the grass
Of growth luxuriant, or the humid bank
In fair profusion decks.

The movement of the paragraph continues this visual mixture of large impression (the 'extended field', the 'purple heath') and sudden definition (the bees sucking from the flowers with 'inserted tube') that establishes the lovers' involvement in walking and registering the landscape.

Johnson's observation that Thomson's was a mind that at once comprehended the vast and attended to the minute is particularly just here. It points to Thomson's skill in recreating human participation in natural scenery, which probably comprises, as in this passage, general memories and isolated, clear details. It is a further characteristic of this passage that Thomson does not seek to link its description of the beneficent natural process to 'the God of the Seasons'; such theo-physical meditations tend, by their very nature, to be generalized. Instead he relates the landscape to his passion for Amanda; since this motive is secondary to the structure of the country walk, it functions as a consequence more subtly. The enthusiasm of the random sampling of nature's 'lavish stores' intimates the happiness of Thomson's imagined excursion more vividly than some allegorical figure of Contentment. The luxuriance and extensiveness of the scenery are more explicitly linked to Amanda: 'Nor is the mead unworthy of thy feet'; mention of her feet releases the memory of where she trod, the field's 'unnumbered flowers'. Amanda, too, presumably exemplifies the limitless beauty of nature unmediated by mimic art. Yet these parallels and equations are allowed to emerge more easily and unobtrusively than they did in the generalized iconography of the passage from *Summer*.

The Finished Garden

In the country walk with Amanda Thomson seems to shape his descriptions of landscape and feeling by a subtle imitation of excited human recollection. But like all Augustan poets, Thomson elsewhere relies more usually upon organizing his ideas and feelings in some available artificial structure—the deliberate imitation of classical poets, for example, often in recent English versions. Two visual forms also provided Thomson with patterns: the picturesque—seeing some landscape in the manner of a Dughet or Claude and then finding a verbal equivalent for the effect upon a spectator of one of their pictures; and the gardenist—never differentiated by the poet's critics as a significant structure, but one, as we shall see, of some consequence to both Thomson and later poetry.

The poet's walk with Amanda takes the lovers from the 'negligence of Nature wide and wild' to the controlled effects of a landscape garden:

At length the finished garden to the view
Its vistas open and its alleys green.
Snatched through the verdant maze, the hurried eye
Distracted wanders; now the bowery walk
Of covert close, where scarce a speck of day
Falls on the lengthened gloom, protracted sweeps;
Now meets the bending sky, the river now
Dimpling along, the breezy ruffled lake,
The forest darkening round, the glittering spire,
The ethereal mountains, and the distant main.

The garden is 'finished' not only in the sense of a perfected nature but a completed artifact. The elements of nature have been employed, but shaped to exercise certain predetermined effects, to elicit and contain certain anticipated reactions from its visitors as they explore its four-dimensional structure. Yet, curiously, Thomson neglects to respond to that fundamental aspect of this garden. He treats it instead like some picture, over whose illusionary depths his 'hurried eye / Distracted wanders'; his visual attention is 'Snatched' hither and thither—'now the bowery walk. . . . Now . . . the bending sky . . . the river now—until, as in a Claude painting, it gluts itself on the 'ethereal mountain, and the distant main.' No wonder Thomson immediately asks, 'But why so far excursive?', and returns, almost Cowley-like, to a catalogue of botanical specimens close at hand and under his eye—if not, at this point, under his microscope.

Yet there lurks in this description of the garden, which appeared in the first edition of *Spring* in 1728, hints of how gardens could be experienced, both for their own sakes and subsequently as some formal metaphor for Thomson's mental activity. The poet tells us that 'Its vistas open', which should tempt visitors to explore, according to their mood and present inclination, either the 'verdant maze' or the 'lengthened gloom'. The word 'maze' has sufficient affinities with 'amaze' to contrive the proper suggestion of a garden's psychological manipulation of visitors; this is echoed by 'Distracted', though its application to a solely visual exploration is curiously limiting. The 'Dimpling river' and the 'ruffled lake' provide further deliberate alternatives—designed for the garden and recognized in the poetry's syntax—as do the 'alleys green' and the 'forest darkening round', which are themselves ingredients of yet another, larger scheme of the garden's design, namely the bringing into visitors' mental range the idea of an explorable landscape immediately around them and an inaccessible, hence 'ethereal', territory on the horizon. This was the basic design of such a garden as Rousham, for example, where Kent during the 1730's softened the lines of an earlier plan by Charles Bridgeman: the results provided both distant features, like the 'Eyecatcher' upon a northern hill, that was not intended to be reached, and direct invitations for visitors upon the bowling-green before the house to turn away from the prospect over the river and explore the glades and terraces immediately to their left.

These notions of garden design and psychology seem to be registered by Thomson's paragraph, yet their potential is neglected. His treatment of the garden as a picture with visual relationships and harmonies recognizes of course an essential inspiration, as we saw, to early landscapists and one often enough adumbrated in their writings. But even if, as Pope thought, 'All gardening is landscape painting', the experience of a garden, as Bolingbroke found at Twickenham, was also the movement *through* multiplied scenes. Thomson learns these gardenist possibilities later. But already in 1730 Kent's illustrations for *Spring* and *Autumn* contain hints of the consequent development of the poem: the buildings disposed carefully in the lower landscapes catch the eye and tempt the curious, as it were, towards them. That the domed building in *Autumn* roughly resembles Lord Burlington's Palladian villa at Chiswick might be an added allusion to an early garden in which provision was made for psychological exploration.

It was in 1743 that Thomson first visited Hagley Park, the estate of his friend and patron, Lord Lyttelton. It was at Hagley that *The Seasons* were enlarged and revised and the Park figures in one of the major additions to the text of 1744. It is a long passage (*Spring*, ll. 904–62) but the section immediately following Thomson's apostrophe to Lyttelton is worth detailed study:

Thy passions thus
And meditations vary, as at large,
Courting the muse, through Hagley Park you stray—
Thy British Tempe! There along the dale
With woods o'erhung, and shagged with mossy rocks
Whence on each hand the gushing waters play,
And down the rough cascade white-dashing fall
Or gleam in lengthened vista through the trees,
You silent steal; or sit beneath the shade
Of solemn oaks, that tuft the swelling mounts
Thrown graceful round by Nature's careless hand,
And pensive listen to the various voice
Of rural peace—the herds, the flocks, the birds,
The hollow-whispering breeze, the plaint of rills,
That, purling down amid the twisted roots
Which creep around, their dewy murmurs shake
On the soothed ear. From these abstracted oft,
You wander through the philosophic world;
Where in bright train continual wonders rise
Or to the curious or the pious eye.

Lyttelton's feelings and thoughts are seen to be closely related to particular spots in his park, and they 'vary' as he strays. The poetry follows him down the valley, its syntax forcing us to attend to the various elements of this part of the landscape ('woods . . . mossy rocks . . . cascade') before we realize ('You silent steal') that these have been the objects of *his* vision during the stroll. The alternative to the sublime scenery of hanging woods, rough rocks, and waterfalls is the shade of solemn oaks and the 'various voice / Of rural peace'. The close relationship of context to meditation, announced at the start of the passage, is suggested, too, by Lyttelton's attentiveness to these voices of nature, from whom he hears of the idea of 'peace', or by the breeze and rills that whisper and complain to the 'soothed ear'. The last three and a half lines of the passage quoted work even more carefully to describe the meditative habits of garden visitors: the *sequence* of scenes promotes a 'bright *train*' of 'continual wonders', the noun stressing the mental participation in the exterior world.

Parallel with these empirical adventures Lyttelton moves also 'through the philosophic world': their close connection is signalled by that 'abstracted oft' (implying both his abstraction and the ideas his mind abstracts from the images seen around him) and by the bright wonders presenting themselves 'to the curious or the pious eye'. Yet the garden's congruence with the human mind and feelings is not necessarily simple or transmitted in one direction only. Designed to stimulate certain ideas, Hagley Park was also, as we shall see, a garden flexible enough to yield different impressions to different human moods. Thus, some lines later, Thomson sees Lyttelton walking with his wife and notes how 'Then Nature all / Wears to the lover's eye a look of love'. That a garden could be read according to the temper of a particular mood as well as teach its visitors to respond to its 'finished' ideas was probably something that Thomson learnt from Hagley Park.

We have sufficient independent testimony of Lyttelton's estate to be able to judge how thoroughly Thomson responded to the possibilities of its gardenist structure. But it is also worth remarking how he still slips from a proper response to a garden into a picturesque mode when he describes how Lyttelton, though still within his estate, reaches the brow of a hill and takes in the 'bursting prospect'. At that point the poetry of the garden, which notices different vistas and varying scenes and lets them image 'man's continual changes' of mood and idea, gives way to a poetry which attempts to recreate our scrutiny of a landscape painting: the eye 'excursive roams', enjoying the various configurations of illusionary scenes, but always outside them:

Meantime you gain the height, from whose fair brow
The bursting prospect spreads immense around;
And, snatched o'er hill and dale, and wood and lawn,
And verdant field, and darkening heath between,
And villages embosomed soft in trees,
And spiry towns by surging columns marked
Of household smoke, your eye excursive roams—
Wide-stretching from the Hall in whose kind haunt
The hospitable Genius lingers still,
To where the broken landscape, by degrees
Ascending, roughens into rigid hills
O'er which the Cambrian mountains, like far clouds
That skirt the blue horizon, dusky rise.

The prospect is seen from a fixed point of view some height above it, thus creating a space between Lyttelton and the landscape. There is no sense here of the mind either registering particular items or being involved in any dialogue with the scenery around it: indeed, the garden landscape *through* which Lyttelton walks in the preceding passage and in which elements were particularized by their relationship to his mind is now replaced by one *over* which it is the eye that has almost exclusive control and in which nothing is particularized: 'hill and dale, and wood and lawn' rather than 'gushing waters play' or 'plaint of rills'. It is a pattern quite appropriate for our survey of distant countryside; its contrast with the garden sequence is psychologically accurate. Moreover, its one specific moment—the couple of lines on the Hall—implies a familiar enough human instinct, that of reading intimate detail into distant objects with which one is familiar (though Thomson's flattery is also an obtrusive element here).

The whole prospect passage borrows its 'grammar of patterns and structures' from Claudean landscapes. The eye is at first hurried hither and thither over a painting (and over real landscapes that painterly tastes have instinctively come to read as paintings) until it either knows the full repertoire of incidents or finds some centre or focus—often with Claude, as Michael Kitson has suggested, this is the horizon. Only then does the eye start to linger over specific items, for their own sakes as well as for their place in the total pattern. Thomson's syntax recreates this process. We read hurriedly from 'And, snatched o'er hill' through the catalogue of items in order to discover the subject ('your eye') and then slacken our speed ('roams') to sample particular details ('the Hall') and relate them gradually ('by degrees') to the whole impression of a structure in which sky and earth seem of a piece, which in a painting of course they are.

Thomson manages such imitative picture-reading with enormous sophistication in this passage of 1744 and, as already mentioned, skilfully juxtaposes this sort of visual encounter with landscape to that visual-cum-introspective narration of a garden's spaces. The apt discrimination between these structures was, however, not always maintained by Thomson himself nor by the many 'descriptive' poets who strove to imitate his achievements later in the century. Their frequent confusion hampered verse which sought to describe the mind's meetings with landscape: painterly imitations in verbal form tend to be accounts primarily of visual experience and concentrate upon transcribing excursions of the eye over large terrain; the gardenist structure, by responding to local incidents, to the details of a garden's changing vistas as they strike the mind, provided a different and more flexible syntax for introspective poetry.

The poetic possibilities may be assessed perhaps best in the first place by looking at a prose account of Hagley Park. Joseph Heely published his *Letters on the Beauties of Hagley, Envil and the Leasowes* nearly thirty years after Thomson's death. Yet, even allowing for fresh developments in garden design—those accomplished by 'Capability' Brown, in particular—Heely's account jibes well with that in *Spring*, and it is evident that the skill Thomson acquired in reading a garden like Hagley during the 1740's remained typical of sensitive and alert visitors for several decades.

Towards the end of his many leisurely pages on Hagley, Heely notices the seat which Lyttelton erected to Thomson 'in secessu, quem vivus dilexit'. He continues immediately:

For variety—for almost every principal feature that distinguishes the beauty of landscape, perhaps not one place in the whole park, holds the eye so much in pleasure as this—the favourite one of the ingenious and descriptive *Thomson*.

This variety at Hagley and its carefully managed contrasts have been Heely's constant theme: 'it not only affords a multiplicity of scenes, but every one rises somewhat different in character'. Yet, as that remark makes clear, the character of scenes is as crucial as their diversity. Elsewhere, Heely can praise 'an endless prospect, enriched with every variety [that] held me for some time in much pleasure', where it appears that variousness alone is what gives the view its 'character' and attracts the visitor—just as Lyttelton in Thomson's poem is seen absorbing the panorama of various scenery from his hilltop. But Heely makes it abundantly clear in his detailed itinerary that within the garden these many different scenes have been designed to exert their respective characters one after the other upon a visitor as he explores its spaces: 'Pursuing the path, . . . almost every step called for a pause.'

Heely's narrative of a walk through Hagley Park illustrates finely the opinion of Pope that variety, 'one of the chief rules of landscape design, is 'included mostly in the contrasts'. Heely's way is along

a narrow easy waving path, by the side of a pebbly rill, that led me to a rude, gloomy hollow, with every appearance of its being left in that state, by some violent concussion, or inundation. . . . I stepped into the midst of it, to a simple bench under a tree; and from the gaity of a park, open, and filled with chearful objects, found myself in a moment immersed in a wild, disordered, and savage solitude.

And upon leaving this spot, 'after climbing a bank of a few paces, you find yourself, in an instant, borne from the regions of gloom and melancholy, to the roseate bowers of paradise'. The character of each spot is quite properly described by Heely in terms of his own emotional response to it ('gloom and melancholy'), though the tendency to generalize these responses is probably a result of Heely's writing less in his own person than in the role of any sensitive visitor. The emotional terms, however, answer the covert design that the garden has upon those who explore it. Thus at the first glimpse of the Ruin, Heely 'cannot resist an involuntary pause' during which the mind 'struck with its character, . . . naturally falls into reflections'.

There are times when these different characters are organized in some sequence of pleasantly planned surprises: 'Your attention will be called in this busy part of the park, almost every step you take. —— In advancing a few paces from the last seat, to another, you will find the face of every thing changed again'. But there is a different psychological pattern of alternative invitations: 'every step I took, whether I descended into the obscure, or rose again to the more sprightly'. And so, just before Heely reaches the Ruin,

a seat within a knot of old and crooked alders will invite you to it, where your eye will best be led over the grove that skirts the park, up the green sublime sides of the Clent hills, to their fir-crowned summit, in lofty eminence; —— or will delighted, repose at its foot, on the remains of an old dusky building, solemn and venerable, rearing its gothic turret among the bushy trees.

At that point Heely chooses to visit the Ruin. The word 'invitation' or its surrogates becomes integral to Heely's sense of the garden: from a bench somewhere along his progress he can see 'another deep glen, running into the pool, and beautifully studded with tall oaks', in the middle of which stood an urn 'too inviting, to be passed without a nearer inspection. —— I indulged my curiosity'. Elsewhere 'a bench, under an amazingly large oak, stopped me to look at a portico, through a leafy opening'; or again, from his seat near a grotesque and ruined lime tree 'I was invited . . . to explore other beauties'.

It is obvious enough that Heely's aim is to celebrate Hagley Park's imaginative design, its control of our responses, and 'its intention . . . to fill the mind with the most romantic ideas'. He dutifully falls under the spell of each particular spot and is equally attentive to the unfolding sequence of these landscape characters. His approach to and departure from the Grotto constitute perhaps the most carefully composed passage—composed, first, in the actual garden and, then, in his own prose. He has been following

an easy winding path, shady, and well conducted, till it opened to a sweep of lawn, skirted every way by groves, and subordinate clumps of well grown elms. An elegant temple, rising in a circular bend, on a brow that gradually slopes to the foot, will fasten your attention, and compel you to acknowledge, no building ever stood more powerfully conducive to the pleasure of landscape.

This prospect surrenders quickly to the 'solemn opake cast' of the Grotto, where 'for some time I musingly walked within the umbrage of gloomy yews, and other ever-greens, crowded, and in negligent confusion'. But Heely's taste for gardens is acute and sophisticated, and he suspects that his present solemn and gloomy situation 'was meant to contrast the more lively features of some approaching effort of the designer's genius'. His conjectures, as he tells us, 'were soon confirmed':

From a small bench under an oak of surprising magnitude, the scene began to open—to shew something so inexpressibly pleasing—that I could not help forming ideas of an immediate transition into Arcadian felicity—into fairy land; where fancy might possibly prompt me to imagine the little dapper inhabitants were surrounding my steps; and I, a spectator of their mystic revels.

The idea of the first was realized; and, to fill the beautiful picture, I fondled the other in the true spirit of Quixote enthusiasm.

Probably Heely's most personal and, as *he* says, enthusiastic moment in the *Letters*, this reveals how once a garden has initiated certain ideas and moods the visitor himself can improve upon its suggestions by his own fancy. The park at Hagley, by the time Heely comes to describe it, is one that demonstrates

the excellence of the present mode of gardening . . . in being subject to no manner of form, nor to any confinement whatever — that every place has *capability*; and beauty, with an enterprizing judgement, may be introduced, though, perhaps not to appear in such captivating features as in some others.

Heely means, most obviously, that landscape gardening is no longer organized into a priori shapes of parterres or terraces or arcades; yet the force of his remark is also to reveal the opportunities for individual interpretation of a garden's forms and character. Unlike an introspective poet such as Thomson, whose role it is to disclose his imaginative experience, Heely is just a reporter; but even in his mainly factual account lurk clues to the possibilities of subjective response to a landscape. When he describes a 'sombrous glen' as a 'face of the deepest solitude, yet not without a certain cheerfulness hanging about it, extremely pleasing', he identifies alternative characters, to either of which, given his mood, a man might respond.

This account of Hagley Park suggests that Thomson's vision of it added to *The Seasons* in 1744, although much briefer and circumscribed, nevertheless responded to its various structure. A stranger at Hagley, says Heely, 'stands in rapture—he gazes —contemplates'. So Thomson, more intimate with its owner than any tourist, learnt not only to gaze and contemplate but to forge some poetic and imaginative connections between these activities. In particular, I suggest, he learnt at Hagley that 'Real landscape, and canvas landscape are two things' (the observation is Heely's). The 'extreme difference' between 'painting and designing' also extends to the different activities of reading a picture and exploring a garden. It is a distinction that Thomson demonstrates he has appreciated not only by further additions to the 1744 text of *The Seasons* but by his visit to another garden near Hagley.

This visit is recorded by William Shenstone, to whose garden at The Leasowes, Thomson came with William Lyttelton. They had all passed, Shenstone tells us,

into Virgil's Grove. What a delightful place, says he, is this for a person of a poetical genius. I don't wonder you're a devotee to the Muses. —— This place, says Mr L[yttelton] will *improve* a poetical genius. —— Aye, replied Mr T. and a poetical genius will improve this place.

Shenstone's account of this visit, which took place in 1746, reveals Thomson is by this time a connoisseur of the finer points of garden art. He had been 'particularly struck with the valley and brook *by which he had passed*' (my italics) and at a later stage recommended another walk up the valley from Virgil's Grove: he is, in other words, attentive to the exploratory as well as the picturesque structures of a garden. He also, according to Shenstone, approved plans for a model of Virgil's Tomb, an obelisk and various mottoes selected from Virgil and was eager to establish the precise idea and character of the Grove: 'He denominated my Virgil's Grove there Le Vallon occuls. —— Sombre, says Mr L. —— No, not sombre occuls. —— This must evidently be the idea of Petrarch's Valclusa'.

Thy Villas Shine

In one of the characteristic passages of Whig patriotism in which Thomson indulges, he celebrates the 'goodly prospect' that greets him from Richmond Hill:

hills, and dales, and woods, and lawns, and spires,
And glittering towns, and gilded streams, till all
The stretching landscape into smoke decays!
Happy Britannia! where the Queen of Arts,
Inspiring vigour, Liberty, abroad
Walks unconfined.

[*Summer*, ll. 1439–44]

The whole Thames Valley seems to become one large landscape garden: the oaks are 'unmatched', the valleys float with golden waves, the meadows glow, and 'On every hand / Thy villas shine'.

    This panegyric was augmented in the 1744 revisions, and nearly seventy lines (ll. 1371–1437) inserted into *Summer* just before it. This addition declares Thomson's increasing authority as a connoisseur and historian of the English garden and suggests once again that he was finding the structures of a garden useful to him as a meditative poet. The first section of the new passage is not, in fact, about any garden; but what I want to argue is that Thomson applies his insights about such a place as Hagley to a landscape that might otherwise have tempted him into some picturesque structure. The introduction to the evening walk immediately stresses the congruence between the contemplative man and natural scenery:

Now the soft hour
Of walking comes for him who lonely loves
To seek the distant hills, and there converse
With nature, there to harmonize his heart,
And in pathetic song to breathe around
The harmony to others.

There is still something distinctly Augustan and Shaftesburian in that sharing of solitary meditation and song. But the song is presumably sympathetic ('pathetic') to nature, just as immediately before it the chiaroscuro of evening clouds assumed 'romantic shapes' for those whose 'waking fancy' was capable of dreaming them. These privileged imaginations are capable of new insights in 'nature's vast Lyceum', and Thomson's poetry subtly works at intimating the encounter of their minds with the visible world.

These 'social friends' register a 'fairer world' than ordinary mortals because their eye not merely looks but 'exalts'. The motives and capabilities they bring to their encounter with the natural world enhance both their minds and their vision of phenomena: the phrase, 'Improving and improved', attempts to convey that simultaneous process by which educated and educative spirits understand and are manipulated by some natural context. This 'happy unison' is equally between nature and man as between 'social friends'. But the references to 'improvement' also signal the gardenist structures which Thomson next applies to the lover's walk:

Which way, Amanda, shall we bend our course?
The choice perplexes. Wherefore should we choose?
All is the same with thee. Say, shall we wind
Along the streams? or walk the smiling mead?
Or court the forest glades? or wander wild
Among the waving harvests? or ascend
While radiant Summer opens all its pride,
Thy hill, delightful Shene?

This congruence of this varied landscape with the lover's moods is reflected in the adjectives ('smiling', 'radiant') and verbs ('court', 'opens'). Their delight is transferred to Shene, which Thomson himself glossed as the 'old name for Richmond, signifying in Saxon shining or splendour'. Lovers, it is true, are predictably single-minded, especially such generic ones as this passage produces; but Thomson insists, despite this 'All is the same with thee', that their particular mood may call for a specific context which will match or augment it. His reading of such possibilities at Hagley Park is here transferred to a larger landscape: no doubt the reference to 'Lyceum' may include an allusion to the fact that it was in a *garden* at Athens that Aristotle also taught philosophy.

Even the prospect from Richmond Hill is less remarkably picturesque than the situation would admit. Indeed, the main feature of the view is a mental excursion to various landscape gardens. It is mental, not merely visual, an imaginative or 'raptured eye', because it pretends to visions that could not literally be seen: various figures at home in their appropriate landscapes. Just as the poet and Amanda may choose their path according to the temper of their present affections, so the creators of some of the most renowned gardens of the early eighteenth century are envisaged in the contexts that they have made particularly their own:

> the pendent woods
>
> That nodding hang o'er Harrington's retreat;
> And, stooping thence to Ham's embowering walks,
> Beneath whose shades, in spotless peace retired,
> With her the pleasing partner of his heart,
> The worthy Queensberry yet laments his Gay,
> And polished Cornbury woos the willing muse,
> Slow let us trace the matchless vale of Thames;
> Fair-winding up to where the muses haunt
> In Twit'nam's bowers, and for their Pope implore
> The healing god; to royal Hampton's pile,
> To Clermont's terraced height, and Esher's groves,
> Where in the sweetest solitude, embraced
> By the soft windings of the silent Mole,
> From courts and senates Pelham finds repose.

It is a catalogue that most informed observers in the 1740's might have compiled, though Thomson reveals himself a knowledgeable historian of English gardens by his citation of Harrington's retreat, Petersham Lodge, where the 'pendant woods' were part of one of the very first landscape gardens.

There is a further addition in 1744 that concerns a landscape garden: the vision of 'The fair majestic paradise of Stowe' added to the text of *Autumn* (ll. 1037–81). It was fitted into the poem not only at a crucial moment of its introspective theme but into a section over which Thomson had already worked in 1730, moving lines from *Winter* and enlarging them (ll. 957–75 and 1030–36). It seems evident that as he grew more knowledgeable about gardens he sought to focus those parts of his evolving poem where the solitary imagination encounters natural phenomena by invoking the structures that landscape gardens had made peculiarly their own. The passage on Stowe must therefore be read as the much deliberated culmination of the whole movement of lines from l. 950, when we are first introduced to the 'lonesome muse'.

He steals away from the 'degenerate crowd' to 'soar above this little scene of things'. It is, in the first place, a straightforward praise of those who raise themselves above 'low-thoughted Vice' and 'throbbing passions'; but it contrives also to suggest how the solitary muse visits a different scenery by virtue of his sympathetic imagination. The 'lonesome muse' is in fact introduced as one to whose eye the colours of autumn appear most sharply and most variously and to whose ear alone they whisper:

But see the fading many-coloured woods,
Shade deepening over shade, the country round
Imbrown; a crowded umbrage, dusk and dun,
Of every hue from wan declining green
To sooty dark. These now the lonesome muse
Low-whispering, lead into their leaf-strown walks,
And give the season in its latest view.

The emphasis on 'view' and the autumnal colouring suggests a merely visual prospect; but the hints of 'Low-whispering' are picked up—though Thomson's connection ('Meanwhile') is yet another example of his difficulties with these transitions and developments—and attached to the 'philosophic' scrutiny of meteorological phenomena. The passage, as it stood originally in *Winter*, merely proposed a visual description:

Sometimes, a fleece
Of clouds, wide-scattering, with a lucid veil,
Soft, shadow o'er th'unruffled face of heaven;
And, through their dewy sluices, shed the sun,
With temper'd influence down.

But the revision seems to attempt a penetration of the interpreting consciousness into, even as it discusses, the phenomenon:

light shadowing all, a sober calm
Fleeces unbounded ether; whose least wave
Stands tremulous, uncertain where to turn
The gentle current; while, illumined wide,
The dewy-skirted clouds imbibe the sun,
And through their lucid veil his softened force
Shed o'er the peaceful world.

An accurate, objective vision (the 'Fleeces' of cirrus clouds) is now joined with introspective mood ('sober calm'). Yet Thomson is somewhat hampered in that mingling of inward and outward worlds by either a mimetic instinct or a too generalized formulation of the subjective, perceiving mind. Thomson is by no means dedicated to imitating exactly what he sees; but compared with, say, Gay's *Rural Sports* or Pope's *Windsor Forest*, *The Seasons* manifest a frequent delight in precisely registered phenomena. On the other hand, the person who actually registers the details of the natural world is often, as we shall see later, rather impersonal. The 'lonesome muse', like the 'lone

Quiet in her silent walks' whom he meets later, is too general and too studiously eloquent of a universal condition to bring to its encounter with landscape any very personal energy.

Thomson does modulate into a more individual voice with the next paragraph:

Thus solitary, and in pensive guise,
Oft let me wander o'er the russet mead,
And through the saddened grove, where scarce is heard
One dying strain to cheer the woodman's toil.

There is at once the possibility of alternative scenes ('russet mead' or 'saddened grove') that already imply their emotional correlatives. But he neglects to explore them immediately and invokes—perhaps by analogy with his own song—the 'music of the swarming shades'. These birds are seen to connect their assumed feeling ('some widowed songster pours his plaint') with an apt scenery ('the dead tree'). Thomson returns, however, to human sympathy in the following passage: 'The pale descending year, yet pleasing still, / A gentler mood inspires'. The 'mournful grove' answers, as it instigates, human sadness; the rustling leaf even draws the attention of the abstracted wanderer and adds its specific resonance to his studies. Yet this scene can itself yield a different character: as the 'quicker breeze' announces the expressive change by some hint of its human relevance ('sobs'), the gales spring up and strip from nature the last leaves and flowers: 'And — woods, fields, gardens, and orchards all around — / The desolated prospect thrills the soul'.

What follows is perhaps one of Thomson's more impressive attempts to explain how the imagination presides over encounters between prospect and soul. With the invocation of a pale iconographical image of Melancholy, whose outward aspect the poet acquires like a contagious disease, Thomson perhaps betrays the hesitations and experimental nature of his search for an adequate introspective poetry. But the 'sacred influence' of this figure having once inflamed his imagination, the process of creation is offered without its aid:

Ten thousand thousand fleet ideas, such
As never mingled with the vulgar dream,
Crowd fast into the mind's creative eye.
As fast the correspondent passions rise,
As varied, and as high — devotion raised
To rapture, and divine astonishment;
The love of nature unconfined, and, chief,
Of human race.

After over fifty lines more or less directed to images of the exterior, autumnal world, the 'mind's creative eye'—itself a most vital phrase—assumes, albeit brief, control. The word 'eye' retains the visual element of the process, without insisting upon its primacy, and the mind creates the thousands of 'fleet ideas'. In the terms of a Lockean psychology, upon which Thomson draws here, the images of autumn already canvassed yield the ideas. The imaginative and creative activity amalgamates, under the pressure of emotional and spiritual excitement, images, ideas, and 'correspondent passions'. As he says elsewhere, the mind becomes 'The varied scene of quick-compounded thought, / And where the mixing passions endless shift'.

It is, however, one of the disappointments of *The Seasons* that such moments are always side-tracked or just displaced by another of Thomson's many projects in the poem. We have already noticed in *Summer* (l. 1748) and could also find in *Spring* (l. 925) the inert connective words that Thomson relies upon: 'while' and 'or to the curious or the pious eye' are sleights of hand to evade explaining the relationships between his two dominant motives. In this passage from *Autumn* the insight into the creative imagination is transposed via that series of analogies (As fast . . . As varied, and as high') into a Shaftesburian celebration of the 'social offspring of the heart'. And just as unexpectedly (signalled only by a 'then') Thomson returns to scenes where the mind's creative eye would discover imagery for its 'swelling thought'.

The invitation to Melancholy (l. 1030) to bear the poet

> to vast embowering shades,
> To twilight groves, and visionary vales,
> To weeping grottoes, and prophetic glooms

was inserted here from *Winter* in the edition of 1730. It combines allusions to a selection of landscape garden ingredients with some recognition of how their 'character' works upon the human visitor: thus the grottoes are 'weeping', glooms 'prophetic', and the vales conducive to visions. There is little sense yet of the different contexts a garden might provide or of any positive role for the answering imagination. For the gloomy vales alone seem responsible for the 'angel forms athwart the solemn dusk'; the 'enthusiastic ear' is merely passive in its reception of 'voices more than human'. But what Thomson contrives in the edition of 1744 is to suggest that those 'vast embowering shades' were but part of a various landscape:

> Or is this gloom too much? Then lead, ye Powers
> That o'er the garden and the rural seat
> Preside

> · · · · · · · · · · · ·
> Oh! lead me to the wide extended walks,
> The fair majestic paradise of Stowe!

Thus Cobham's gardens offer the poet, still in the role created for him at line 970 ('solitary, and in pensive guise') and elaborated at lines 1004 onwards ('exalts the swelling thought'), another territory of exceptional scope for his particular genius.

Thomson imagines himself with Pitt walking and talking among the gardens at Stowe—exactly that dual activity for which Pope uses the verb 'expatiate' at the start of the *Essay on Man*:

While there with thee the enchanted round I walk,
The regulated wild, gay fancy then
Will tread in thought the groves of Attic land.

The 'round' of Stowe's landscape, itself implying certain predetermined patterns in the 'finished garden', is answered by, just as it initiates, the phrase 'tread in thought'. Later the same congruence is rehearsed: 'While thus we talk, and through Elysian vales / Delighted rove'. The specific allusions to Stowe's design are particularly apt and reinforce Thomson's sense of how garden structures can provide a form for meditation. The vision of Pitt's political career—

thy pathetic eloquence, that moulds
The attentive senate, charms, persuades, exalts,
Of honest zeal the indignant lightning throws,
And shakes Corruption on her venal throne

—is stimulated by their surroundings in the Elysian Fields: that we learn this subsequently ('While thus we talk, and through Elysian vales') reveals some subtlety in Thomson's handling of a garden's associative patterns in his poetry.

In the legendary Elysium those mortals favoured by the gods enjoyed their existence after death; in Stowe's Elysian Fields their example was commemorated by statues in the Temple of Ancient Virtue and their continuing relevance by the busts in the niches of the Temple of British Worthies. It is doubtless this last that Thomson designs a knowing reader to recall as the relevant item that would have provoked his meditation on Pitt's public career. And certainly it is an equally apt transition to reflect upon Cobham's, whose dismissal from the army in 1713 had first allowed him to turn his attention to his Buckinghamshire estate. The frustrations and insecurities of public service and the frequent disregard of British worth were a pervasive theme of the gardens at Stowe; indeed the whole creation of the landscape dotted with its various temples [plate 47] was a realization of the family motto—*Templa Quam Dilecta*—and so reminded its visitors at almost every vista that private worth could sometimes be sustained only in private elysiums. Thomson alludes directly to these ideas perhaps when he proposes to Pitt that they 'sit beneath the sheltered slopes, / Or in that Temple'—presumably they have reached the Temple of Friendship, finished in 1739, five years before Thomson added these lines to *The Seasons*: Pitt's bust was inside among those of

The Gate-way by Kent.

The Witch House.

The Temple of Modern Virtue.

The Temple of Antient Virtue.

The Shell Bridge.

PLATE 47

Temples at Stowe.
Engraved page from Bernard Seeley (publisher), *Stowe, the Gardens of the Rt Honourable the Lord Viscount Cobham* (1751 ed.).

opposition Whigs to whom the Temple was dedicated. The scenery answers this specific context—'with thy converse blest, catch the last smiles / Of Autumn beaming o'er the yellow woods'—uniting both the political retreat and the warmth of shared interests and friendship with the sadness and colouring of autumn.

The Stowe passage as a whole contains most of the gardenist ideas we have encountered so far: the theme of meaningful retreat—meaningful, above all, in its dialogue with the public world; the mental delight in adjudicating the careful contest between art and nature; the 'various' scenery that allows such a full repertoire to match 'the varied movements of the heart'. Thomson manages, too, a more intricate mingling of his reflection and allusions to Stowe's gardens: the thoughts on how the landscape 'enchants' the imagination and stimulates its literary ambitions can also be read as a meditation upon the art of landscaping:

While there with thee the enchanted round I walk,
The regulated wild, gay fancy then
Will tread in thought the groves of Attic land;
Will from thy standard taste refine her own,
Correct her pencil to the purest truth
Of Nature, or, the unimpassioned shades
Forsaking, raise it to the human mind.
Oh, if hereafter she with juster hand
Shall draw the tragic scene, instruct her thou
To mark the varied movements of the heart,
What every decent character requires.

It is partly the convolutions of syntax that engineer these ambiguities: 'thy . . . taste' refers back three lines to 'thee' (i.e., Pitt); but those intervening lines are occupied by landscape images that seem to usurp the antecedent, so that in the forward momentum of reading the passage it is the garden as much as his friend that seems to refine Thomson's fancy. The punctuation itself allows 'The regulated wild' to be both in apposition to the 'enchanted round' and an adjectival phrase that modifies 'fancy'; so that the garden provides a pure truth for Thomson in its natural groves: and its expressive 'shades', which are already finished and shaped by art and design, offer his imagination a model to 'raise . . . to the human mind'. Even the following passage on Thomson's dramatic work plays with 'scene' and 'character' to suggest that Stowe's mimic Attic groves as much as Pitt's example will guide him.

The ambiguities of the passage may arguably owe more to luck or muddle than judgement, though their persistence and their apt realization of gardenist themes and aims suggest some effort by Thomson to relate his thoughts to the garden. But unlike the usual poetry on gardens—for example, Gilbert West's *Stowe* of 1732—and unlike some of Thomson's own picturesque prospects, the mind is not merely led by what the eye sees. This is most evident in his refusal to give a complete account of the circuit at Stowe, which West offers; instead he selects certain spots in the landscape—the Elysian Fields or the Temple of Friendship—by which to order and form the 'internal world' of his own thoughts.

It remains to consider Thomson's notions of this 'internal world', a phrase that he uses in his apostrophe to John Locke, 'Who made the whole internal world his own' (*Summer*, l. 1559). The psychological activity by which Thomson's wide-ranging interest in nature is registered is the topic of a passage in the 1728 edition of *Spring*, later omitted:

> Thus the glad skies,
> The wide-rejoicing earth, the woods, the streams,
> With every life they hold, down to the flower
> That paints the lowly vale, or insect-wing
> Wav'd o'er the Shepherd's slumber, touch the mind
> To Nature tun'd, with a light-flying Hand,
> Invisible; quick-urging, thro' the Nerves,
> The glittering Spirits, in a flood of day.
>
> [*Spring* (1728), p. 43]

The omnivorous appetite for phenomena, large and small, is well conveyed, and so is the susceptibility of the mind to these sights. Less satisfactory is the lingering presence of allegorical machinery—the 'light-flying Hand' of some goddess Nature, who urges the 'glittering spirits' along a shaft of daylight on some baroque ceiling. Equally awkward, because unresolved, is the 'Invisible' process of the mind's reception of natural items which the first four lines of the passage have made palpable and visual.

Two other passages that did survive revision manage to remove the iconographical forms and clear up the ambiguity at the expense of the mystery and nervous excitement which are the strengths of the rejected lines from *Spring*. The first comes in *Autumn* (ll. 1359 ff.):

> the mineral strata there;
> Thrust blooming thence the vegetable world;
> O'er that the rising system, more complex,
> Of animals; and, higher still, the mind,
> The varied scene of quick-compounded thought,
> And where the mixing passions endless shift;
> These ever open to my ravished eye.

Like the revolving seasons and the tracts of nature it contemplates, the poet's mind is also a 'scene', a theatre of action: the eye mediates between them. But unlike the 'scenes' of Marvell's Nun Appleton House, Thomson's 'quick-compounded' is too mechanical an explanation of the mental drama, not surprisingly since this phrase is one of Thomson's debts to Locke, who was concerned to explain rather than increase the sense of mystery of mental experience. The inertness of the following line may also suggest that Thomson sacrifices any sense of the tensions and excitements to controlled explanations of the mind: this is supported generally by his delight in visible signs of the 'directing hand of Art' or of science and by a specific passage in *Spring*, where 'ever-changing views of good and ill, / Formed infinitely various, *vex the mind*' (ll. 298–99, my italics). In comparison with Pope, who delighted in these Montaignean visions of mental changeableness and who presented Eloisa's anguish with a keen attention to its contrary motions, Thomson is just not interested in or delighted enough by what he calls 'inward-eating change' (*Spring*, l. 333).

The final paragraphs of *Summer*, after his invocation of Locke's contributions to 'true Philosophy', offer another exploration of mental life, and have already been quoted at the start of this chapter. Thomson distinguishes between reason's eye which traces the 'chain of causes and effects to Him' and fancy's eye which

> receives
> The whole magnificence of heaven and earth,
> And every beauty, delicate or bold,
> Obvious or more remote, with livelier sense,
> Diffusive painted on the rapid mind.

Nature here merely 'displays' itself to fancy, which adopts in consequence a rather passive role ('receives' as opposed to reason's active 'tracing'). The agent of the painting is unclear, further contributing to the mind's passivity, though allowing its agility ('rapid'): if it is the 'livelier sense' that paints the mind, which Lockean psychology would suggest it was, then the mechanical emphasis overwhelms the creative.

But for Thomson the larger meaning of his seasonal explorations resides anyway in what he calls 'Philosophy' rather than the imagination. 'Tutored' by science, he says (*Summer*, ll. 1753–54, my italics), '*hence* Poetry exalts / Her voice'; he continues by demonstrating the role of Lockean science in providing an 'inward view' of the human mind, just as other lessons of the scientific revolution have been learnt in the exterior world:

> With inward view,
> Thence on the ideal kingdom swift she turns
> Her eye; and instant, at her powerful glance,
> The obedient phantoms vanish or appear;
> Compound, divide, and into order shift,
> Each to his rank, from plain perception up
> To the fair forms of fancy's fleeting train.

Satisfaction lies again in the subjection to the scientific understanding of this mental kingdom: science's glance is 'powerful', the dangerous phantoms of the human mind instantly 'obedient', and the variety of mental existence ranged from 'plain perception' to 'forms of fancy's fleeting train' in such ranks that the two activities appear to be kept mutually exclusive. Thomson seems to allow fancy a premier role in that gradation of mental skills, it is true. But his mistrust of imagination is taken, along with the explanations of its processes, from Locke:

But, when with these the serious thought is foiled,
We, shifting for relief, would play the shapes
Of frolic fancy; and incessant form
Those rapid pictures, that assembled train
Of fleet ideas, never joined before,
Whence lively Wit excites to gay surprise,
Or folly-painting Humour, grave himself,
Calls laughter forth, deep-shaking every nerve.

[Winter, ll. 609-16]

Fancy is but a frolic, however joined by wit, and provides 'relief' from the mind's 'endless growth and infinite ascent' towards the 'world-producing Essence' celebrated throughout the poem.

Thomson's is by no means either a simple outlook or a simple poetry. What has been called the 'palimpsest' of *The Seasons* seeks to contain many ideas and many attitudes, not always successfully united with each other. Among this debate and jostle the ideas and visions that concern this particular study, as they interested many later poets, are often overwhelmed or at least misdirected. His evident fascination with the private world of imagination and introspection is side-tracked or absorbed by his scientific admiration, his Augustan conviction about a public role for poetry, and his own choice for that role of the psalmist of the 'God of Seasons'. What should concern us at this stage is to isolate those former elements that become of special importance to literary history in the later eighteenth century, without neglecting how the other impulses condition them.

Thomson's instincts are—as we have seen—largely for order, control, harmony. He points out 'Where lavish Nature the directing hand / Of Art demanded' (*Autumn*, ll. 75-76) and obviously admires landscape gardens in part because in them that demand is answered. He celebrates 'Rural confusion' when it is 'composed' of herds and flocks (*Summer*, ll. 485-86). He can 'lose himself' best in the 'green delightful walks' of Dodington's seat at Eastbury in Dorset, one of the most spectacularly controlled landscapes of Vanbrugh and Bridgeman [plate 48]. The emblem of all this delight in control is probably the fisherman in *Spring* (ll. 394 ff.), whose 'art' subdues the 'springing game'. Very rarely does Thomson commit himself to chaos, and only then with a confidence that either human or at best divine order can be discovered in it: 'In cheerful error let us tread the maze / Of Autumn unconfined' (ll. 626-27). He cheers himself with the anticipation of a schematic and regulated nature; for the image of 'maze' signals this apparent labyrinth

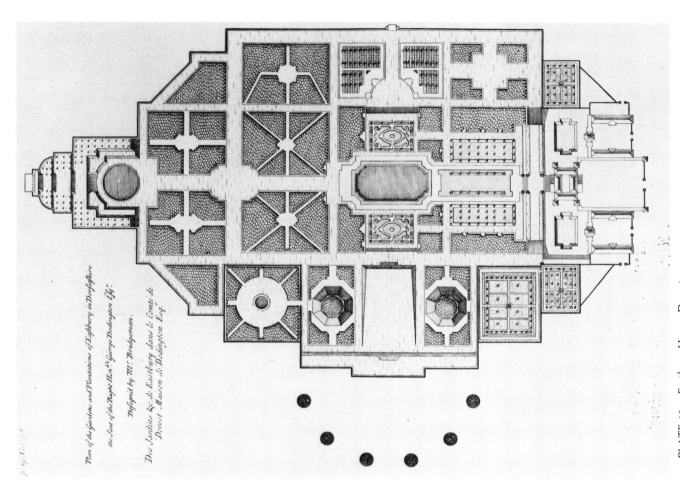

Plan of the garden and Plantations of Eastbury in Dorsetshire
the Seat of the Right Honble George Dodington Esqr.

Designed by Mr Bridgeman.

Des Jardins &c: de Eastbury dans le Comte de
Dorset Maison de Dodington Esqr.

PLATE 48   Eastbury House, Dorset.
Engraving from 1731 edition of Colin Campbell, *Vitruvius Britannicus*.

133   THE INGENIOUS AND DESCRIPTIVE THOMSON

which has yet been constructed to lead the persevering and the patient to its centre. 'Verdant maze' at *Spring*, line 105, signifies the same confidence in the identification of ultimate design; so, I believe, do such phrases as 'dewy gems' (*Spring*, l. 196) where the punning allusion to *Georgics* II. 335 invokes the word *gemma*, that in Latin means both bud and jewel, and allows Thomson to identify nature and art in the same object.

The etymological play is also in the interests of another control, that of the scientific, empirical observer, who notices how sunlight catches the moisture on plants. This control is, of course, a major theme in the poem. It provokes much scientific explanation, much ordering of the world in lists and catalogues. Even when this is declared impossible—

Then spring the living herbs, profusely wild,
O'er all the deep-green earth, beyond the power
Of botanist to number

—we are led to feel more the force of hyperbole than the defeat of empirical scrutiny. The 'cherished eye' (*Spring*, l. 89), the 'sage-instructed eye' (*Spring*, l. 210) of science, is constantly evident in a poem that is firmly aware of the achievements of the Royal Society and such of its members as Locke, Cowley, and Evelyn in emancipating 'Philosophy' from 'the magic chain of words and forms / And definition void' (*Summer*, ll. 1546–47). The primacy of sight as a mediating and controlling agency is made clear at that point in *Autumn* (ll. 1138 ff.) when night falls:

Now black and deep the night begins to fall,
A shade immense! Sunk in the quenching gloom,
Magnificent and vast, are heaven and earth.
Order confounded lies, all beauty void,
Distinction lost, and gay variety
One universal blot—such the fair power
Of light to kindle and create the whole.

Thomson aligns himself there with *The Dunciad*, momentarily sharing Pope's horror at 'universal darkness' rather than Edward Young's fascination with *Night Thoughts*.

But there are rival instincts at work in *The Seasons*. And the eye, the steady agent of Newton, Locke, and Cowley, lends its vision alike to personal, intimate moments and to 'larger prospects'. Both, certainly, avoid the 'pale fancies and chimeras huge' that come with the dark, preferring the clear daylight of the 'moral world'. A search for the 'Eternal Mind' is one activity by which Thomson holds at bay the 'winter-glooms':

Hence larger prospects of the beauteous whole
Would gradual open on our opening minds;
And each diffusive harmony unite
In full perfection to the astonished eye.

[*Winter*, ll. 579–82]

The sight is aptly 'astonished' here, for it is the means of apprehending the 'beauteous whole'—though the imagery of sight and landscape reminds us ambiguously that these insights are meant to be grounded in a firmly empirical regard of natural phenomena. It is the clear eye of reason, we are told later, that sees beyond details of seasonal change:

> The great eternal scheme
> Involving all, and in a perfect whole
> Uniting, as the prospect wider spreads,
> To reason's eye refined clears up apace.   [ll. 1045–49]

So the philosophic man is able to see beyond Winter's 'latest glooms', where 'Horror wide extends / His desolate domain', to a metaphoric 'prospect' of the mind.

This large regard, however, is sometimes less urgent and less authentic than the sensibility that finds in nature's immediate and local moods a sympathetic echo of Thomson's private vision. And at such moments the coherence of psychological explanation is implicitly called in question by the poet's sense of the mysteries and confusion of certain mental and imaginative acts. Thomson's main difficulty in effecting this alternative, more private poetry is his inability to put off the public tone and discover a poetic personality individual enough to energize encounters with the objective world. Whenever he loses himself in his love for God or in deistic admiration, he ceases to maintain his own identity:

> Nature! great Parent! whose unceasing hand
> Rolls round the Seasons of the changeful year,
> How mighty, how majestic are thy works!
> With what a pleasing dread they swell the soul,
> That sees astonished, and astonished sings!
> Ye too, ye winds! that now begin to blow
> With boisterous sweep, I raise my voice to you.   [Winter, ll. 106–12]

The 'I' is a mere agent of the larger praise. The solitary contemplative in Summer (l. 282) who

> muses through the woods at noon,
> Or drowsy shepherd as he lies reclined,
> With half-shut eyes, beneath the floating shade
> Of willows grey, close-crowding o'er the brook —

these figures are ornamental, enhancing the atmosphere of the scene rather than focusing the values in it. We may register the absence of an effective and ordering subject in Thomson's poem in two ways: first, by the largeness of view expected of his 'Muse', an aerial photography of the imagination:

> The muse expands her solitary flight;
> And, hovering o'er the wild stupendous scene,
> Beholds new seas beneath another sky.   [Winter, ll. 891–93]

This 'much-transported Muse' (*Summer*, l. 171) is worked too briskly over too many concerns:

> As rising from the vegetable world
> My theme ascends, with equal wing ascend,
> My panting Muse
>
> [*Spring*, ll. 572–74]

But a second symptom of Thomson's surrender of personal or subjective focus to more universal perspectives is simply the frequent change of this focus. The progress of each poem involves seeing the scope and deeper significance of its season from many points of view—hence the tale of Lavinia and Palemon (*Autumn*, ll. 177 ff.) or the switch from 'The swain / Disastered' to the 'studious' poet in *Winter* (ll. 278–79, 431). Thomson obviously intends the various angles to complete a larger knowledge than is possible to his solitary imagination or to any other single person's. But just as the figures in Kent's illustrations seem generally unrelated to each other, Thomson's various mouthpieces and eyepieces make their discrete contributions from different stations. It is as if the illustrations were Kent's criticism of this literary fact: his divinities and humans are unconnected (the sickles that both hold in *Autumn* have little force) and the figures within the landscape are disposed with more of an eye to the balance and lines of composition than to their thematic relationships. As we shall see in the next two chapters, introspective poetry and landscape painting needed to learn (in part from garden design) the advantages of a less diffuse focus and of a more single-minded attention to their subject matter.

Thomson himself is occasionally forced to 'recall his wandering song' (*Autumn*, l. 150); yet it does not always return to a scrutiny or meditation where we can feel the controlling intensity of a strong imagination over the meeting of exterior and interior worlds. The phrase with which in *Winter* (l. 29) he seems to summarize his work in the poem, 'With bold description and with manly thought', begs the question of their connection. But some of his solutions have already been noticed: the pageants of baroque allegories (see *Winter*, ll. 1030–33) where the traditional representation of our notions of the natural world in human form connects the two; the emblematic recognition of wisdom by the virtuous man (see *Summer*, l. 465); the description of landscape in terms of an eye scanning a picture by Claude or Rosa (see *Summer*, ll. 590 ff.), where the process of interpreting a landscape becomes part of its structure; the focus of meditation by relating it to the calculated effects or sequences of a landscape garden. These last two are certainly Thomson's most considerable achievements.

Thomson's own accounts of the imagination involve an equally varied repertoire. In 1744 he added a passage to *Spring* (ll. 455–66) immediately after he has catalogued some of the sights of this particular season:

There let the classic page thy fancy lead
Through rural scenes, such as the Mantuan swain
Paints in the matchless harmony of song;
Or catch thyself the landscape, gliding swift
Athwart imagination's vivid eye;
Or, by the vocal woods and waters lulled,
And lost in lonely musing, in a dream
Confused of careless solitude where mix
Ten thousand wandering images of things
Soothe every gust of passion into peace—
All but the swellings of the softened heart,
That waken, not disturb, the tranquil mind.

The possibilities, then, declared after eighteen years' work on his poem, are three. First, a tradition of imitation, newly authorized by the endeavours of the Royal Society; this mimetic effort by an art ('paints . . . song') reproduces the known world either directly or—more usually—by the roundabout process of imitating predecessors who seem to have lent themselves to such a task. Second, an apparently independent exercise of the 'imagination's vivid eye'. Third, a detached or 'abstracted' reflection among natural scenery that is not necessarily an immediate part or object of meditation. Again, the connections between these three modes seem to be ignored in favour of Thomson's penchant for a schematic itemizing of the categories of vision. The reader is left with the sense that the human consciousness involves itself with natural scenery rather by an association of all three modes than by their use one at a time.

Thomson frequently invokes the idea of mimesis: especially at moments of difficulty ('But who can paint the lover' or 'who can paint / Like Nature') his anxiety settles for one of the confusions of the *ut pictura poesis* theory, which describes the poet's verbal task in painterly ways:

Behold yon breathing prospect bids the Muse
Throw all her beauty forth. But who can paint
Like Nature? Can imagination boast,
Amid its gay creation, hues like hers?
Or can it mix them with that matchless skill,
And lose them in each other, as appears
In every bud that blows?

[Spring, ll. 467–73]

The verbal imagination is identified with the art that is most concerned to reproduce the exterior world—painting. And consequently the passage continues by begging the question of language's own special resources:

If fancy then
Unequal fails beneath the pleasing task,

Ah, what shall language do? ah, where find words
Tinged with so many colours, and whose power,
To life approaching.

At other times he can seem merely evasive about poetry's
'translation' of Nature's copybook:

> To me be Nature's volume broad displayed;
> And to peruse its all-instructing page,
> Or, haply catching inspiration thence,
> Some easy passage, raptured, to translate,
> My sole delight, as through the falling glooms
> Pensive I stray, or with the rising dawn
> On fancy's eagle-wing excursive soar.
>
> [*Summer*, 192–98]

'Pensive' at least implies a proper territory for meditation and
the mind's identification of sympathetic images ('falling
glooms') in nature; we might compare the phrase in *Autumn* (ll.
670–71) 'meditate the book / Of Nature'. But the fancy is seen to
depart upon excursions which depend little if at all upon the
locale of their inspiration.

The second of his list of approaches to landscape—'catch
thyself the landscape'—can hardly be free of mimetic impulse.
Yet *The Seasons* frequently testify, alongside the imitations of
Virgil or Claude, to that marvellous clarity of apparently
unmediated sight. Here the poet does see for himself and uses
language to announce his direct treaty with the natural world,
innocent alike of mimetic worries or theological purpose: 'And
from the bladed field the fearful hare / Limps awkward' (*Summer*,
ll. 57–58). On at least one occasion this personal sharpness of
vision focuses on the landscape of Thomson's own youth in
Scotland (*Autumn*, ll. 878 ff.). The passage reminds one how
infrequently in *The Seasons* we are made aware of the memory's
role in landscape, a role which will become central to later
introspective poetry. Thomson usually likes the scientific regard, appearing to record his direct apprehension of nature;
whereas landscapes of memory make us, if only implicitly,
aware of the poet's mental life.

The third category of imaginative life is more ambiguous.
The solitary is said to be '*lost* in lonely musing, in a dream /
Confused', yet Thomson salvages from this a fine sense of what
we might today call 'stream of consciousness', a process compact
of many 'wandering images of *things*', distinct but disjunct, and
the 'swellings' of emotion. As offered, this does not seem to be a
version of association. It is too attentive to the mysterious-
ness of mental process to be anything but a very subtle version
of what Pope describes in a note to his translation of *The Iliad*:

the descriptions of places and images raised by the poet are still tending
to some hint, or leading onto some reflection upon moral life or
political institution, much in the same manner as the real sight of such

scenes and prospects is apt to give the mind a composed turn, and incline it to thoughts and contemplations that have a relation to the object.

For Thomson allows what elsewhere he calls an 'exalted eye'—the vision that is both sight and insight, thing and thought blended. Rarely perhaps does his poetry achieve this in practice as well as in theory: we wish for more of those moments like the glimpse of the 'sprightly youth' beside the pool in *Summer*:

> Awhile he stands
> Gazing the inverted landscape, half afraid
> To meditate the blue profound below.   [ll. 1246–48]

The energy that makes *gaze* and *meditate* transitive verbs also links the figure's mind to the landscape. The suggestion of Narcissus confirms the introspective force of the lines, and 'half afraid' declares both Narcissus' and the poet's hesitations in face of their own thoughts. The 'inverted landscape' at which the figure gazes (there are many similar moments in Wordsworth) recalls the process by which our retinas receive their impressions of our surroundings upside-down, like reflections in a pool of water.

Thomson's most ambiguous responses in the poem are to mental experiences over which we appear to exercise little or no control. They constitute his night thoughts, meditations that occur after the sun of the 'moral world' has set: in *Summer* (ll. 1603 ff.) the passage of day is compared to a fleeting

> vision o'er the formful brain,
> This moment hurrying wild the impassioned soul,
> The next in nothing lost.

The confusion of images in the mind ('formful brain'), their rapidity and involvement with the emotions, and their final evaporation seem to fascinate Thomson and repel him: the vestiges of Lockean terminology sustain the one, the identification of disorder and nullity the other. At times the disapproval is more pronounced:

> interrupted by distracted dreams
> That o'er the sick imagination rise
> And in black colours paint the mimic scene.

These lines occur during *Spring's* account of the distractions of love (ll. 1004 ff.). Thomson is generally tolerant of what he calls its 'charming agonies' and the fluctuating affections of the lover in the passage are seen to seek a corresponding scenery at every turn. Thus in his waking melancholy he

> restless runs
> To glimmering shades and sympathetic glooms,

Where the dun umbrage o'er the falling stream
Romantic hangs; there through the pensive dusk
Strays, in heart-thrilling meditation lost,
Indulging all to love.

But the same scenery, more violent and Rosa-like, becomes the territory of his downright despair when he dreams of 'desolation brown' and

    shrinks aghast
Back from the bending precipice; or wades
The turbid stream below.

The 'sick imagination' and the 'distracted dreams' invent a 'mimic scene' as an apt corollary of their own despair and this solipsist fantasy seems to earn Thomson's disapproval. Yet the mid-eighteenth-century fascination with sleep and night leads Thomson on other occasions to yield himself to the same world as the distracted lover's:

    As yet 'tis midnight deep. The weary clouds
Slow-meeting, mingle into solid gloom.
Now, while the drowsy world lies lost in sleep,
Let me associate with the serious Night,
And Contemplation, her sedate compeer;
Let me shake off the intrusive cares of day,
And lay the meddling senses all aside.

                    [*Winter*, ll. 202–8]

The rejection of 'meddling senses' is a strange reaction from a poet who invokes them so warmly elsewhere in the poem; but the implication is certainly that he seeks to enter a world of almost pure contemplation, for which 'serious Night' is the appropriate territory and correlative.

The 'midnight deep' and a landscape of 'wildest largest' groves is where Thomson celebrates the 'ancient bards' in a long passage in *Summer* (ll. 515–606). The congruence of their strong visionary imagination and the place they inhabit is established at once: these are the

    scenes where ancient bards the inspiring breath
Ecstatic felt, and, from this world retired,
Conversed with angels and immortal forms.

Thomson obviously reverences their special perspectives on 'Nature . . . and Nature's God' that he has himself to win by different means. In their surroundings, where 'A thousand shapes or glide athwart the dusk / Or stalk majestic on', he experiences something of their bardic trance and rapt enthusiasm:

    Deep-roused, I feel
A sacred terror, a severe delight,
Creep through my mortal frame; and thus, methinks,

A voice, than human more, the abstracted ear
Of fancy strikes.

This visitation urges Thomson to link his 'responsive song' with that of the bards and with the genius of their special landscape and to hear

voices chaunting from the wood-crown'd hill,
The deepening dale, or inmost sylvan glade:
A privilege bestow'd by us alone
On contemplation, or the hallow'd ear
Of poet swelling to seraphic strain.

Then, after a rather disarming enquiry of Miss Elizabeth Stanley whether she belongs to the heavenly choir, Thomson concludes:

Thus up the mount, in airy vision rapt,
I stray, regardless whither; till the sound
Of a near fall of water every sense
Wakes from the charm of thought: swift-shrinking back,
I check my steps and view the broken scene.

The 'airy vision' signals the poet's momentary emancipation from mere description, yet his recall to the sensual world reminds us of the power over his imagination of such 'broken scenes'. In the text of 1744 the following description of the waterfall was made more sublime, perhaps to match its 'impetuous torrent' with the bardic presences that have just visited Thomson and its *genius loci* with their *genius furens*. Later in *Summer* (ll. 1158 ff.) he returns to similar scenes in Snowdonia, to what we shall identify in the next chapter as a landscape of the bard. It is obvious that his fascination for such 'hideous' mountains, as for the tempests of winter, cannot always be explained by his delight in subduing them to larger and more benevolent perspectives. For they image for him a faculty of the imagination that is itself disturbing and, despite the invocation of Inspiration at the start of *Summer*, that does not always seem amenable to 'surrounding Heaven'.

In a passage (ll. 550–54) which Thomson introduced first into *Winter* in 1730 he claims that Pope's 'life [is] the more enduring song'. Thomson has been meditating upon the pleasures of 'society', of a 'few chosen friends' beneath his 'humble roof', just as Pope himself also came close to thinking that what he did with his private life, virtue, and estate was a more enduring contribution than participation in the public arena of politics and Grub Street. But the poetical consequences of the claim are more sharply felt in Thomson and the poets who followed what they took to be his example than in Pope.

The More Enduring Song

THE INGENIOUS AND DESCRIPTIVE THOMSON

For Pope poetry was always a public voice, however slyly and subtly it used, privately derived personae, and so became an 'enduring song' freed from distractions of biography. But if you believe that your life is the 'more enduring song' then its presence in your poetry must be felt more strongly and as a more energizing subject matter. Now this for various reasons Thomson did not allow to happen. The tone of his personal involvement is not spread throughout *The Seasons*; partly he had larger and more public ambitions, to trace 'the kind art of forming Heaven' (*Summer*, l. 312), which required its own tone; partly because he had not settled upon a suitable structure or language for personal poetry.

But in landscape gardens Thomson did find a structure by which to focus more personal meditation. No doubt the paradisal associations of a garden gave its forms a divine sanction, and certainly its 'Order in variety' held a special appeal for the poet of the 'God of Seasons'. But landscape gardens like Stowe and Hagley Park provided above all contexts for meditation where the mind was allowed an illusion of creative power. Though natural effects were managed ('finished') by art and even augmented by temples, statues, and inscriptions, the associative power of garden scenes upon the mind initiated patterns of thought in suitably responsive visitors. The Elysian Fields with its Temple of Ancient Virtue, satirically set off next door with a ruined Temple of Modern Virtue [plate 47], and both facing the Temple of British Worthies across the waters of the 'Styx', were a scene designed to foster reflections; yet those who reflected there, as Thomson and as Gilpin's *Dialogue Upon the Gardens . . . at Stowe* (1748) reveal, could enjoy meditative patterns beyond the immediate scope of their setting. And there were other parts of Stowe, and of Hagley, where the mind was even less directed and could read its own expressive ideas into landscape.

Thomson would have found some of these notions in what is obviously one of his favourite authors, Shaftesbury, who asks in *Miscellaneous Reflections* 'Who can admire the outward beauties and not recur instantly to the inward . . . ?' Shaftesbury was sceptical whether a garden's order—and he is thinking of French and Dutch gardens at the turn of the century—could ever find an answering harmony within the minds of their owners:

A parterre, cypresses, groves, wildernesses. Statues here and there of virtue, fortitude, temperance. Heroes' busts, philosophers' heads, with suitable mottoes and inscriptions. Solemn representations of things deeply natural—caves, grottoes, rocks, urns and obelisks in retired places and disposed at proper distances and points of sight, with all those symmetries which silently express a reigning order, peace, harmony, and beauty! . . . But what is there answerable to this in the minds of the possessors?

Thomson, as we have seen, was generally disposed to proclaim that there was much answering to their gardens in the spirits of Lord Cobham and Lyttelton.

Gardens further taught Thomson the excitements of space. Unlike landscape pictures and unlike the grand perspectives of French gardening that are designed to be taken in at one admiring glance and are thus aptly celebrated in engravings, the English garden asked to be explored, its surprises and unsuspected corners to be discovered on foot. It is an art about whose particular, individual ingredients we learn before we understand and see the whole in the mind's eye. So that if, as Ralph Cohen has argued, *The Seasons* is a poetry of space rather than sight, its events observed in the arena of a four-dimensional world, then the art of English gardening of which Thomson gradually became fully aware contributed a distinctive structure to that poetry. And, taking all nature for his garden like Kent, he applied the habits and forms of association and meditation that were learnt within a Stowe or Hagley Park beyond the haha. Sometimes it is difficult to decide whether Thomson's language of garden design identifies a 'finished' landscape or merely that the rural topography is seen in gardenist patterns, just as prospects were read as painted landscapes: thus *Autumn's* version of the *beatus ille* theme (ll. 1235 ff.) notes among the 'pure pleasures of a rural life' the presence 'of prospect, grove, or song, / Dim grottoes, gleaming lakes, and fountain clear'.

But what gardens could not contain in sufficiently sublime intensity were those bardic landscapes of mountain and torrent. These, too, had been commended by Shaftesbury and the famous passage in *The Moralists* will help to establish this chapter's final point:

Tis true, said I, Theocles, I own it. Your genius, the genius of the place, and the Great Genius have at last prevailed. I shall no longer resist the passion growing in me for things of a natural kind, where neither art nor the conceit or caprice of man has spoiled their genuine order by breaking in upon that primitive state. Even the rude rocks, the mossy caverns, the irregular unwrought grottoes and broken falls of waters, with all the horrid graces of the wilderness itself, as representing Nature more, will be the more engaging, and appear with a magnificence beyond the formal mockery of princely gardens. . . . But tell me, I entreat you, how comes it that, except a few philosophers of your sort, the only people who are enamoured in this way, and seek the woods, the rivers, or seashores, are your poor vulgar lovers?

The engaging of Philocles' mind by the 'primitive state' of nature is the harmonizing of his genius with the genius loci. Less adventurous and radical than Shaftesbury, Pope had still insisted that landscape designers consult the 'Genius of the Place', so that their realizations of the presiding *numen* of a garden scene might in their turn prompt visitors to appreciate its special qualities. This injunction of Pope's was a part of that larger movement, in which Thomson also shares, by which the Protestant Enlightenment sought to temper the demonic or extrarational imagination by naturalizing it upon British soil. And of this Geoffrey Hartman has written in a brilliant essay: 'This conversion of the demon meant that the poetical genius would coincide with the genius loci of England; and this meant, in practice, a meditation on English landscape as alma mater —where landscape is storied England, its legends, history, and rural-reflective spirit. The poem becomes, in a sense, a seduction of the poetical genius by the genius loci: the latter invites —subtly compels—the former to live within via media charms'. The 'new structure of fusion' that these invitations require of poetry was tentatively explored by Thomson throughout *The Seasons*, but never engages his full attention. It is the poetry discussed in the next chapter that displays most prominently the theme which Geoffrey Hartman announces. Gray's bard, whose death if not his life might be claimed as the 'more enduring song', is an apt representative of a visionary whose personal resonance is fused with that of his surrounding scenery.

FOUR

The Landscape of the Bard

Wild and British

Gray's ode on "The Bard", if not his best or his most famous poem, was important to many in the second half of the eighteenth century because it represented a new poetics. One of those who saw it in that way was Joseph Warton, who invoked it in his *Essay on the Writings and Genius of Mr. Pope:*

There is nothing in so sublime a style as *The Bard* of Gray. This is a matter of *fact*, not of *reasoning*; and means to point out, what Pope *has actually done*, not what, if he had put out his full strength, he was *capable of doing*. No man can possibly think, or can hint, that the Author of *The Rape of the Lock*, and the *Eloisa*, wanted *imagination*, or *sensibility*, or *pathetic;* but he certainly did not so often indulge and exert those talents, nor give so many proofs of them, as he did of strong sense and judgement. . . . He stuck to describing *modern manners;* but those *manners,* because they are *familiar, uniform, artificial, and polished,* are, for these four reasons, in their very nature *unfit* for any lofty effort of the Muse. . . . Whatever poetical enthusiasm he actually possessed, he with-held and suppressed. The perusal of him . . . affects not our minds with such strong emotions as we feel from *Homer* or *Milton* so that no man, of a true poetical spirit, is master of himself while he reads them. Hence he is a writer fit for universal perusal, and of general utility; adapted to all ages and all stations; for the old and for the young; the man of business and the scholar. He who would think, and there are many such, the *Faerie Queene, Palamon and Arcite, The Tempest,* or *Comus,* childish and romantic, may relish Pope.

The deficiency Warton finds in Pope, his suppression of sublime imagination, the absence of poetical enthusiasm, is remedied in "The Bard". The ode's importance seems to have had less to do with its intrinsic merits than with its success in giving specific expression to a whole area of cultural history that seemed to the mid-eighteenth century a fresh and exciting territory for the imagination: not only critics like Warton, but poets and painters looked to its special ideas and energies for a means of revivifying their art. As Gray wrote to Mason about some images in *Caractacus,* one of his friend's own efforts in this new vein, 'you may dress them at pleasure, so they do but look wild and British' (*Correspondence*, p. 603). And Mason, much more of a gardenist than Gray, must have been well aware that such images represented rival ideas to those that could be accommodated within a landscape garden. It is this challenge to the Augustan art of gardening that this chapter examines.

Gray's ode was written between 1755 and 1757. It concerns the apocryphal slaughter of the Welsh bards by Edward I and the fate of the sole survivor, details of which Gray had taken from Thomas Carte's *General History of England* (Vol. 2, 1750). But he contributed from his own resources the lines on the mountain landscape:

On a rock, whose haughty brow
Frowns o'er old Conway's foaming flood,
Robed in the sable garb of woe,
With haggard eyes the Poet stood;
Loose his beard, and hoary hair
Stream'd, like a meteor, to the troubled air
And with a Master's hand, and Prophet's fire,
Struck the deep sorrows of his lyre.
'Hark, how each giant-oak, and desert cave,
Sighs to the torrent's aweful voice beneath

Not only does the landscape re-echo the torrent's noise, it exactly images the prophetic utterance and passionate vision of the bard himself. The scenery's human characteristics—the rock's haughty frown, the torrent's voice—announce from the start the relationship of scenery to human passion: this congruence is further emphasized by the comparison of his beard and hair to a trailing meteor.

The printing of the ode, together with another, "The Progress of Poetry", was undertaken by Walpole at his Strawberry Hill Press. Earlier, after seeing drafts of the ode in 1755, Walpole had commissioned some illustrations from Richard Bentley:

Nothing but you, or Salvator Rosa, and Nicolo Poussin, can paint up to the expressive horror and dignity of it. . . . Now the two latter are dead, you must of necessity be Gray's painter.

Gray, however, would not allow the finished drawings to be used, and this refusal focuses what is perhaps a crucial difference between poetry and painting. Bentley's drawings provide the basic narrative facts, but they lack what Walpole called the 'expressive' power of the poem; they fail to discover an adequate visual language either in human gesture, as Loutherbourg and Fuseli did in their versions of "The Bard", or in the landscape setting, as Rosa or Dughet would have done and as Gray's poem itself does. Bentley's failure lies partly in his sense of scale, partly in his bland treatment of the landscape setting which is used merely to fill the spaces of the paper [plate 49]: neither succeed in conveying the Bard's visionary glimpse of history and passionate involvement in his vision, which the ode virtually states is mirrored by the sublime scenery. Apart from Bentley's Rosa-like tree in his "close-up" version of the bard's encounter

PLATE 49   Richard Bentley, drawing for Gray's "The Bard" (?1757).

PLATE 50   Richard Bentley, drawing for Gray's "The Bard" (?1757).

with Edward [plate 50], he neglects the relationship between the figure and the landscape.

Probably the most famous version of Gray's ode is that by John Martin, painted in the early nineteenth century. Though we are asked by the very forceful organization of the picture

PLATE 51   Thomas Jones, *The Bard*.
Oil painting (1774).

—the bard's stance above all—to accept the scenery as the apt image of his sublime imagination, the bravura prospect of crags and mountains overwhelms the figure of the bard. A less well-known picture by Thomas Jones, exhibited in 1774, captures the relationship of figure to landscape and the expressive energy of Gray's poem with more fidelity to landscape ideas in the second half of the eighteenth century. Jones thought his picture [plate 51] 'taken from Gray's *Ode* . . ., one of the best I ever painted'.

The bard is prominent, the focus of the painting as he was of the ode: solitary, melancholy, passionate, and eloquent of that 'ravishing Harmony' which Gray heard first when the blind Welsh harper, Parry, visited Cambridge in 1757 and spurred the poet to finish his ode. The lines of Jones's figure—his 'stream-ing' hair and the gesture of his right arm—are echoed by the blasted tree behind him and draw our attention into the land-scape beyond, a powerful, crowded scene of chiaroscuro. To the bard's left Jones introduces the ravine into which he hurls himself, an important (and for a painting, more difficult) narra-tive device that alludes to Gray's second introduction of lands-cape imagery—

He spoke, and headlong from the mountain's height
Deep in the roaring tide he plung'd to endless night—

Jones's landscape imagery—with one notable exception—derives from his master, Richard Wilson: the shattered tree is reminiscent of Wilson's *The Destruction of Niobe's Children* of 1760, and the fall of cliffs in the background recalls such landscapes as *Cader Idris*. But his masterstroke is original: the removal to Snowdonia of Stonehenge, an appropriately Druidical temple (as it was then thought to be) for the bard; it both solemnizes his prophetic vision and, in painterly terms, gives it expression. Jones had visited Stonehenge some years before painting *The Bard* and had recorded its grandeur and magnificence, which he thought were heightened by the surrounding void

not affording any thing to disturb the Eye, or divert the imagination . . . . Whereas, were this wonderful Mass situated amidst high rocks, lofty mountains, and hanging Woods—however it might contribute to the richness of the scene in general—would lose much of its own grandeur as a single object—the Experiment is easily tried upon Canvas.

That he tried the experiment when painting Gray's bard suggests his peculiar sympathy for the poem: Gray had called it 'the British Ode'—itself, as we shall see, a complex claim—and an ancient British temple was a perfect emblem for this visual commentary upon Gray's poem. Another painting by Paul Sandby, had it survived, might have shown the same insight into Gray's imagination: Mason arranged for Sandby to paint it and thought it the best picture of the century when it was exhibited in 1761. Gray's own estimation of Sandby's art, that he 'excells in landscapes, with figures, Views of Building, ruins, etc.', obviously led him to anticipate a 'great picture of Snowden in which the Bard and Edward I make their appearance'.

Sandby's picture was described in the exhibition catalogue as 'An Historical Landskip'. The phrase signals at least one basic ingredient of "The Bard"'s prestige: Gray afforded a British historical subject susceptible to treatment in the manner of Rosa, Poussin, or Claude. More particularly for poets he provided an example of landscape which was expressive, even emblematic, of a passionate imagination that was to tempt many from Augustan poetic concerns and from Augustan gardens. His bard sanctions most of the sublime introspection of the second half of the century, and it is his ghostly successor, bearing on his 'branded arm . . . / What seem'd the poet's harp of yore', who leads Wordsworth from "The Vale of Esthwaite" into 'Helvellyn's inmost womb' where he is initiated.

Gray's imagination joined together the mythical possibilities of British history and the taste for a landscape appropriate to it. He was by no means alone in this endeavour. In 1769 he received from James Beattie a specimen of the latter's poem, "The Minstrel", and a letter which linked the character of the minstrel), as Bishop Percy had sketched it in his essay prefixed to *The Reliques of Ancient English Poetry* (1765), with the 'solitary and mountainous country'. Gray responded that Beattie's 'ideas are new, and borrowed from a mountainous country, the only one that can furnish truly picturesque scenery' (pp. 1140–41).

Yet Gray displays some uncertainties in his reactions to the new 'British' landscape poetry. In the same letter to Beattie he advises against making description—'always . . . the most graceful ornament of poetry'—the subject matter. It is characteristic of Gray that he would not subscribe to mere description: in this he resembles Joshua Reynolds, who would not allow the highest place to landscape painting. But Gray can still think Joseph Warton's *The Enthusiast, or the Lover of Nature* 'all pure description' and Akenside's *Pleasures of the Imagination* 'above the middleing, & now & then (but for a little while) rises even to the best, particularly in Description' (pp. 223–24). And his own letters reveal a skill with and a dedication to description that he obviously did not allow himself in poetry. But as his "Bard" suggests and as his letter to Beattie confirms, description was allowed if it served a larger purpose, as when poetry came to include the 'truly picturesque' associations of British myth and landscape. His habits of looking at scenery, in its wilder forms especially, were also fraught with ambiguities. He often looks at a scene and describes it to a correspondent as if it were a landscape garden; yet he also learnt to reject, or at least extensively revise his opinions of, the very Augustan art of landscape gardening. Again, he was not the only poet of mid-century to move out of the garden. But before the extent of these new attitudes is discussed it will be worth examining Gray's representative, if particularly personal and sometimes ambiguous, contribution to them.

In 1758 he wrote to his friend, William Palgrave, who was visiting Scotland, a letter that must be quoted at length, not least because it is so eloquent of its writer's half-serious, half-mocking approach:

I do not know how to make amends, having neither rock, ruin, or precipice near me to send you; they do not grow in the south: but only say the word, if you would have a compact neat box of red brick with sash windows, or a grotto made of flints and shellwork, or a wallnut-tree with three molehills under it, stuck with honey-suckles round a bason of gold-fishes, and you shall be satisfied; they shall come by the Edinburgh coach.

In the meantime I congratulate you on your new acquaintance with the *savage*, the *rude*, and the *tremendous*. Pray, tell me, is it anything like what you had read in your book, or seen in two-shilling prints? Do not you think a man may be the wiser (I had almost said the better) for going a hundred or two of miles; and that the mind has more room in it than most people seem to think, if you will but furnish the apartments? I almost envy your last month, being in a very insipid situation myself;

and desire you would not fail to send me some furniture for my Gothic apartment, which is very cold at present. It will be the easier task, as you have nothing to do but transcribe your little red books, if they are not rubbed out; for I conclude you have not trusted everything to memory, which is ten times worse than a lead pencil: Half a word fixed upon or near the spot, is worth a cart-load of recollection. When we trust to the picture that objects draw of themselves on our mind, we deceive ourselves; without accurate and particular observation, it is but ill-drawn at first, the outlines are soon blurred, the colours every day grow fainter; and at last, when we would produce it to any body, we are forced to supply its defects with a few strokes of our own imagination.

[pp. 586–87]

This revealing document offers various perspectives upon Gray's imaginative habits: his scepticism with the more precious and rococo elements of landscape gardens, mainly because they ape so ridiculously the world of nature outside the garden; his conviction that no vicarious knowledge of places—via engravings, for instance—can communicate their real genius loci; his subscription to Lockean psychology—for if thought is seeing, if (in Bishop Berkeley's version) the 'objects intromitted by sight . . . are no other than a new set of thoughts and sensations', then what the eye sees become the constituents of a vocabulary and the intelligent man will endeavour to increase its mental and emotional range; the joint role of memory and precise memoranda in defining for subsequent use this mental 'furniture', yet the necessary, even if reprehensible, aid that comes from the imagination to augment original experience.

Seven years later Gray was himself in the Highlands and described the experience in a letter to Mason:

the Lowlands are worth seeing once, but the Mountains are extatic, & ought to be visited in pilgrimage once a year. none but those monstrous creatures of God know how to join so much beauty with so much horror, a fig for your Poets, Painters, Gardiners, & Clergymen, that have not been among them: their imagination can be made up of nothing but bowling-greens, flowering shrubs, horse-ponds, Fleet-ditches, shell-grottoes, & Chinee-rails.

[p. 899]

Since he goes on to say that 'Italy could hardly produce a nobler scene', his refusal to take the English garden very seriously probably dates from his early visit to Italy with Walpole. The ironies (especially the self-ironies) and the gentle mockeries in his correspondence make any interpretation of his ideas rather tricky; but those two letters to Palgrave and Mason suggest his underlying concern with a mental stimulation and storehouse of poetic imagery that the landscape garden did not yield.

Gray defended the 'skill in gardening, & laying out grounds' as England's one 'original talent' (p. 814). It is obvious, too, that he appreciated the direction of a visitor's mind by a landscape garden: he quotes some verses by Matthew Green on Merlin's Cave at Richmond:

Needless it is the Busts to name
Of Men, Monopolists of Fame;
Four Chiefs adorn the modest Stone
For Virtue, as for Learning, known.
The thinking Sculpture helps to raise
Deep Thoughts, the Genii of the Place:
To the Mind's Ear, & inward Sight,
There Silence speaks

[p. 301]

But it is equally evident that Gray prefers not to be hampered by preconceived ideas, especially when they are ill-conceived as well. Doubtless his admiration for Woburn Farm and for Esher owes something to Walpole's enthusiasm, but his comments are particularly his own when he writes to Thomas Wharton: 'I am glad you agree with me in admiring Mr Southcote's Paradise, wch whenever you see it again, will improve upon you. . . . you do not say enough of Esher. it is my other favorite place. it was a Villa of Cardinal Wolsey's, of wch nothing but a part of the Gateway remain'd. Mr Kent supplied the rest, but I think with you, that he had not read the Gothic Classicks with taste or attention. he introduced a mix'd Style, wch goes by the name of *Battey Langley Manner*' (pp. 403–4). He responded to the associations of a landscape garden and his own historical imagination was evidently offended by anything inauthentic. Yet he recommends the effects upon the 'Mind's . . . inward sight' of a second visit to Woburn. He seems always ambiguous in his response to landscaped grounds—quick to be humorous at the expense of their rococo fantasies, yet ready to explore their associative patterns: thus he writes parodically to Walpole that the ghost of John Dennis recounted to him the discovery of a 'mead of Asphodel':

Betwixt the confines of the light and dark
It lies, of 'Lysium the St James's Park.
Here spirit-beaux flutter along the Mall,
And shadows in disguise skate o'er the iced Canal;
Here groves embowered and more sequestered shades,
Frequented by the ghosts of ancient maids,
Are seen to rise. The melancholy scene,
With gloomy haunts and twilight walks between,
Conceals the wayward band: here spend their time
Greensickness girls that died in youthful prime,
Virgins forlorn, all dressed in willow-green-i,
With Queen Elizabeth and Nicolini.

[pp. 15–16]

Yet the sceptical half of his response is sometimes restrained, as when his visit to hear *King Arthur, or the British Worthy*, an opera by Purcell and Dryden, is rewarded, among much that merely entertained him, by 'the inchanted part of the play . . . not Machinery, but actual magick: the second scene is a British temple enough to make one go back a thousand years, & really be in ancient Britain' (p. 37).

It is probably on his visit to Italy that Gray strengthened the habits of mind learnt in landscape gardens at the same time as he discovered larger territories in which to use them, these in their turn confirming his scepticisms about the English garden. Some years before he left for Italy with Walpole he wrote to his future travelling companion about a visit to the common and beech woods at Burnham: he saw its unimproved features as if they were organized into some landscape park and was particularly insistent as well as witty about the associations which his mind pretended to discover in the scenery. But on his European travels he seems to have found the scenery commensurate with his ideas: 'Not a precipice, not a torrent, not a cliff, but is pregnant with religion and poetry' (p. 128). From Italy he tells his friend, West, that 'Mr Walpole says, our memory sees more than our eyes in this country'. He finds Albano and Frascati are 'infinitely preferable' to the 'realities' of Windsor or Richmond Hill because they give free scope to this imaginative memory (p. 161). A typical experience is recounted by Walpole and Gray in a joint letter to West; but what is significant about their visit to the temple of Minerva Medica is the organization of their memories and impressions of a classical landscape into patterns borrowed from a garden like Chiswick or Stowe:

You have seen prints of the ruins of the temple of Minerva Medica; you shall only hear its situation, and then figure what a villa might be laid out there. 'Tis in the middle of a garden: at a little distance are two subterraneous grottos, which were the burial place of the liberti of Augustus. There are all the niches and covers of the urns with the inscriptions remaining; and in one, very considerable remains of an ancient stucco ceiling with paintings in grotesque. Some of the walks would terminate upon the Castellum Aquae Martiae, St John Lateran, and St. Maria Maggiore, besides other churches; the walls of the garden would be two aqueducts, and the entrance through one of the old gates of Rome.

[p. 148]

The organization of a visitor's responses within a landscape garden had itself been based upon paintings of precisely such Roman remains, and the tradition of such pictures continued. In the decade after Gray's visit to Italy Richard Wilson painted the same temple of Minerva Medica [plate 52]. But the difference between their visual and verbal accounts signals the extent to which the literary imagination was learning to emancipate itself from imitative word-painting: Gray's response is to a landscape seen along various axes, a multi-directional impression of the whole site, which a garden but not a picture allows; moreover, even his topographical motive cannot conceal his associations

THE LANDSCAPE OF THE BARD

PLATE 52　Richard Wilson, *The Temple of Minerva Medica, Rome.* Oil painting (1750's).

with the Roman scene, and it is the opportunity to reveal and discuss these mental images and ideas that also distinguishes Gray's landscape from Wilson's.

Gray obviously appreciated this opportunity to suggest or define his impressions and associations. It is strikingly displayed in the two letters he wrote to his mother and to West about the alpine crossing. To Mrs. Gray he sends a detailed, topographical account, only slightly coloured by any emotional response—a precipice is *monstrous*, the views *astonishing*, *solemn* or *romantic* (pp. 122–23). A month later, perhaps because his mind has had time to marshall the ideas alongside the images, it is an account of a mental just as much as of a physical ascent:

I do not remember to have gone ten paces without an exclamation, that there was no restraining: Not a precipice, not a torrent, not a cliff, but is pregnant with religion and poetry. There are certain scenes that would awe an atheist into belief, without the help of other argument. One need not have a very fantastic imagination to see spirits there at noon-day: You have Death perpetually before your eyes, only so far removed, as to compose the mind without frighting it. I am well persuaded St Bruno was a man of no common genius, to choose such a situation for his retirement . . . You may believe Abelard and Heloise were not forgot upon this occasion.

[p. 128]

The remaining, Italian, part of their journey provided yet more opportunities for such 'furnishing of the mind's apartments'.

After his return home Gray's instinct for larger and wilder scenes was satisfied by excursions throughout England and Scotland. He suggested once to Mason—but perhaps only half seriously—that they 'hire a house together in Switzerland . . . it is a fine *poetical* country' (p. 467, my italics). And he seems to have found Lord Holland's imitation of Cicero's villa at Baiae particularly absurd, especially after his own visit to that 'remarkable place . . . and its remains of antiquity' (p. 163):

Art he invokes new horrors still to bring.
New mouldering fanes and battlements arise,
Arches and turrets nodding to their fall,
Unpeopled palaces delude his eyes,
And mimic desolation covers all.

[*Poems*, pp. 262–63]

The organization of scenery in landscaped parks, even if well handled, increasingly bored him and he preferred 'one of the most beautiful Vales here in England to walk in with prospects that change every ten steps, and open something new wherever I turn me, all rude and romantic' (p. 379). In contrast, Oatlands Park, near Weybridge, seemed designed to eliminate the intricacies of his involvement: for Lord Lincoln was

hurting his view by two plantations in front of his terrace, that regularly answer one another, & are of an oval form with rustic buildings in the middle of them . . . & (as they prosper) will join their shade to that of the hills in the horizon, exclude all the immediate scene of enclosures, meadows, and cattle feeding, & reduce that great distance to nothing. this seems to be the advice of some new Gardiner, or Director of my Lord's Taste.

[p. 578]

The echoes of Pope's landscaping advice in the *Epistle to Burlington* only serve to underline Gray's lack of interest. His letter teasing Nicholls, who not only seemed to derive more pleasure from visiting gardens than Gray but actually owned his own, mingles wistfulness and irony:

And so you have a garden of your own, & you plant and transplant & are dirty & amused! are not you ashamed of yourself? why, I have no so such thing, you monster; nor ever shall be either dirty or amused as long as I live! . . . how charming it must be to walk out in one's own gardening, & sit on a bench in the open air with a fountain, & a leaden statue, & a rolling stone, & an arbour!

[p. 1065]

By the date he wrote that (1769) Gray had discovered on trips along the south coast in 1755 and 1764 and into the Highlands in 1765 a much more extensive apparatus to stimulate his mind than fountains and statues.

His appetite for 'what lies within reach, that may be worth seeing' led him to compile a catalogue of the *Antiquities, Houses,*

Parks, Plantations, Scenes and Situations in each county (p. 564). But some sense of his priorities may be gathered from his note to Wharton that, having gone out of his way in the rain to see Richmond Castle and Swaledale, 'some faint gleams of sunshine gave me an opportunity of walking over Studley, & descending into the ruins of Fountains Abbey'—and it is the latter rather than Aislabie's gardens that 'I examined with attention' (p. 784).

Gray was, of course, among the pioneers of picturesque travel. It was Gray to whom Gilpin first submitted one of his picturesque tours and Gray who urged publication. And with his *Claude glass* and a taste nurtured upon prints—Gray inherited Thomson's collection of engravings—his attitude towards scenery was often an eagerness for 'Peeps & delightful Openings', where the landscape was framed as in a painted picture, for the blue shading of trees 'as they go off to distance', another painterly effect, and for glimpses of the English countryside as if caught by an artist like Wootton: 'a fine valley with green meadows & hedge-rows, a Gentleman's house peeping forth from a grove of old trees' (pp. 1074–75). Yet just as often Gray neglects the merely visual to record mental activity; like that later picturesque document, Wordsworth's *Guide to the Lakes*, published anonymously in 1810, which is addressed to the 'Minds of Persons of taste, and feeling for Landscape'.

Gray's mental adventures along his picturesque routes may be glimpsed in the hints of letters and the uses he makes of landscape to sustain and express ideas in his poetry. The poet's mind found in scenery that provided a 'changing prospect at every ten paces' (p. 1079) a wealth of imagery and ideas that the more studied and separated vistas of a landscape garden could not match. Only in the Highlands did he talk in terms of landscaping, as he had at the temple of Minerva Medica in Rome; perhaps a gardenist vocabulary helped to structure his experience of the sublime and 'prodigious' scenery—at Glamis Castle (pp. 890–891) he envisages the scene that 'a very little art' would improve in such a way that nature's own forms would be recognized and used. Likewise he can still describe natural scenery in gardenist language, see it as in landscaped parks: on the south coast in 1755 he remarked a 'natural Terrass 3 Mile long' (pp. 427–28); and in his journey from Lancashire into Yorkshire in 1770 the Lune valley and later Wharfdale are described in terms that would be perfectly appropriate in Walpole's history of gardening: 'winding in a deep valley, its hanging banks clothed with fine woods, thro' wch you catch long reaches of the water' (p. 1104).

As he had advised Palgrave, Gray's own commentary during his excursions consists largely of memoranda 'fixed upon or near the spot'. But images can still have ideas attached to them: at Gordale Scar he quotes *Lear*. More interestingly, ideas emerge from the images, loosened from them by an allusive phrase or submerged memory of something else: in the Lake District the 'ancient kingdom' of the mountains around Honister is the 'reign of Chaos & old Night', and the moonlight upon Derwent Water recalls something in *Samson Agonistes* (pp. 1088–89). The mental interest is always to summon, as he says in Hampshire, the 'Idea' of a place (p. 427); on return visits this becomes noticeably easier, so that at Netley Abbey for the second time his mind focuses more swiftly and subtly upon its sense of arcane mystery (p. 843). But at other times the letters record only the more mechanical function of his associations: in the Lakes he is much reminded of the Alps, or 'a great rock like some ancient tower nodding to its fall' (p. 1079) releases an echo of his own verses on Lord Holland's villa.

Gray's example, in short, reminds us that the picturesque mode was simply a mechanism for ordering the *mind's* impressions; there was always some painterly imitation, some scene shaped in words; but an adept literary imagination could recognize its own special workings. Above all in Scotland Gray was fascinated with the literary ideas prompted by the visual experience of the Highlands. At one point he notes how the mountains look down from 'a most aweful height . . . on the tomb of Fingal'; some pages later he tells of a hill 'cover'd with oak, with grotesque masses of rock staring from among their trunks, like the sullen countenances of Fingal and all his family frowning on the little mortals of modern days' (pp. 892, 894). But even before he went to the Highlands he connected their landscape and the bardic imagination in a letter of 1763: *Ossian*, he told Brown, showed that 'Imagination dwelt many hundred years agoe in all her pomp on the cold and barren mountains of Scotland' (p. 797). Though Gray was sceptical about the authenticity of Macpherson's writings, he admired in them the meeting of a strong imagination and a landscape instinct with poetry. So he was prepared at Glamis to hear Highlanders 'singing Ersesongs all day long' (p. 890).

Unlike some of his contemporaries, to whom the next sections are devoted, Gray's own poetry did not readily accommodate the interests which his letters display. To move from these, especially the later ones that narrate his northern journeys, back into his odes is to experience that same descent, which his own Latin verses recount, from rugged alpine passes to the milder and classical shores of Genoa:

Horridos tractus, Boreaeque linquens
Regna Taurini fera, molliorem
Advehor brumam, Genuaeque amantes
    Litora soles.

[*Poems*, p. 309]

In his unfinished 'essay' on the "Alliance of Education and Government" Gray took up a familiar theme, the relationship

The Gentler Genius of the Plain

between environment, especially climate, and government and national character. In the large public gestures of the poem he demands:

Say then, through ages by what fate confined
To different climes seem different souls assigned?   [*Poems*, p. 95]

For a while he rehearses the answer that reason and resolution can help the soul to triumph over her native element; but he also argues a contrary view:

Not but the human fabric from the birth
Imbibes a flavour of its parent earth:
As various tracts enforce a various toil,
The manners speak the idiom of the soil.
An iron-race the mountain-cliffs maintain,
Foes to the gentler genius of the plain.   [*Poems*, p. 98]

The debate between alternative characters of mountain and plain and the vacillations of argument, which establish an ambiguity central to Gray's poetic thought, are notably his own. In the Alcaic Ode which he inscribed in the album of the monastery of the Grande Chartreuse in August 1741 he characteristically follows an enthusiastic appeal to the genius of that forbidding place ('O Tu, severi religio loci') with the recognition that fortune will doubtless remove him from such sublime scenery—

Per invias rupes, fera per iuga,
Clivosque praeruptos, sonantes
      Inter aquas, nemorumque noctem   [*Poems*, p. 317]

—in which case he begs only 'some secluded corner'. His poetic output is equally divided: sometimes an 'Ode in the Greek Manner'; sometimes what his commonplace book recorded as his 'Gothic', 'Erse' or 'Welsh' poems. But if he was uncertain as to the progress of his own poetry ('Oh! lyre divine, what daring spirit / Wakes thee now?'—p. 176), he appeared always to seek some identification of the particular spirit or soul of a poem with its appropriate landscape.

The Latin poems composed on his Italian journey are especially attentive to the memories and associations which we have seen crowded upon him. The genius loci of Tusculum, of the impetuous Anio, of the Alban hills actually promote and endorse Gray's own muse:

Mirare nec tu me citherae rudem
Claudis laborantem numeris: loca
      Amoena, iucundumque ver in-
Compositum docuere carmen.
Haerent sub omni nam folio nigri
Phoebea luci (credite) somnia;

Argutiusque et lympha, et aurae
Nescio quid solito loquuntur.

[*Poems*, p. 311]

The streams speak with an eloquence that is one with Gray's articulation of their ambience. Similarly, his Welsh bard declaims with a passion that is instinct in the scenery; it is an identification that was, as we saw, Gray's specific contribution to his sources. In other 'Gothic' pieces similar landscape suggestions emerge. The flood ('diluvium') of his source for "The Death of Hoel" is slightly but significantly metamorphosed into 'the torrent's might, / With headlong rage and wild affright'. "The Fatal Sisters" set their own appropriate scene—storms, darkness, sleet, 'Clouds of carnage [that] blot the sun'. Owen is celebrated in his symbolic landscape of rocky shore, and Conan's name elicits in the 'Sacred tribute of the bard' brief glimpses of a landscape devoured by flames, whirlwind, and thunder where the 'shivered oak' is again Gray's own addition. It can only be speculated how much his poetry on these generally 'Gothic' topics could have used the 'mental furniture' of his visit to Scotland had it occurred before such compositions. Yet the 'bard divine' of the "Ode For Music", written four years *after* his Scottish tour, is still unlocated in 'yonder realms of empyrean day' (*Poems*, p. 268).

That vagueness perhaps signals Gray's uncertainties, even pessimism, as to the progress of poetry. In its Grecian landscape the imagination had occupied a certain territory: 'each old poetic mountain / Inspiration breathed around'; Helicon, with its sacred springs, had provided a various landscape where the 'stream of music' was echoed by the surrounding rocks and groves. But in its progress to Britain, poetry since Milton and Dryden had failed to discover any appropriate and sacred scenery. The 'genii of the stream', in Gray's "Ode on the Death of a Favourite Cat", are a humorous valediction to a natural mythology which England could not seem to accommodate. It was in the work of contemporaries, with whom Gray obviously sympathized, that British poetry was joined with the spirit of its own places—Fingal and his children staring from Highland cliffs.

In three non-'Gothic' poems, however, Gray does explore the encounter between his imagination and the natural scenery of his own country: in the famous "Elegy", and in the odes on Spring and Eton College. In the Alcaic Ode he had acknowledged that no negligible divinity ruled the streams and forests of the Grande Chartreuse: but in England, as Geoffrey Hartman has observed, an appeal to Father Thames ('an inauthentic figure of speech') becomes the invocation of 'an authentic figure of silence'. For the Etonian scenery does not abide Gray's question. The prospect is distant in time as well as place, and this nostalgic visitation of a ghostly territory secures no firm rapport between the poet and any genius loci. Similarly, in "Ode on the Spring" the moralizing poet first establishes an exact equation between himself and the landscape of spring:

Where'er the oak's thick branches stretch
A broader browner shade;
Where'er the rude and moss-grown beech
O'er-canopies the glade,
Beside some water's rushy brink
With me the Muse shall sit, and think
(At ease reclined in rustic state)

[*Poems*, p. 50]

But this traditional and reciprocal relationship is undermined by the least suspected 'genii of the stream', the sportive insects, whose perspective allows only that the poet's 'sun is set, thy spring is gone'.

Although much of Gray's poetic richness in these odes derives from his allusions to earlier poetry, the echoes and evocations of the classics, Milton, and Shakespeare are also a means of calling Gray's response to landscape into question. (Similarly, his 'British' poetry invokes other literature: the landscape of "The Fatal Sisters", which sprang from Gray's researches into the history of British poetry and which was, according to Walpole, 'to be encased in a history of English bards', echoes *Paradise Lost* and *The Aeneid*, just as the 'yawning steep' of Hela's 'dread abode' in "The Descent of Odin" echoes Milton's hell, and its winter scenery, Dryden's *King Arthur*.) But paradoxically these borrowed attributes seem to sustain only while the vision which they serve lasts. The palimpsest of allusion to Milton, Pope, Spenser, and Dyer in the opening prospect of Eton ('Ye distant spires, ye antique towers, / That crown the watery glade') inspires Gray quite literally ('I feel the gales, that from ye blow') only as long as the prelapsarian vision continues. It is part of the elegaic tone of both the odes on spring and Eton that an atavistic landscape of poetic memory contrives to withhold its support from some continuing rapport between poet and place.

The "Elegy" in its early drafts explored the 'gentler genius of the plain', meaning both the spirit of place and of the poet, with more security. The two are brought to their encounter from the start:

The curfew tolls the knell of parting day,
The lowing herd wind slowly o'er the lea,
The ploughman homeward plods his weary way,
And leaves the world to darkness and to me.

[*Poems*, p. 117 ff]

Gray's distinctive version of the *beatus ille* and *O fortunatos nimium* themes transposes literary allusion into a fabric of personal meditation. His night thoughts are focused upon items of local topography, and the syntax ('*yonder* ivy-mantled tower'—'*that* yew-tree') gestures from poet to landscape, just as the pointing figure in a painted landscape leads us into its special meaning. Unlike the two odes, this "Elegy" establishes its imagery of 'straw-built shed', 'blazing hearth' and georgic activity, not to deny their power (either in fact or in literary history), but to consolidate the poet's involvement with the obscure villagers and to approve his final preference for peace and obscurity to the perils of the great world:

And thou, who mindful of the unhonour'd Dead
Dost in these notes thy artless Tale relate
By Night and lonely Contemplation led
To linger in the gloomy Walks of Fate

Hark how the sacred Calm, that broods around
Bids ev'ry fierce tumultuous Passion cease
In still small Accents whisp'ring from the Ground
A grateful Earnest of eternal Peace

No more with Reason & thyself at strife;
Give anxious Cares & endless Wishes room
But thro' the cool sequester's Vale of Life
Pursue the silent Tenour of thy Doom.

With these stanzas from the Eton ms. the "Elegy" was at some stage in its composition supposed to end.

Gray's alteration and extension of the poem represent, among many complex motives, a refusal to accept such a simple identification of poet with landscape. The firm declaration of the poet's belief in the genii loci which initiate his understanding of the place ('by Night and lonely Contemplation led') is hedged in the later version ('If chance, by lonely Contemplation led'). Correspondingly, the figure of the poet is represented as one less 'at home', more of an outsider, with a sensibility (which the literary allusions now support in quite a different way) and an imagination that preclude any simple identification with the rural scene. The picture, offered through the mouth of 'some hoary-headed swain', shows a melancholy Narcissus-figure ('And pore upon the brook that babbles by'), who is replaced when he departs ('Another came'). His relationship to the landscape, still seen by one who is really part of it, becomes faintly ridiculous, that of a connoisseur of moodscapes:

Oft have we seen him at the peep of dawn
Brushing with hasty steps the dews away
To meet the sun upon the upland lawn.

There at the foot of yonder nodding beech
That wreathes its old fantastic roots so high
His listless length at noontide would he stretch
And pore upon the brook that babbles by.

Hard by yon wood, now smiling as in scorn,
Muttering his wayward fancies he would rove

And his epitaph commemorates, we could say, precisely the simple sentimentalist of the poem's first version: one for whom the graveyard is a 'lap of earth' (the Virgilian allusion notwithstanding), for whom benevolence was a straightforward affair and to whom (in a manner of speaking) the sportive insects had never addressed their complicating taunts. The "Elegy" is too subtle and intricate—and at some points too unclearly phrased—to allow this interpretation to preside exclusively. But I suggest that Gray's final vision of the poet in the country churchyard is one which is characteristically ambiguous: attentive to the encounter between a poetic imagination and the presences of a landscape, but also too sceptical of the poet's role (Oh! lyre divine, what daring spirit / Wakes thee now?') to acknowledge with any confidence that its sensibility may be emphatically trusted.

The poet of the "Elegy" and the later bard obviously represent for Gray, susceptible always to vacillation and doubt, alternative habits of the imagination. We know that he told Nicholls that 'I felt myself the Bard' during its composition (*Correspondence*, p. 1290).; there is also an unused drawing for the "Elegy" by Bentley which distinctly portrays Gray among the churchyard scenery [plate 53]. These poems also focused for the second half of the century rival, if not mutually exclusive, visions of poetry. This chapter is concerned mainly with the bardic role, while the final one will take up the other. However, it is worth distinguishing at this point one, broadly generalized, difference between them.

The poet in the "Elegy" and in the odes on Spring and Eton is rebuffed in his attempts to read the moralized landscape; Gray dramatises his meditative pose and we are led to see his attitudes in a more problematic light. For if 'manners speak the idiom of the soil', it is perhaps significant that neither in the country churchyard nor in the spring landscape is the poet anything but an interloper—in contrast, the bard is endemic to his terrain. Nor, at all securely, does the "Elegy" identify a divinity in the landscape, a spirit of place that answers the poet's, as Gray himself had experienced in the alps or as the bard does in Snowdonia. Though his Empedoclean plunge into the 'roaring tide' does not instill confidence in his imaginative example, the bard is allowed a 'Rapture' and 'Noble incantations' which do not need to interpret a landscape in their own image or ascribe some melancholy meaning to its topographical items. Rather they consort aptly with the sublime mountains which in their turn endorse his 'truth severe'; his poetry revives an ancient magic of connection:

PLATE 53   Richard Bentley, unused drawing for *Designs . . . for Six Poems*
by Mr. T. Gray (1753).

Mountains, ye mourn in vain
Modred, whose magic song
Made huge Plinlimmon bow his cloud-topped head.   [*Poems*, p. 187]

If the bard became the more exciting figure of a poet for the
later eighteenth century, it was due to his novelty and that
confident and magical identity with his landscape. Also, despite
Gray's scholarly insistence upon the proper mode of Pindarics,
his bard encouraged an affective rather than a formal poetry,
one which invoked a daring and expressive language for passion
and sublime feeling.

THE LANDSCAPE OF THE BARD

*Descriptive
and
Allegoric*

Gray, it will be remembered, advised Beattie never to let descriptions become the subject-matter of his poetry. In 'A Long Story' he mocks the 'versifying tribe' with 'Your history whither are you spinning? / Can you do nothing but describe?' (*Poems*, p. 145). The temptations to describe increased in proportion as the use of older, allegorical structures for describing the passions and sublime states that were the subjects of the bardic muse declined:

The verse adorn again
Fierce War, and faithful Love,
And Truth severe, by fairy Fiction drest.
In buskin'd measures move
Pale Grief, and pleasing Pain,
With Horrour, Tyrant of the throbbing breast

[*Poems*, pp. 198–99]

Gray was himself, as his bard is in those lines, predictably conservative. The images of the 'fury passions' which molest the Etonian youth or of the virtues that attend upon Adversity are the same traditional personifications, derived from *Aeneid* IV. 273–81 and mediated by the Renaissance painter's iconography:

Wisdom in sable garb arrayed,
Immersed in rapturous thought profound,
And Melancholy, silent maid
With leaden eye that loves the ground,
Still on thy solemn steps attend:
Warm Charity, the general friend,
With Justice to herself severe,
And Pity, dropping soft the sadly-pleasing tear.

[*Poems*, p. 72]

It is perhaps this painterly mode to which Gray points in his lines on Bentley's art: 'in their course, each transitory thought / Fixed by his touch a lasting essence take' (*Poems*, p. 154). Yet Gray's own predilections for ambiguity and variable attitudes, which echo Pope's in the *Moral Essays*, must have led him to suspect the permanence which Bentley's *language* would give to psychological states. His own emblems, too, share that stultifying effect, though they are put to purposeful account in the "Elegy":

Can storied urn or animated bust
Back to its mansion call the fleeting breath?
Can Honour's voice provoke the silent dust,
Or Flattery soothe the dull cold ear of Death?

The empty, statuesque personifications are used there to accentuate the hollowness of church memorials.

A less inflexible alternative to the emblematic was Gray's rejected 'description', which, in fact, he himself uses in carefully subservient ways throughout his poetry. But its possibilities are more palpable in one of his contemporaries, whose version of the same Melancholy is rather different:

With eyes up-raised, as one inspired,
Pale Melancholy sat retired,
And from her wild sequestered seat,
In notes by distance made more sweet,
Poured through the mellow horn her pensive soul:
And dashing soft from rocks around,
Bubbling runnels joined the sound;
Through glades and glooms the mingled measure stole,
Or o'er some haunted stream with fond delay,
Round an holy calm diffusing,
Love of peace and lonely musing,
In hollow murmurs died away.

[*Poems*, p. 483]

The landscape, described in order to express the ideas of pensive melancholy, and with a verbal music that prevents it from aping the merely pictorial, comes from William Collins's *Odes on Several Descriptive and Allegoric Subjects*, which appeared in 1746. His more flexible treatment of iconographical images, mixing them with apt and expressive landscapes, earned him the label of 'picturesque genius' from James Grainger. Pope, as we saw in the second chapter, did the same with the figure of melancholy in "Eloisa to Abelard". What distinguishes Collins and other poets who flourished in the years just after Pope's death is the frequency with which they chose to refurbish older allegorical fictions by providing them with images drawn from contemporary landscape taste. Thus Collins's "Ode to Fear" presents Danger,

　　　　whose limbs of giant mould
What mortal eye can fixed behold?
Who stalks his round, an hideous form,
Howling amidst the midnight storm,
Or throws him on the ridgy steep
Of some loose hanging rock to sleep.

[*Poems*, p. 419]

Like Gray, Collins contrives various literary allusions in such lines, but the specific description of a relevant landscape is his own.

Collins's painterly taste obviously determined those devices of landscape description. His lines, 'Ye genii who, in secret state', are dedicated to three painters—Ruisdael, Rosa, and Claude—whose work has taught him to appreciate the various characters of scenery. Yet he concludes that neither their pictorial skills nor his verbal imagination can finally do justice to either the effects of moonlight upon a landscape (precisely what a painting *can* achieve, of course) or its effective qualities (which, equally, a poem may attempt). Gray, too, had felt the same dissatisfactions with artistic versions of scenes he knew at first hand: at Gordale Scar he stayed '(not without shuddering) a quarter of an hour, & thought my trouble richly paid, for the impression will last for life' (p. 1107); later at his inn he notes that François Vivares, Smith of Derby, and William Bellers had all been painting Gordale, yet implies that his own *impression* will be worth any number of their engravings [see plate 57]. What both Gray and Collins suggest is that they value their own unmediated contact with a natural scene:

Let me, where'er wild nature leads
    My sight, enamoured look
And choose my hymning pipe from reeds
    That roughen o'er the brook.

[*Poems*, p. 543]

It is a prelude to Collins's final hyperbole (that no art can express his experience of nature) that he is led by 'wild nature'. But the very expressions of his stanza deny that claim. Wild nature is only another appearance of the genius loci, different clearly from those tutelary spirits who begin the poem and are confined to the squares and streets of the 'thronged city', but still a proper and traditional verbal structure. What is fascinating is, first, Collins's refusal of visual analogies and modes and, second, his merging of an emblematic figure with its expressive territory *in the same phrase*: 'wild nature' is both a presiding spirit and a wild scene that draws his eyes into its mysteries.

Another form Collins's descriptions take is to provide for his allegorical figures a temple or shrine, whose situation and decoration are recorded:

Come, Pity, come, by Fancy's aid,
Even now my thoughts, relenting maid,
    Thy temple's pride design:
Its southern site, its truth complete,
Shall raise a wild enthusiast heat
    In all who view the shrine.

There Picture's toils shall well relate
How chance or hard involving fate
    O'er mortal bliss prevail

. . . .

There let me oft, retired by day,
In dreams of passion melt away,
    Allowed with thee to dwell

[*Poems*, p. 417]

It is a variation of the 'instructions to a painter' formula, now directed at the landscape designer, who was well versed in the erection of temples to Piety (at Studley Royal) or to Friendship and Liberty (at Stowe). By providing his allegorical characters with their appropriate *paysage sacré* Collins converts them into the more subtle role of a tutelary spirit. And offering such landscapes in the by now familiar form of garden designs he is able to borrow a vocabulary of numinous description, inherited from classical literature certainly, but given fresh point on the English country estate. The particular diety celebrated by a temple determined the character of that part of the landscape, which may then be described with that in mind. It was a habit, as we shall see, that elicited innumerable inscriptions for gardens, each eager to invent and articulate the 'genius loci separti'. In other odes Collins suggests similar descriptions, offering Liberty, on one occasion, a 'roseate bower'.

An extension of this gardenist habit is to seek appropriate buildings in the larger landscape beyond the ha-ha. A more compelling moment of the "Ode to Liberty", for instance, involves the search for Druid temples:

Then too, 'tis said, an hoary pile
Midst the green navel of our isle,
Thy shrine in some religious wood,
O soul-enforcing goddess stood!
There oft the painted native's feet
Were wont thy form celestial meet:
Though now with hopeless toil we trace
Time's backward rolls to find its place.

[*Poems*, p. 451]

In such spots the spirit of Liberty enforces the soul, extending her particular effects over the (even imaginary) visitor. Such a Temple of Liberty had been designed by Gibbs for Stowe in 1741—a fine gothic triangular building [plate 54]. But it is evident that for many mid-century poets the idea of Liberty needed a larger and wilder landscape; a distinctly British landscape for a redolently British virtù and not, what Gray in "A Long Story" called, 'a small closet in the garden'.

This taste for landscapes, which in their turn rendered the garden too confined a domain for the poetic imagination, is linked by Collins and similar spirits to their tastes for what his "Epistle . . . to Sir Thomas Hanmer" (*Poems*, pp. 389 ff.) called 'wilder . . . and less artful' visions. In that "Epistle" it is Shakespeare who is the proffered exemplum:

But stronger Shakespeare felt for man alone:
Drawn by his pen, our ruder passions stand
The unrivalled picture of his early hand.

With an appropriate echo of Milton (another sublime genius) Collins hears Shakespeare's 'Fancy,' 'wild of wing,' calling the responsive soul to rove 'With humbler nature in the rural grove'. An older bardic figure, Orpheus, is also seen amid 'lonely cliffs and caves', drawing his audience 'From hollow oak, or mountain-den' (though the lines are only doubtfully ascribed to Collins [*Poems*, p. 562], this imagery is precisely his). This need to identify high emotions with expressive imagery had led Collins, while still at school, to compose his *Persian Eclogues* (*Poems*, pp. 371 ff.). It is his motives for these bland concoctions rather than their neglible intrinsic value that merit our interest. For he was drawn, his Preface explains, by the 'elegancy and wildness of thought' in Arabic literature and by its 'figurative' style. Its ideas and images are matched in ways quite opposite to 'our geniuses [which] are as much too cold for the entertainment of such sentiments as our climate is for their fruits and spices'. The judgement of Collins's contemporaries was that he had not seized the opportunities forcibly enough: William Shenstone told Thomas Percy in 1760 that 'Poor Collins' had not 'availd himself of their many local peculiarities'. Such strictures, in fact, were only judging Collins's efforts by his own ambition to join 'new images and sentiments' and to explore the 'wild and local' possibilities of Arabia's 'silent horror o'er the desert-waste'. The Arabic imagination—'predominant . . . wild, vast, and un-bridled' to Thomas Rhymer as early as 1674—perhaps proved too exotic, too unknown for the young poet to emulate. The taste for wildness and sublimity had to be rooted in native soil.

Collins turned to British ideas and images for his *Odes*, praised by one of his early editors for their 'luxuriance of imagination, a wild sublimity of fancy, and a felicity of expres-sion'. Today it is probably only his "Ode to Evening" that

PLATE 54   The Temple of Liberty, or Gothic Temple, Stowe.

justifies this claim. Yet the whole sequence of odes, uneven, dense, more enthusiastic than measured, provides a patterned scheme of related reflections on the creative imagination and its specifically British territory. Sometimes, as in the "Ode to Simplicity", there are only glimpses of landscape background; at others, as in the "Ode on the Poetical Character" the 'visions wild' are accorded a specific and expressive scenery:

Where is the bard, whose soul can now
Its high presuming hopes avow?
Where he who thinks, with rapture blind,
This hallowed work for him designed?

High on some cliff to Heaven up-piled,
Of rude access, of prospect wild,
Where, tangled round the jealous steep,
Strange shades o'erbrow the valleys deep,
And holy genii guard the rock,
Its glooms embrown, its springs unlock,
While on its rich ambitious head,
An Eden, like his own, lies spread

[*Poems*, pp. 433–34]

The landscape is instinct with literary presence and, doubtless, with reminiscences of paintings, but the "Ode" ends with the admission that Milton's imagination, with its vast Edenic landscape, is beyond the modern poet. Collins succeeds in localizing 'Britannia's Genius' (*Poems*, p. 457) and matching it with his own poetic skills only in the "Ode to Evening". Not exclusively a bardic production, it may be considered here for its marvellous ability to localize a sublime feeling. The analogy in painting, as Lord Clark has noted, is Richard Wilson's attention to such English scenes as *Hounslow Heath* or *Penn Ponds*, where he naturalizes the landscape tastes acquired in Italy.

What Collins achieves by way of original vision, I believe, is a more intricate involvement of his own imagination with that of the evening landscape; this has little to do with his occasional imitation of pictorial imagery and is more dependent upon the texture of literary allusion redeployed in ways that the landscape garden suggested. The first edition of the "Ode" had declared:

Then let me rove some wild and heathy Scene,
Or find some Ruin 'midst its dreary Dells,
    Whose Walls more awful nod
    By thy religious Gleams.

Two years later Collins alters this to a more complicated address to the spirit of place and, in this case, time also:

Then lead, calm vot'ress, where some sheety lake
Cheers the lone heath, or some time-hallowed pile,
    Or upland fallows grey,
    Reflect its last cool gleam.

[*Poems*, pp. 465–66]

The new lines establish the deliberate surrender of the poet to the tutelary spirit in place of the casual and haphazard 'roving' of the first version. Yet they keep the sense of the various landscape itself tempting him onwards, with the result that arguments over syntactical ambiguities at line 32 seem unnecessary: 'its last cool gleam' is both the lights off the lake touching some 'time-hallowed pile' and the reflections of evening's car. In other words, we have a mingling of the real and the local, what a painter could depict, with the literary and tutelary spirit of evening; a marriage of the visible and seen with the imaginary and inventive. So in the exploration of a garden's scenery, the poet is led or forbidden by spirits given local form (temples and inscriptions in gardens, the ruins or hut in Collins's scene) at the same time as he feels he alone is responsible for discovering its expressive components:

But when chill blustering winds or driving rain
Forbid my willing feet, be mine the hut
    That from the mountain's side
    Views wilds and swelling floods,
And hamlets brown, and dim-discovered spires,
And hears their simple bell, and marks o'er all
    Thy dewy fingers draw
    The gradual dusky veil.

[*Poems*, p. 466]

PLATE 55
William Gilpin,
Lake Scene with Castle.
Watercolour (1780's).

The descriptive and allegoric elements work to make this a distinct affirmation of a properly verbal expression of the idea of evening.

The Idiom of the Soil

In the "Ode to Evening" the poet moves from some picturesque lakeside that Gilpin's pencil might have drawn [plate 55] to a hut upon the mountain's side; the spirit of evening is thereby traced from its calmer to its wilder character. In the terms that Burke was to make definitive eleven years after Collins published his *Odes*, evening modulates from the beautiful to the sublime. Burke lent his authority to a host of (often indifferent) poems, a circumstance to which he maybe alluded in 1783 when he objected to the 'miserable rhapsodies' of MacPherson's *Ossian*. However, he had in 1761 reviewed that work, found it sublime, and noted its characteristics as strangeness, wildness, and lack of restraint. The coincidence of Burke's distinction between beauty and sublimity, especially of the *terms* of his analyses, with the search for a new poetics undoubtedly confirmed his influence. It will suggest something of this conjunction between aesthetics and literary history to note that Burke's *Enquiry* appeared only one year after Joseph Warton first issued his *Essay on Pope*, where, as we have seen, "The Bard" eventually became the test of true imagination. Some of the poetry that is discussed in this and the following section was, of course, published before Burke; yet it serves to remind us of the distinct search in mid-century for fresh imaginative modes of which they are all, the *Enquiry* and the poems, symptomatic.

Burke provided several relevant perspectives upon the landscape of the bard. He consistently valued poetry above painting, because it wields more power over the emotions and the passions, which are the favoured territory of the new poetry. He contended that sublime language was not based upon a mere picturesque, image-raising capacity: hitherto, as Burke's editor has shown, the best poetry had been held to be that 'most picturesque and clearest' in its imagery, which Burke's new insistence upon specifically verbal structures denied:

The truth is, all verbal description, merely as naked description, though never so exact, conveys so poor and insufficient an idea of the thing described, that it could scarcely have the smallest effect, if the speaker did not call in to his aid those modes of speech that mark a strong and lively feeling in himself. Then, by the contagion of our passions, we catch a fire already kindled in another, which probably might never have been struck out by the object described.

That such emphasis licensed grandiloquent vagueness is unhappily true; yet it also offered to release poetry from the notion to which Joseph Warton gives succinct expression: "The use, the force and the excellence of language, certainly consists in raising *clear*, *complete*, and *circumstantial* images, and in turning *readers* into *spectators*'. Such prescriptions only locked eighteenth-century poets in a more and more debilitating homage to 'ut pictura poesis' and finally earned Wordsworth's famous scorn of poetry's 'mimic art' in *The Prelude*. Burke chose to distinguish between 'a clear expression and a strong expression' ('the first regards the understanding; the latter belongs to the passions. The one describes a thing as it is; the other describes it as it is felt'); this could have released a properly literary attention to human emotion. Yet at the very point when his example could have led writers away from Rosa and Ruisdael (Collins's rejection of them in "Ye Genii" anticipated this) Burke's analysis of the sublime in landscape inevitably pushed them back into precisely the territories that painters had excelled in depicting; as his disciple, Hugh Blair, explained:

What are the scenes of nature that elevate the mind in the highest degree, and produce the sublime sensation? Not the gay landscape, the flowery field, or the flourishing city; but the hoary mountain, and the solitary lake; the aged forest, and the torrent falling over the rock.

Such scenes were, by definition, the territory of solitary figures like James Beattie's minstrel:

Concourse, and noise, and toil he ever fled;
Nor cared to mingle in the clamorous fray
Of squabbling imps; but to the forest sped,
Or roamed at large the lonely mountain's head,
Or, where the maze of some bewildered stream
To deep untrodden groves his footsteps led,
There would he wander wild

[ll. 146-52]

The minstrel certainly attends to both the beauty of 'verdure warbling' and the sublime of 'silent mountains' (ll. 530 & 527), but his solitude marks him as essentially an exponent of the sublime. It is here perhaps above all that Burke influenced the cause of the late eighteenth-century landscape poem: by dividing the social and selfish passions between the beautiful and the sublime respectively, by linking beauty with 'society in general' and sublimity with 'absolute and entire solitude', he authorized anew the lonely melancholy or enthusiastic poet which the Warton brothers had already celebrated. Burke confirmed, in other words, the mode of "Eloisa to Abelard" over that of *An Essay on Man*, of 'deep solitudes and awful cells' and 'dear horrors of all-conscious night' over 'Together let us beat this ample field'.

Collins's "Ode on the Popular Superstitions of the Highlands of Scotland" (again before Burke) invoked this opposition of society and solitude in addressing John Home on his departure from London for Scotland. Home, who was later to encourage

Macpherson in his Gaelic enthusiasms, leaves both a society and a peopled landscape:

thou return'st from Thames, whose Naiads long
Have seen thee lingering, with a fond delay,
Mid those soft friends whose hearts, some future day,
Shall melt, perhaps, to hear thy tragic song.   [p. 501]

And he returns to a landscape that is noticeably free of such social structures and classical deities:

Fresh to that soil thou turn'st, whose every vale
Shall prompt the poet and his song demand:
To thee thy copious subjects ne'er shall fail;
Thou need'st but take the pencil to thy hand,
And paint what all believe who own thy genial land.   [p. 503]

The conventional juxtaposition of city and country is turned to an encomium upon a scenery which promotes the arts. Though Collins still offers inert painterly advice to the poet, and though his fascination for 'Fancy's land' is not at all straightforward, he clearly chooses to see the Highlands as predominantly a landscape of sublime poetry:

Even yet preserved, how often may'st thou hear,
Where to the pole the Boreal mountains run,
Taught by the father to his listening son
Strange lays, whose power had charmed a Spenser's ear.
At every pause, before thy mind possessed,
Old Runic bards shall seem to rise around
With uncouth lyres, in many-coloured vest,
Their matted hair with boughs fantastic crowned.   [pp. 504–5]

The bardic muse is not all 'sober Truth', Collins admits, but Scottish scenes are 'still to Nature true' and 'call forth fresh delights to Fancy's view'—which Shakespeare's witches are invoked to support. Collins's ambiguous attitude and his uncertain (self-mocking?) commitment to superstition do not prevent him welcoming it as a proper subject for poetry and one which will benefit especially from a sublime scenery:

'Tis thine to sing how, framing hideous spells,
In Skye's lone isle the gifted wizard seer,
Lodged in the wintry cave with [   ]
Or in the depths of Uist's dark forests dwells;
How they, whose sight such dreary dreams engross,
With their own visions oft astonished droop,
When o'er the watery strath or quaggy moss
They see the gliding ghosts unbodied troop.   [pp. 506–7]

The imprecisions both of fear and the shadowy landscape ('some dim hill that seems uprising near') conform to Burke's later insistence upon sublime obscurity:

Every one will be sensible of this, who considers how greatly night adds to our dread, in all cases of danger, and how much the notions of ghosts and goblins, of which none can form clear ideas, affect minds, which give credit to the popular tales concerning such sorts of beings. Those despotic governments, which are founded on the passions of men, and principally upon the passion of fear, keep their chief as much as may be from the public eye. The policy has been the same in many cases of religion. Almost all the heathen temples were dark.

Even Collins's final preference for the insights and forms of the poetic rather than the pictorial imagination are in accord with Burke's:

[p. 516]

Proceed, in forceful sounds and colours bold
The native legends of thy land rehearse;
To such adapt thy lyre and suit thy powerful verse.

Home, whom Collins addresses, did obey the command after a fashion, for he encouraged Macpherson: though *The Poems of Ossian* are in prose, they purport to be translations of Gaelic poetry. In essays prefixed to his 'versions' Macpherson clearly endorses the connections and emphases Collins had made: he links the traditions and songs of the Celtic states to a people who dwelt 'among the mountains and inaccessible parts of a country' (1: 29); like Gray in the "Alliance of Education and Government", Macpherson makes explicit the influence of climate and landscape upon literary culture (1:49) and praises the '*locality* of their description and sentiment' (1:53, my italics). In 1762 Macpherson issued his *Fingal, An Ancient Epic Poem*, on whose title page [plate 56] a bard with his harp is seated in the appropriately wild scenery. The use of landscape in *Fingal* is, as Hugh Blair was to insist in his *Critical Dissertation on the Poems of Ossian*, 'always suited to the occasion' (1:154). It is used with some skill and economy, in fact, being instinctively part of Ossian's own supposed utterance as it is of his heroic characters: an example from *Fingal*—

"I beheld their chief", says Moran, "tall as a glittering rock. His spear is a blasted pine. His shield the rising moon! He sat on the shore, like a cloud of mist on the silent hill! Many, chief of heroes! I said, many are our hands of war. Well art thou named, the Mighty Man: but many mighty men are seen from Tura's windy walls."

He spoke, like a wave on a rock. "Who in this land appears like me? Heroes stand not in my presence: they fall to earth from my hand. Who can meet Swaran in fight? Who but Fingal king of Selma of storms? Once we wrestled on Malmor: our heels overturned the woods. Rocks fell from their place; rivulets, changing their course, fled murmuring from our side."

[2: 260–61]

These images are probably the most satisfying moments still of Macpherson's interminable fictions. And as Blair properly remarked, the landscapes are endemic to the supposed poet's

PLATE 56   Samuel Wale, from title page of *Fingal*.
Engraved by I. Taylor (1761).

habits of thinking (the occasional allusion to Milton apart!): the 'figurative cast' of his language eschews abstract ideas which

extended little farther than to the objects he saw around him. A public, a community, the universe, were conceptions beyond his sphere. Even a mountain, a sea, or a lake, which he has occasion to mention, though only in a simile, are for the most part particularized; it is the hill of Cromla, the storm of the sea of Malmor, or the reeds of the lake of Lego. A mode of expression, which whilst it is characteristic of ancient ages, is at the same time highly favourable to descriptive poetry.

[1: 121]

Yet the elimination of 'descriptive poetry' per se is perhaps one of Macpherson's accomplishments; what glimpses we have of sublime scenery are already part of the characters' minds, not deployed for their own sakes. Blair again:

everywhere the same face of rude nature appears; a country wholly uncultivated, thinly inhabited, and recently peopled. The grass of the rock, the flower of the heath, the thistle with its beard, are the chief ornaments of his landscapes. "The desert", says Fingal, "is enough for me, with all its woods and deer".

[1:118]

Macpherson, then, provided an enormously influential example of landscape *used* by the literary imagination (both his own and that of his supposed bards). Thomas Warton actually listed landscapes among his reasons for doubting the authenticity of Macpherson's work; but in his *History of English Poetry* he seems to have reconciled such awkward glimpses of neoclassical apparatus (especially, genii loci) with traditions of northern literatures: 'The allusions in the songs of Ossian to spirits, who preside over the different parts and direct the various operations of nature . . . correspond with the Runic system, and breathe the spirit of its poetry'.

Macpherson's contribution was certainly to eliminate merely pictorial descriptions, simply (perhaps) because there were no painterly precedents, and to concentrate upon a psychological scenery which connects what Blair calls 'the state in which human nature shoots wild and free' (1:80) and 'the mountain shaded with the mist; the torrent rushing through a solitary valley; the scattered oaks, and the tombs of warriors overgrown with moss [which] all produce a solemn attention in the mind, and prepare it for great and extraordinary events' (1:125). These Ossian *paysages intérieurs* must have been given fresh authority (and ultimately of course a more scholarly imprimatur) by the publication of Percy's *Reliques of English Poetry* in 1765. Again, landscape description figures little in the collections, but when it does occur, as in "Sir Patrick Spens"—

Late, late yestreen I saw the new moone
Wi' the auld moone in hir arme;
And I feir, I feir, my deir master,
That we will com to harme

[ll. 469–77]

—its economy of *mental* imagery was a forcible reminder to poetry of how to use local description. Such is certainly the lesson that Beattie, whose *Minstrel* was issued in 1771 and 1774, thought he had learnt from Percy:

Whate'er of lore tradition could supply
From Gothic tale, or song, or fable old,
Roused him, still keen to listen and to pry.

[ll. 518–20]

Beattie's subtitle *The Minstrel; or, the Progress of Genius* locates his account of gothic poetics firmly among those inquiries of Gray and Collins into the British destinies of classical tradition. His theme of some 'soul sublime' (l. 3) is a *Bildungsroman* of the bardic muse, in the first book above all an education in landscape (ll. 190 ff.) and solitude (l. 522). Yet his best insights into the sublime scenery of his childhood, like Wordsworth's (though less carefully realized), allow the mind—imagination and fantasy—to usurp the preeminence of mere sight:

Oft when the winter storm had ceased to rave,
He roamed the snowy waste at even, to view
The cloud stupendous, from th'Atlantic wave
High-towering, sail along th'horizon blue:
Where, midst the changeful scenery, ever new,
Fancy a thousand wondrous forms descries,
More wildly great than ever pencil drew,
Rocks, torrents, gulfs, and shades of giant size,
And glittering cliffs on cliffs, and fiery ramparts rise.

The minstrel's 'thoughtful eye' led some to believe him mad (ll. 137–44); but it is precisely this instinct for *wonder* rather than for a merely pictorial vision that sustains the better passages of Beattie's poem:

Lo! where the stripling, wrapt in wonder, roves
Beneath the precipice o'er hung with pine;
And sees, on high, amidst th'encircling groves,
From cliff to cliff the foaming torrents shine:
While waters, woods, and winds, in concert join,
And Echo swells the chorus to the skies.
Would Edwin this majestic scene resign
For aught the huntsman's puny craft supplies?
Ah! no: he better knows great Nature's charms to prize.

And oft he traced the uplands, to survey,
When o'er the sky advanced the kindling dawn,
The crimson cloud, blue main, and mountain grey,
And lake, dim-gleaming on the smoky lawn;
Far to the west the long long vale withdrawn,
Where twilight loves to linger for a while;
And now he faintly kens the bounding fawn,
And villager abroad at early toil.
But, lo! the Sun appears! and heaven, earth, ocean, smile.

And oft the craggy cliff he loved to climb,
When all in mist the world below was lost.
What dreadful pleasure! there to stand sublime,
Like shipwrecked mariner on desert coast,
And view th'enormous waste of vapour, tost
In billows, lengthening to th'horizon round,
Now scooped in gulfs, with mountains now embossed! [ll. 163–87]

What withholds from Beattie, I think, any greater success is that his poem tells rather than shows; it *recounts* a process by which a young mind echoes the images of nature and rarely ventures any more inward vision in which, for instance, 'the visible scene / Would enter unawares into his mind / With all its solemn imagery'.

The Minstrel, then, is a prime example of what Beattie calls the 'gothic lyre' (l. 532). It has, in addition, debts to two related themes in the bardic landscapes: melancholy and enthusiasm, for which the Warton brothers had early provided the basic texts. The minstrel is both the 'lone enthusiast' (l. 479), musing 'with pleasing dread' among nature's solitudes and rather self-consciously following in the footsteps of Joseph Warton's *The Enthusiast; or the Lover of Nature* (1744). Similarly, his fascination with 'Even sad vicissitude' and his frequenting 'th'unsightly slime and sluggish pool' (ll. 195, 210) mark him of the elect company of Thomas Warton's visionary in *The Pleasure of Melancholy* (1747). In that poem the melancholy poet celebrates the figure of Contemplation, 'whom, as tradition tells, / Once in his evening walk a Druid found, / Far in a hollow glade of Mona's woods' (ll. 306–8). Beattie follows Warton in devoting another poem to "The Triumph of Melancholy", where he finally admits its power over his 'bewildered soul' and records its particular compulsion in sublime scenery:

The traveller thus, that o'er the midnight waste
Through many a lonesome path is doomed to roam,
Wildered and weary sits him down at last;
For long the night, and distant far his home.

The melancholy muse ranged the full spectrum of expressive landscapes; sometimes, as Macpherson records of the Druids, 'retired to the dark recesses of their groves, and the caves they had formerly used for their meditations' (1.9); sometimes, as Thomas Warton preferred, the stronger experiences of sublime vertigo 'upon the topmost rock of Teneriff'. But the melancholic imagination, whatever the temper of its local habit, always continued to seek an appropriate landscape, as Coleridge's tribute to Joseph Cottle reveals:

Not there the cloud-climb'd rock, sublime and vast,
That like some giant king o'erglooms the hill;
Nor there the pine-grove to the midnight blast
Makes solemn music! But th'unceasing rill
To the soft wren or lark's descending trill
Murmurs sweet under-song 'mid jasmine bowers,
In this same pleasant meadow . . .

And Keats, too, locates his own special vision of melancholy in scenery where details are praeternaturally defined ('the globed peonies', for instance) or, as Collins did, in landscapes with shadowy temples where 'Veiled Melancholy has her sovrane shrine'.

The Ossianic imagination was not loth to surrender to mist and darkness. For in them the private genius discovers its own vocabulary; the melancholic identifies his own inward obscurities in the clouds, 'Blackening the landscape's face, that grove and hill / In formless vapours undistinguish'd swim'. The analogue in the novel, as Earl Wasserman pointed out, is 'the blank page [in *Tristram Shandy*] at which each of us is to stare in order to visualize in his own private way the Widow Wadman'—Was ever anything in Nature so sweet?—so exquisite!'".

Night Thoughts

But this vogue for solipsist and obscure sublimity, sanctioned by Burke in 1756, had been not long since of (at best) only ambiguous appeal to Pope. In *The Dunciad* he locates with relish the absurdities of the dunces—their taste for bardic trance ('In lofty madness meditating song; / Her tresses staring from

Poetic dreams'); their predilection for opiate-induced dreams and the visionary worlds released by sleep; their love of the gothic past ('bold Ostrogoths . . . fierce Visigoths') and of the gloomy private realm of enthusiasm and night thoughts.

Pope certainly knew the enemy he was attacking. The opening to the final book of *The Dunciad* (published in 1742), which enacts the total disintegration of civilization, prophetically anticipates Edward Young's *Night Thoughts*, which began to appear later in 1742. This long, rambling poem is dedicated to exactly those visions that Pope denounced. Pope fends off the darkness of unreason as long as possible:

Yet, yet a moment, one dim ray of light
Indulge dread Chaos, and eternal night
. . . .
Suspend a while your force inertly strong,
Then take at once the poet and the Song.

The generalizing effect of 'the Poet and the Song' implies not merely Pope's own annihilation by darkness but the total intellectual death 'when Wit and Humour are no more':

Nor public flame, nor private, dares to shine;
Nor human spark is left, nor glimpse divine!
Lo thy dread Empire, Chaos is restored;
Light dies before thy uncreating word:
Thy hand, great Anarch, lets the curtain fall;
And universal darkness buries all.

That final engulfing darkness is Pope's great enemy and he has attacked all the dunces' activities that promote it.

Yet Edward Young actually invokes the fate, in his case propitious for poetry, to which Pope had condemned the dunces a few months before: 'Canst thou, O Night indulge one labour more? / One labour more indulge; then sleep my strain'. In a further passage Young apostrophizes the world of sleep which had recently gathered Pope's dunces to its depths:

While o'er my limbs sleep's soft dominion spread,
What though my soul fantastic measures trod
O'er fairy fields; or mourn'd along the gloom
Of pathless woods; or down the craggy steep
Hurl'd headlong . . . .
Or scaled the cliff; or danced on hollow winds,
With antic shapes, wild natives of the brain?

My song the midnight raven has outwinged,
And shot, ambitious of unbounded scenes,
Beyond the flaming limits of the world
Her gloomy flight.

What is immediately striking, not only about Young's indifferent poem but others like it, is that it reaches its best moments in such visions of expressive landscapes that emerge as metaphors of the poet's meditations. That might explain Pope's ambiguous attitude: he devastates, yet his own poetry has created for the dunces' gothic nightmare an epic energy which cannot but be admired and which is attended with imaginative skills utterly denied to Young. And Pope had himself, as we have seen, indulged these visionary moments in the seclusion of his own grotto. There were Augustan traditions of night thoughts—sanctioned, for instance, by Virgil's picture of the deserted Dido and Milton's "Il Penseroso"—and Pope had encountered the ghost of an Unfortunate Lady 'along the moonlight glade'. But what *The Dunciad* would seem to be ridiculing (even as it renders them sublime) are the lack of precision, the merely sensational aspects of night thoughts, and their uncontrollable parade of personal emotion. These are the ingredients from which, in 1756, Burke constituted the sublime and which the bardic landscape this chapter has explored also employed.

One of the earliest night pieces was the Countess of Winchilsea's "A Nocturnal Reverie", a favourite poem for Wordsworth. Published in 1713, it used the freshly observed details of a natural scene to mirror a 'sedate content', which even the most awful moments of her night walk do not threaten:

When darken'd Groves their softest Shadows wear,
And falling Waters we distinctly hear;
When thro' the Gloom more venerable shows
Some antient Fabrick, awful in Repose.

A personal observation, though, is modulated into a social, public recitation ('we fear'), and this reluctance to record the working of private sensibilities among natural scenery has, of course, a strong hold on the Augustan poet: as Pope wrote in 'The Design' of *An Essay on Man*,

more good will accrue to mankind by attending to the large, open, and perceptible parts, than by studying too much such finer nerves and vessels, the conformations and uses of which will forever escape our observation.

[*Poems*, 3/i:7]

The experience of a landscape garden, too, was both an essentially public affair, as the 1739 engravings of Stowe reveal [see plate 43], and a social exchange of impressions, as Gilpin's *Dialogue* (1748) upon the gardens at Stowe demonstrates. We shall see in the next and final section of this chapter how the garden first began to tempt the solitary genius and later failed to hold him. This flight from the garden corresponded approximately in motive and in date with the poet's explorations of the solitary and personal dimensions of night poetry.

The literary history of the night piece stretches from Thomas Parnell's "A Night Piece on Death", published posthumously by Pope in 1722, to Coleridge's "Frost At Midnight" of 1798. Its progress, somewhat unsteady, is marked by poets' concern to find a vocabulary in the outside world for their inward experience and to 'behold' (in Akenside's lines)

in lifeless things,
The inexpressive semblance of himself
Of thought and passion.

Many methods and experiments concurred: the steady elimination of a social syntax (Parnell's 'our Eyes'); the mistrust of merely descriptive verses, whether in imitation of paintings or not, because they did not involve the passions which poetry was dedicated to arouse:

Illustrious objects strike the gazer's mind
With feeble bliss, and but allure the sight,
Nor rouse with impulse quick th'unfeeling heart.

Yet there is a strong refusal to abandon the seen world, not only because its frequent absence in poetry like *Night Thoughts* contributed to the failures of communication, but because it was the actual *treaty* between outside and inside that was at stake—hence Warton's 'haply' in the following lines, signalling his reorientation among the natural elements:

And now no more th'abstracted ear attends
The water's murm'ring lapse, th'entranced eye
Pierces no longer thro' th'extended rows
Of thick-rang'd trees; till haply from the depth
The woodman's stroke, or distant tinkling team,
Or heifers rustling thro' the brake, alarms
Th'illuded sense, and mars the golden dream.

Only the congruence of the senses with the imagination could discover modes of poetry that allow an inward landscape of introspection—the 'secret ministry' of frost—or sudden visions of meaning located still in the visible world—

The moon, preceded by the breeze
That bade the clouds retire,
Appears amongst the tufted trees,
A Phoenix nest on fire.

The more awkward searches for meaning in natural phenomena often, as with Parnell, entail voices speaking to him from a yew tree or

Those Graves, with bending Osier bound,
That nameless heave the crumbled Ground,
Quick to the glancing Thought disclose
Where *Toil* and *Poverty* repose.

The recitation, too, of the constituent parts of 'solemn glooms' / Congenial to my soul' rarely illuminated the specifically inward feeling; the dogged elaboration of analogues —Johnson's' addition [to a landscape description] of such embellishment as may be supplied by historical retrospection, or incidental meditation'—again usually evaded the actual *process* of the mind's encounter with the outside world, as did the assumption that only to name a certain scenery and link it to the names of Spenser or Milton produced a felt landscape. We may, in short, mark the progress of the enthusiastic, melancholy muse by comparing Akenside's search for the nightingale with Keats's: in the former's "To the Evening Star" the 'plaintive Syren' admonishes the poet to contemplate 'man's uncertain lot:

O sacred bird, let me at eve,
    Thus wandering all alone,
Thy tender counsel oft receive,
Bear witness to thy pensive airs,
And pity nature's common cares
    Till I forget my own.

In contrast, Keats's "Ode" not only becomes itself the process of such reception but the distinctions between subject and object are dissolved in the 'high requiem' that is both poet's and bird's.

Two metaphoric tactics of this poetry deserve special commentary. The first begins as simple description of reflections in water—Parnell's

The Lake is smooth and clear beneath,
Where once again the spangled Show
Descends to meet our Eyes below.

Perhaps the fascination with reversed images of nature derives from our unconscious recollection of the upside-down impressions of the world received upon our retinas. Certainly for the eighteenth-century poet this allowed scope for at least implied puns on 'reflections': merely exterior impressions—descriptive images—slide into imaginative ideal dramas—mental images. A later passage, of Wordsworth's, resumes these earlier poetic concerns in its distinctive way:

                all the distant grove
That rises to the summit of the steep
Shows like a mountain built of silver light.
See yonder the same pageant, and again
Behold the universal imagery
Inverted, all its sun-bright features touched
As with the varnish, and the gloss of dreams;
Dreamlike the blending also of the whole
Harmonious landscape, all along the shore
The boundary lost, the line invisible
That parts the image from reality;

And the clear hills, as high as they ascend
Heavenward, so piercing deep the lake below.

A more radical method of achieving an inward imagery was to insist upon visionary landscapes, upon a purely subjective vision that colours, even creates, whole landscapes after its own imagination. Of course, earlier landscape descriptions by Thomson, Gay, or Pope all involve imaginative, idealizing vision; none of them pretend to offer 'real' scenery; but their painterly references at least imply the actual landscapes that the artists had gazed upon as well as the idealizing power of their transformation into art. A later poet who implies that nature is the greater artist suggests the same:

Now he sets behind the hill,
    Sinking from a golden sky:
Can the pencil's mimic skill,
    Copy the refulgent dye?

Such landscapes allude to the realities that inspire them. But other poets chose to emphasize the eidetic imagery of which Blake was to speak, when he referred to his painting of *The Bard, from Gray*: 'The painter of this work asserts that all his imaginations appear to him infinitely more perfect and more minutely organized than any thing seen by his mental eye'. Such are the frequent allusions to magical and disappearing landscapes, like Alcina's island in Ariosto or Armida's garden in Tasso. And it is presumably something like those that Thomas Warton has in mind in his "Ode Sent to a Friend on his Leaving a Favourite Village in Hampshire":

For lo! the Bard who rapture found
In every rural sight or sound;
Whose genius warm, and judgement chaste,
No charm of genuine nature pass'd;
Who felt the Muse's purest fires,
Far from thy favour'd haunt retires:
Who peopled all thy vocal bowers
With shadowy shapes, and airy powers

. . . .
So by some sage inchanter's spell,
(As old Arabian fablers tell)
Amid the solitary wild,
Luxuriant gardens gaily smil'd:
From sapphire rocks the fountains stream'd,
With golden fruit the branches beam'd;
Fair forms, in every wondrous wood,
Or lightly tripp'd, or solemn stood;
And oft, retreating from the view,
Betray'd, at distance, beauties new:
While gleaming o'er the crisped bowers
Rich spires arose, and sparkling towers.

If bound on service new to go,
The master of the magic show,
His transitory charm withdrew,
Away th'illusive landscape flew:
Dun clouds obscur'd the groves of gold,
Blue lightning smote the blooming mold:
In visionary glory rear'd,
The gorgeous castle disappear'd;
And a bare heath's unfruitful plain
Usurp'd the wizard's proud domain.

Such *imaginations* (in Blake's idiom) were endemic to the poetry of the night. For in the 'visionary shades', where Robert Blair encounters 'nought but Silence . . . and Night, dark Night', the visionary imagination is free to fill the stillness with its voice and form the surrounding void into its shapes. Blair's *The Grave* (1743) is one among much 'graveyard' literature, including Gray's *Elegy* and James Hervey's *Meditations Among the Tombs* (London, 1746), which explores this penumbra of half-seen, half-imagined scenes. When 'fades the glimmering Landscape on the sight', the obligations of the imagination to known landscapes are less strong. Beattie's minstrel typically experiences a similar chain of thoughts, first dreaming of 'graves, and corpses pale' in the dim evening light, and then, at the haunted stream, succumbing to a Fancy-induced sleep which yielded 'A Vision . . . to his entranced sight' (l. 280–97).

Away from the bright and defining light of day, a poet like Young is forced backwards into his own introspection:

Darkness has more divinity for me;
It strikes thought inward; it drives back the soul
To settle on herself, our point supreme!
There his own theatre! There sits the judge.
Darkness the curtain drops o'er life's dull scene.

But this theatre, too, needs its scenery and this is provided by the half-visual, half-inventive powers of the human mind; Young's lines were to find an echo in the heart of Wordsworth at Tintern Abbey fifty years later; for Young the senses

Take in at once, the landscape of the world,
At a small inlet, which a grain might close,
And half create the wondrous world they see.
Our senses, as our reason, are divine.
But for the magic organ's powerful charm,
Earth were a rude, uncolor'd chaos, still.
Objects are but th'occasion; ours th'exploit.

Not always is the precision of his verse as exciting; too often his poem justly earns George Eliot's criticism that one of Young's most striking characteristics is his 'radical insincerity as a poetic artist'. One sees too frequently exactly what she means:

Young's dedication to the 'divinely inspired enthusiast' who crosses 'all publick roads into fresh untrodden grounds' (this, from his *Conjectures on Original Composition*) endorses any extravagance that may be appropriate. In *Conjectures* Young had argued that 'In the fairyland of fancy, genius may wander wild; there it has a creative power, and may reign over its own empire of chimeras'. This may, on the one hand, promote literal explorations of untrodden natural scenery, a study of landscapes hitherto unvisited in order to provide forms into which personal feelings are released and which thus offer a mode of expression that Augustan poetry did not provide. It may, alternatively, authorize fantasies with few objective correlatives by which the chimeras may be registered. The most fruitful way for poetry, as the final chapter will show, lay in some new compromise by which the eye and the imagination learnt to cohabit.

Walpole disliked the vogue which he thought Macpherson had released—'The giantry of Ossian had introduced mountainous horrors'. Yet he contributed to them with *The Castle of Otranto*. And that essay in gothic sublime may remind us that the novel (undeniably the form which best satisfied the major creative impulses of the late eighteenth century) was just as ready as the poetry to invoke landscape as the expression of feelings. Its role in fiction, especially but not exclusively gothic fiction, and the skills with which it is managed become extraordinarily sophisticated by the time, say, of Ann Radcliffe's *The Italian* (1797). But however much the characters of a gothic novel are deliberately abandoned in solitary confinement, or sublime wastes, fiction is still generally concerned with the social resolution of an action. The bardic muse, examined here, had the advantage (in its eyes) of virtually complete dedication to solitude and private melancholy without those 'social' obligations.

In *The Italian* Ann Radcliffe rewards Vivaldi and Ellena, after their vicissitudes among mountains, ruins, and solitary retreats, by bringing them for their nuptials into the pleasure grounds of a villa: 'The style of the gardens, where lawns and groves, and woods varied the undulating surface, was that of England, and of the present day, rather than of Italy'. The characters' recovery of social experience is, then, linked specifically to the English landscape garden of the late eighteenth century. Mrs. Radcliffe's covert symbolism corresponds with that of many participants in the bardic landscape, who did not feel that their poetry could look to the garden for its landscapes. Joseph Warton, for example, opens his *Enthusiast* with a rejection of Stowe:

Can Stow
Such Raptures
Raise?

Ye green-robed Dryads, oft at dusky eve
By wondering shepherds seen; to forests brown,
To unfrequented meads, and pathless wilds,
Lead me from gardens deck'd with art's vain pomps.

Can gilt alcoves, can marble mimic gods,
Parterres embroider'd, obelisks, and urns
Of high relief; can the long spreading lake,
Or vista lessening to the sight; can Stow,
With all her attic fanes, such raptures raise,
As the thrush haunted copse

And he associated this flight from the garden to hollow oak and pensive rill with the ancient poetry of Britain ('The bards of old . . . sought such retreats').

Some visitors to gardens chose to read these new tastes into existing landscapes: thus Walpole, at Castle Howard in 1772, exclaimed that 'Nobody had informed me that at one view I should see a palace, a town, a fortified city, temples on high places, *woods worthy of being each a metropolis of the Druids*, the noblest lawn in the world fenced by half the horizon, and a mausoleum that would tempt one to be buried alive; in short, I have seen gigantic palaces before, but never *a sublime one*'. Walpole's cousin, General Conway, actually set out to provoke such reactions at Park Place, Henley on Thames, with forty-five prehistoric stones from Jersey. Later in the century at Swinton Park in North Yorkshire William Danby provided a Druids' Temple in the form of a small-scale replica of Stonehenge.

In the decade after Warton rejected Stowe, Gibbs designed the gothic Temple of Liberty [plate 54] to crown the hill to the southeast of its main pleasure gardens. Even earlier there had been at various points along the garden itinerary a Hermitage, which Kent introduced into one of his illustrations for Spenser, a Witch House, St Augustine's Cave, a Sleeping Parlour, and Dido's Cave [see plate 47]—an eclectic assortment of associations, if brought together, but separately contributing their own special brands of solitary or gothic *frisson*. A representative response to them is recorded in Gilpin's *Dialogue*, where one of the characters praises 'the exceeding good invention' of the Witch House. The garden is generally admired in the same dialogue for the opportunities it affords 'disconsolate lover' or 'romantic Genius', who 'may entertain itself with several beautiful Objects in its own Taste, and grow wild with Ideas of the inchanted kind'. In the third edition Gilpin adds a more explicit commendation of these 'rude Appearances of Nature':

'You Enthusiasts are fond of Solitude; and you transfer this Fondness to such Scenes as will most probably afford it—Scenes, where no Human Footsteps, except your Own, are likely to be found. . . .

'I would distinguish [replies the other character] between Pleasures of a moral kind, and those of the imagination: The former we enjoy, when we contemplate a Country smiling in the midst of Plenty. Houses well built, Plantations regular, every thing commodious: But such Regularity excites little Pleasure in the Imagination, which is struck only by Things uncommon, Things odd and surprising. I remember,

PLATE 57　Francis Vivares, *A View in Yorkshire* (Bolton Park). Engraving (1753).

says he, when you and I made a Tour into the North of *England*, you were then as much pleased with these rude views as I was; and said, our well-cultivated Plains were not comparable to their rough Nature in point of Prospect. . . .'

He continues by enumerating the steep precipices, deep glooms, and cascades of that northern landscape, which already constitute an alternative to the garden [plate 57].

These wilder and larger landscapes were often, as we saw with Gray, experienced in gardenist terms. But landscape gardens in their turn came to be revised in the light of the growing taste for 'natural' scenery. The garden could not of course accommodate a landscape imagery comparable to that of Scotland or the Lake District; but it could adapt itself to appear less artificially contrived. The man largely responsible for such changes in design, perhaps the most radical of all landscape gardeners, was 'Capability' Brown. In the decade after Warton's poem, Brown was head gardener at Stowe and if he did not himself design and implement the Grecian Valley there in the late 1740's it is prophetic of his work elsewhere. On either side of an L-shaped valley were wavy lines of trees, with some clumps pushed out from the flanks; within its groves were wandering paths and isolated statues. In 1764 a temple from elsewhere in the gardens, which had housed some of the busts used in the Temple of British Worthies, was rebuilt among the glades at the head of the valley and renamed the Fane of Pastoral Poetry. Despite the temple and the statues (no longer surviving), the valley was something of a new departure at Stowe: it was far less concerned to direct its visitors' responses and was designed for freer movement and with more private spaces. The earlier parts of Stowe, as the 1739 engravings certainly suggest, were the focus of social activity and response; statues, inscriptions, temples were all susceptible to 'readings' that were doubtless common to all its visitors. In contrast, the Grecian Valley no longer required a learned attention to detailed meaning; it made no claim upon our intellect. The subtle variations of the valley afford a landscape that seems to answer our moods, that allows a unique and individual response by each visitor to its unobtrusive character. It expresses us and our changing moods, or such is the illusion that it encourages.

This psychological effect is matched by fresh design elements that would characterize Brown's influence upon English landscape parks throughout the 1760's and 1770's. They are best described as *formal*, in its precise meaning: for in the Grecian Valley the forms of landscape have been rediscovered. Apart from the scattered statues and the Fane of Pastoral Poetry, all hidden among the trees anyway, it is the basic materials of the site that are emphasized: the lines, shapes, and contours of ground, trees, and water (a lake was originally planned there).

The trouble with Brown's designs proved to be, ironically, their studied elimination of designed elements. It is this aspect of Brown's work that Joshua Reynolds is presumably glancing at in his thirteenth *Discourse*:

Gardening, as far as Gardening is an Art, or entitled to that appellation, is a deviation from nature; for if the true taste consists, as many hold, in banishing every appearance of Art, or any traces of the footsteps of man, it would then be no longer a Garden.

William Chambers found Brown's gardens 'differ very little from common fields, so closely is common nature copied in most of them' [see plate 74]. Chambers is unfair to Brown's best designs, which surreptitiously *do* proclaim the art that recognizes and utilizes nature's forms. But his prejudice represents precisely the great appeal of Brownian landscapes for men of taste like Joseph Warton, who could feel that in them they were outside a garden. The anonymous poet of *The Rise and Progress of* the *Present Taste in Planting* (1767) echoes Warton's wish to escape from old-fashioned gardens:

Lo! two pavilions in a wretched stile
Thro' which we soon to rural meads retreat,
And what these gardens want, in them we meet.

By the end, however, he comes to praise Brown's landscape park at Temple Newsam, near Leeds, for 'the charms of Nature gracefully combin'd':

Sweet waving hills, with woods and verdure crown'd,
And winding vales, where murmuring streams resound:
Slopes fring'd with Oaks which gradual die away,
And all around romantic scenes display.
Delighted still along the Park we rove,
Vary'd with Hill and Dale, with Wood and Grove:
O'er velvet Lawns what noble Prospects rise,
Fair as the Scenes, that Reuben's hand supplies!

It is evident that Brown's landscapes ensured for some that the garden continued to provide suitable contexts for private and (so that anonymous poet claims) sublime meditations; but it must also have fostered in its turn a taste for even less structured scenery outside the garden—the territory which picturesque travellers were steadily exploring.

The new experience of a Brownian garden is conveyed best by a passage of Thomas Whately's, where he commends the expressive character of a garden. He urges designs where the private sensibility is less badgered, less forced through stereo-typed patterns of response:

Character is very reconcileable with beauty; and, even when independent of it, has attracted so much regard, as to occasion several frivolous attempts to produce it; statues, inscriptions, and even paintings, history and mythology, and a variety of devices, have been introduced for this purpose. The heathen deities and heroes have therefore had their several places assigned to them in the woods and the lawns of a garden; natural cascades have been disfigured with river gods, and columns erected only to receive quotations; the compartments of a summer-house have been filled with pictures of gambols and revels, as significant of gaiety; the cypress, because it was once used in funerals, has been thought peculiarly adapted to melancholy; and the decorations, the furniture, and the environs of a building, have been crowded with puerilities, under the pretence of propriety. All these devices are rather *emblematical* than expressive; they may be ingenious contrivances, and recall absent ideas to the recollection, but they make no immediate impression, for they must be examined, compared, perhaps explained, before the whole design of them is well understood; and though an allusion to a favourite or well-known subject of history, of poetry, or of tradition, may now and then animate or dignify a scene, yet as the subject does not naturally belong to a garden, the allusion should not be principal; it should seem to have been suggested by the scene; a transitory image, which irresitibly [sic] occurred; not sought for, not laboured; and have the force of a metaphor, free from the detail of an allegory.

This preference for immediate experience of scenery, for its moods rather than its intellectual matter, is undoubtedly based upon an established taste for Brown's landscapes. Whately's emphasis upon the affective qualities of a garden and their apparently haphazard organization answers the idea of imagination that the gothic poetry championed. Thus Thomas Warton —despite his attention to Spenser's allegory—in fact praises Spenser for some of the same qualities that constituted Whately's expressive garden:

We who live in the days of writing by rule, are apt to try every composition by those laws which we have been taught to think the sole criterion of excellence. Critical taste is universally diffused, and we require the same order and design which every modern performance is expected to have, in poems where they never were regarded or intended. Spenser, and the same may be said of Ariosto, did not live in an age of planning. His poetry is the careless exuberance of a warm imagination and a strong sensibility. It was his business to engage the fancy, and to interest the attention by bold and striking images, in the formation and disposition of which, little labour or art was applied. The various and the marvellous were the chief sources of delight. Hence we find our author ransacking alike the regions of reality and romance, of truth and fiction, to find the proper decorations and furniture for his fairy structure.

The 'gothic machinery', for another writer, 'conveys us to scenes beyond the limits of morality' and, accordingly, beyond the territory of directed and social responses. Brown's landscapes are still undeniably available for social pastimes, but they did ensure a continuing role for the garden as the theatre of a private sensibility. Partly because Brown eliminated architectural elements and paths, sweeping the lawns right up to the mansion, the social associations which Pope had made are also removed:

What are the gay parterre, the chequer'd shade,
The morning bower, the ev'ning colonnade,
But soft recesses of uneasy minds,
To sigh unheard in, to the passing winds?

[Poems, 6:225]

Uneasy minds now sought the chequer'd shade of far less organized scenes where the chances of being overheard were less.

The shift in landscape taste in the second half of the eighteenth century was, then, largely the result of the mind's needing new 'decorations and furniture'. Brown's landscapes endorsed more flexible patterns of association, replacing the directed responses in, say, Stowe's Elysian Fields by a freer associationism of private scope. Some landscapes, like Henry Hoare's at Stourhead or Shenstone's at The Leasowes, seem to have combined both opportunities: the public 'meaning' of Stourhead, with its accessible Claudean and Virgilian theme, was complemented by the notably personal motives and colouring which Hoare's private life gave to and found expression for in his garden. Shenstone, too, provided inscriptions and other items available to all; yet what seems to have been the distinctive feature of The Leasowes was the garden's 'perfect picture of his mind' and his poetic fancy.

For some, however, even these private, freer patterns of association were not satisfying, simply because they were not sublime enough. Brown's gardens tended, for such critics, to represent only Burke's beauty and not his sublime; their dedication to formal composition—notably the serpentine line—linked them inevitably to Hogarth's *Analysis of Beauty:*

The eye hath this sort of enjoyment in winding walks, and serpentine rivers, and all sorts of objects, whose forms . . . are composed principally of what, I call, the *waving* and *serpentine* lines.

Intricacy in form, therefore, I shall define to be that peculiarity in the lines, which compose it, that *leads the eye a wanton kind of chase,* and from the pleasure that it gives the mind, intitles it to the name of beautiful.

Gardens became the conventional idea of beauty in contrast to the sublimity of mountains: in West's account of the Lake District the 'variety with pleasing transition' of the gardens at Levens Hall may be contrasted with the 'terrible' and 'stupendously great' landscape of Borrowdale. Yet some attempts were made to establish the sublime inside gardens, notably by Chambers, Uvedale Price, and Richard Payne Knight. Shenstone, interestingly enough, shared Burke's admiration for the sublime yet did not seem concerned to dedicate his garden solely to images of it: Gray's comment on his poetry being, perhaps, the apt description of his garden—'Mr Shenstone, who trusts to nature and simple sentiment, why does he do no better? he goes hopping along his own gravel-walks, and never deviates from the beaten paths for fear of being lost'.

Chambers's sublimity took a Chinese form. But though his *Dissertation on Oriental Gardening* (1772) announces a whole range of gardenist devices from gibbets and poisonous weeds to 'scenes of terror' that were supposed to characterise gardens in China, his actual designs do not seem to have succeeded in providing a sufficiently convincing taste of sublimity, and the fantasies at Kew were mocked by many for their failure to elicit a serious play of mind. Knight in his poem, *The Landscape* (1794), derided Chambers's Chinese solutions to the problem of boredom in Brown's landscapes:

But false refinement vainly strives to please,
With the thin, fragile bridge of the Chinese;
Light and fantastical, yet still and prim,
The child of barren fancy turn'd to whim:
Whim! whose extravagancies ever try
The vacancies of Fancy to supply.

Wordsworth was to echo this reflection of the Chinese fad in English gardening when he prefers the 'common haunts of the green earth' to 'those resplendent Gardens, with their frame/ Imperial, and elaborate Ornaments'.

Price and Knight provided a far more successful prescription for gardens designed to satisfy what Chambers had called 'a strong imagination'. They proposed both in Price's *Essays on the Picturesque* (London, 1794) and Knight's *The Landscape* (London, 1794) to draw upon a richer and more intricate vocabulary derived from painters; it was above all the more savage land-scapes of Ruisdael and Rosa that were in Knight's mind when he directed the designer of sublime gardens:

'Tis not the giant of unwieldy size,
Piling up hills on hills to scale the skies,
That gives an image of the true sublime,
Or the best subject for the lofty rhyme;
But nature's common works, by genius dress'd,
With art selected, and with taste express'd;
Where sympathy with terror is combined,
To move, to melt, and elevate the mind.

That Knight's own garden at Downton Vale worked upon the minds of its visitors in that way we have the testimony of Humphry Repton:

A narrow, wild, and natural path sometimes creeps under the beetling rocks, close by the margin of a mountain stream. It sometimes ascends to an awful precipice, from whence the foaming waters are heard roaring in the dark abyss below, or each wildly dashing against its opposite banks; while, in other places, the course of the river Teme being impeded by natural ledges of rock, the vale presents a calm, glassy mirror, that reflects the surrounding foliage. The path, in various places, crosses the water by bridges of the most romantic and contrasted forms; and, branching in various directions, including some miles in length, is occasionally varied and enriched by caves and cells, hovels and covered seats, or other buildings, in perfect harmony with the wild but pleasant horrors of the scene.

Though Repton is offering a topographical description, the affective potential of Knight's design is perfectly clear. Knight obviously provides within his landscaped park the sublime frissons that most of his contemporaries were seeking outside gardens.

Knight succeeds in uniting *Walpole's* sister arts in one last collaboration which allows them each their particular working: a garden where the natural forms are 'by genius dress'd', yet inspired by paintings whose two-dimensional forms have been extended to allow passage through their spaces, and designed to promote sensations to which the new poetry was especially susceptible and was seeking to give expression. We can see this collaboration and yet separation of artistic powers at work in *The Landscape*. The engravings that accompany the poem to demonstrate the revisions he would make in a Brownian park have a distinctly visual vocabulary—strongly influenced by paintings and designed to promote associations that were first experienced in front of paintings. But the poem invokes a properly literary, if somewhat flaccid, idiom: for what Knight announces is a continuing commitment to ideas of the genius loci. For if the literary mind is to continue to be involved in gardens and to find in them an inspiring landscape, they must contrive to let nymphs and dryads, who can find no sanctuary among Brown's bare and tidy scenes, return and reinhabit the wilder spaces of a garden:

But here again, ye rural nymphs, oppose
Nature's and Art's confederated foes!
Break their fell scythes, that would these beauties shave.
And sink their iron rollers in the wave!
Your favourite plants, and native haunts protect,
In wild obscurity, and rude neglect;
Or teach proud man his labour to employ
To form and decorate, and not destroy;
Teach him to place, and not remove the stone
On yonder bank, with moss and fern o'er grown;
To cherish, not mow down, the weeds that creep
Along the shore, or overhang the steep;
To break, not level, the slow-rising ground,
And guard, not cut, the fern that shades it round.

The appeal to the 'rural nymphs' is doubtless inert literariness. Yet in its sense of numinous presences it does propose a non-painterly rapport between landscape and the literary art which may voice its special and distinct character.

The efforts of Price and Knight to maintain the sisterhood of arts that 'dress and adorn nature' during the 1780's and 1790's were somewhat outmoded. The bardic landscape was already established beyond the garden, which was itself, under Brown, discovering its own play of formal qualities without any literary or painterly distractions; painting and poetry were each learning new and local idioms. We shall see in the final chapter the consequences for each art of its separate path. But here, in conclusion, it is worth suggesting the readjustments in landscape taste which were made during the middle and later eighteenth

PLATE 58 Rousham, the Vale of Venus.

century; it can be done in miniature and without references across the boundaries of the arts by comparing Claude's *Landscape with Apollo and the Muses* [plate 11] with Wright of Derby's *Brooke Boothby* [plate 28].

Painted in 1652, Claude's is typical of the paintings that formed the taste of both landscape designers and their clients. It is an ideal landscape, instinct with a numinous meaning, which the temple, the animals and swans, Apollo and the Muses, and the reclining river god with his urn all join to establish. Its combination of emblem and consummate expression was recreated at Stowe, Rousham (where Venus is attended by swans [plate 58]) and Stourhead. Like the five mortal poets of Claude's scene who appear behind the group of the Muses, we encounter and learn to understand the landscape as wondering visitors to its mysterious, yet ordered and comprehensible structure. And so in those Augustan gardens; like Gilpin's two visitors at Stowe, exploring the temples and statues and inscriptions of the Elysian Fields, we invoke our whole experience of history and myth to understand the garden's meaning. Claude's landscape, too, requires our verbal extension of its visual meaning before it is fully experienced. We become like the poets of mid-century learning vocabularies for such encounters with landscape, and it is no accident that it was gardens, derived from such pictures, that taught them that language.

Wright places Brooke Boothby, painted in 1780–81, in the same position (though reversed) as Claude's splendid and solitary river god. But no longer is the spirit of place represented, as in Virgil, by a *deus ipse loci*; it is suggested by a man who reads his copy of Rousseau in the woods by himself. The painting, of course, attends magnificently to its own formal harmonies of brown and of light and shade, to which we must contribute our own visual appreciation. Apart from the word 'Rousseau' on Boothby's book, there is nothing in the painting which requires our verbal or literary participation. Boothby's solitary reflections are no longer accommodated within a garden whose apparatus of inscription, iconography, and temple, as in Claude's painting, provides a vocabulary for his thoughts. Wright implies as much by giving him a copy of Rousseau to hold. For by the 1780's the sister arts of poetry, painting, and gardening were learning to take separate paths. Garden designers displayed the formal delights of natural elements. Painters learnt to register afresh the natural world, though still with a firm interest in the moods it promoted. Writers were learning that moods and meditations among natural scenery were excitingly within their verbal province. Even Uvedale Price, with his strong painterly enthusiasms, acknowledged the literary responsibilities for describing this sensibility at large in a landscape: not only does he devote three volumes of *Essays* to precisely that, but he explains Hamilton's garden at Painshill, at least part of which was designed after sketches by Salvator Rosa, as 'a wood, which Rousseau might have dedicated *à la reverie.*'

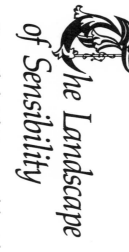

The Landscape of Sensibility

During the last thirty years of the eighteenth century the three sister arts of Walpole's apophthegm, though with some residual instincts for collaboration, were more involved with seeking their individual fortunes. Yet in their separate explorations of form and idea one common theme still survived, variously treated by painters, gardenists, and poets, as by individual members within each group. This was the relationship of figures to landscape.

Not just a formal problem of arrangement, the place and stance of the figure in a landscape may image philosophical ideas of natural scenery as well as emotional attitudes towards it. Yet fresh experiences of landscape continued to be mediated by old patterns of thought: the formulae of hermit and hermitage, as the first chapter described, lingered well into the eighteenth century as a vocabulary for man's perennial need to discover himself among natural solitudes. But the experience both of landscape and of meditation changed so decisively during the century that old structures of seeing and thinking failed to control and order the new territories of spirit. In what Northrop Frye has termed the 'Age of Sensibility' we may watch verbal and visual artists exploring fresh modes and images by which to define the relationship—inward and outward, psychological and physical—of figures to their landscapes.

Though this chapter will end with literary history, certain developments in painting and garden design will be considered first, since they establish some alternative solutions, visual and social, to the place of humans in natural or contrived landscapes. These will provide some historical, some *paideumatic*, context for a discussion of poetry's particular endeavours.

Northrop Frye's 'age of sensibility' is characterized by the view of literature as process not product: a novel like *Tristram Shandy* invites us to watch the author at work writing it; *Pamela* holds emotional suspense in a continuous present; poetry, like Cowper's, Smart's, or Macpherson's, emerges as a record of primitive psychological self-identification, its subconscious association framed in either sharp, momentary lyrics or continuous, oracular, and incantatory forms. Frye's diagnosis and description are often apt for this inquiry into landscape taste; but, just as frequently, they must submit to some revisions.

PLATE 59   Richard Wilson, *Wilton House—Stables and Temple Copse.*
Oil painting (?1758–60).

In painting, which is not a medium most conducive to displaying process, the later eighteenth century did discover an interest in the movement of figures through landscape—*The Market Cart* of Gainsborough, or Rowlandson's *Greenwich Hill.* But more importantly painting found its own means of registering process instead of product. Especially in the application of paint, artists (Gainsborough most conspicuously) drew our attention less to a finished view than to watching the painter at work and being admitted into his apprehension of a landscape. There was an increasing vogue for pictures which showed scenes *being* recorded by sketching connoisseurs [see plate 63]. Artists with minimal interests in the notation of momentary moods or events of landscape are steadily outnumbered by those with a fascination for recording the instantaneous and transitory: hence the increasing respect for sketches as images in their own right rather than as mere notes for later compositions and for paintings like J. C. Ibbetson's *A Phaeton in a Thunderstorm*, which a label on its back tells us is 'An actual scene' and painted by the artist who was a passenger in the carriage. The clear distinctions between figures and landscapes also become blurred, so that Gainsborough's unabashed Mr. and Mrs. Andrews, set *against* rather than *in* their rich georgic scenery, are replaced later in his career by figures identified more equivocally with the textures, colouring, and shapes of surrounding scenery. Paintings which offered finished views of landscape parks—Wilson's *Wilton House* [plate 59], for in-

THE FIGURE IN THE LANDSCAPE

stance—and recorded the products of improvement may come instead to explore the process of alteration—Rowlandson's *A Nobleman Improving his Estate* or, less obviously, Repton's Red Books, where the habit of providing clients with 'before' and 'after' images of their grounds was a means of suggesting the process of transformation. In visual records of gardens this same gradual change of emphasis and perspective is noticeable: Rigaud's views of Stowe, published in 1739 by Sarah Bridgeman [see plate 43], or innumerable Wilson views of Italian villas were all content to see static and (with human activity pushed back into the picture space) generalized participation in the landscape. Whereas a watercolour like Rowlandson's *Stowe Gardens* [plate 60] contrives within its static and 'finished' focus a multiplicity of views, many angles of vision, and (because we are closer to his figures than to Rigaud's) a strong sense of the process of their experiencing the statues and vistas of a garden. His graphic skills allow him to offer what Repton lamented that his Red Books failed to achieve, the impression of movement, process, defining (not definition) of impressions in a garden's spaces.

In garden design the dedication to process rather than product was well in advance of the other arts. The geometrical organization of French or Dutch gardens, best seen at a glance in some bird's eye view, was replaced in England by a style that invited its visitors through a sequence of scenes, where their

PLATE 60   Thomas Rowlandson, *Stowe Gardens*. Watercolour (date unknown).

minds were constantly being provoked by architectural or verbal items and where certain objects were designed to be seen or encountered from various points of view. Even if the sequence of scenes was only a succession of three-dimensional pictures (Walpole's 'An open country is but a canvass on which a landscape might be designed'), there was both the temptation to enter the third dimension and the process of moving between each vista. Gilpin's *Dialogue* comments on this latter experience when Callophilus explains that the 'impertinent Hedge' which suddenly blocks their view is designed to keep the attention awake. Gilpin's later picturesque writings attend to both the finished, pictorial products of travel and the mental processes which his texts narrate; he identified both possibilities on his visit to Stowe in 1747. But a writer like Whately could look back to the Augustan garden from the 1770's and find it too emblematic—that is, too static and eloquent of product—and prefer gardens which encouraged the excitements of mental process. The landscape gardens which best promoted these 'transitory' (Whately's word) ideas and moods were those by Brown. When Repton succeeded Brown, the garden began to recover some of its older, more static forms; for, while Repton certainly disliked picturesque habits of design and insisted upon the need for movement in or through a landscape, he was also intent upon rescuing the garden once again for social purposes. And these were best served by such items as terraces, flower beds, and compartmented gardens. This conservatism probably explains poets' dissatisfaction with a territory increasingly unsuitable for their psychological concerns. In the poetry of landscape we shall see a lingering painterly esteem for product not process, a seduction by pictured stasis even when narrated psychological experience requires more attention to the notation of the stream of consciousness. Christopher Smart announced that 'an IDEA is the mental vision of an object': yet there is some debate, even in Smart, between the pleasure of offering ideas in finished artistic products and the fascination with registering the creative process of that mental vision. Poetry which narrated experiences in landscape and was able to avoid inertly pictorial images necessarily stressed the role of memory or the shaping spirit of its verbal imagination.

Landscape Business

British landscape painting in the eighteenth century, like Gray's notion of the progress of poetry, involved naturalizing foreign forms and modes and achieving various views of native scenery. William Cowper's *The Task* celebrated 'Italian light on English walls'—

None more admires, the painter's magic skill,
Who shows me that which I shall never see,

THE LANDSCAPE OF SENSIBILITY

Conveys a distant country into mine,
And throws Italian light on English walls

—but at the same time he complains of those who prefer
'pencill'd scenes' and 'imitative strokes' to Nature's store:

The air salubrious of her lofty hills,
The cheering fragrance of her dewy vales,
And music of her woods

We respond to these, says Cowper, with every sense, while only the eye is pleased by a painted landscape. Yet his verses do not convince us here that he, any more than a painter who imitates Claude or Dughet, has discovered a language of natural description endemic to a full expression of the 'power' of English scenery. And when Thomas Jones in 1769 complained that 'there was Lambert, and Wilson, and Zuccarelli, and Gainsborough, and Barret, and Richards, and Marlow in full possession of Landscape business', he enumerated artists who were characterized by their dialogue with, even their domination by, foreign painterly traditions.

The landscape painter in the eighteenth century was torn between topography and fantasy, between his instinct for recording actual views and visions of idealized scenery. John Wootton worked in both, yet never seemed to let his attention to English topography in one influence his imitations of Dughet or Berchem in the other. Even the styles of those paintings which offered apparently unmediated views of landscape—topography most evidently, but genre and conversation piece as well on occasion—are generally borrowed from Dutch artists, who were among the first to explore and depict the English countryside. Visual idioms that were the direct outcome of personal observation were extremely rare.

Borrowed habits of looking at nature also contributed ideas about man's relationship to it. Some painterly traditions endorsed enquiries into natural phenomena, after the theories of the Royal Society, and reveal man as an empirical searcher—either as a recorder of topography or an accountant of the detailed textures of wood, rock, water, and sky. Other traditions allowed his sensibility to be exercised or indulged in more or less fancy pictures of natural scenery—nymphs disporting themselves under salmon falls, sublime melodramas of fire or eruption, moodscapes of light and mist, landscapes which imaged various ideas or moods. There were, necessarily, combinations of these. There were private explorations of man's various relationships with nature through the sketch and watercolour, as well as the public statements of the finished canvas. The spectrum of involvement, participation, and experience of natural phenomena is, in fact, wider and more diverse than in poetry or—despite Chambers and Price—in gardening.

PLATE 61   Richard Wilson, *View near Tivoli*.
Oil painting (1760's).

We may gauge something of this range of attitudes by noticing the different positions vis-à-vis scenery that an artist adopted: he may distance the large effects or bring them strangely close; he may soften corners, revise actual scenery in the interests of conventional modes and tastes. And how the artist stands in the scenery that he paints is echoed in the artist's surrogates—the figures shown in the landscapes as passive watchers, artists, actors, victims, incidents of topography, or extensions of natural forms. There may even be scenes empty of human presence. Some examples only, rather than any systematic history, can be examined here.

Richard Wilson's *A View near Tivoli* [plate 61] shows an artist sketching in the foreground, watched by a peasant. He is separated by an invisible fall of ground from the view he is taking of the hilltop of Tivoli on his left and the delicate aerial prospect of the distant plain beyond and to his right. The sense of far perspective is somehow enhanced by the pointing arm of another peasant, nearer to us. Wilson's own image of Tivoli, as presumably his artist's sketch (we have Wilson's sketches of Tivoli as evidence), reveals a nostalgia for a finished landscape. Obviously the levels of 'finish' in an oil painting and a sketch are

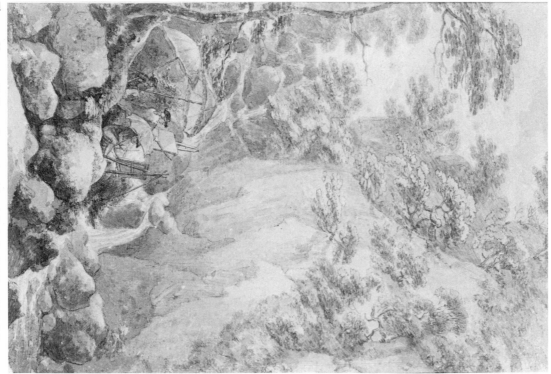

PLATE 62

202

THE FIGURE IN THE LANDSCAPE

Thomas Hearne, *Sir George Beaumont and Joseph Farington Painting a Waterfall.*
Pen and wash (?1777 or '78).

very different, but Wilson's views seem to present the spectator
with a distinct *composition*, in which attention to local sights is
married to the ideal vision of earlier Italian and French landscape art. In contrast, a pen and wash drawing by Thomas
Hearne shows *Sir George Beaumont and Joseph Farington painting a
Waterfall* [plate 62]. Unlike Wilson's artist, distinctly set in the
picture and distinctly separated from the subject of his sketch
just as if were contemplating it in a Claude-glass, Beaumont and
Farington are represented almost as part of the texture of rock,
water and foliage. It is the artificial shapes of their parasols that
betray their presence in the natural scene. One of the artists

PLATE 63   Francis Wheatley, *An Artist and a Lady in a Landscape.* Oil painting (1777).

glances shyly at us from underneath his parasol, aware of our observation. Yet another account of artists in a landscape is provided by Francis Wheatley's pictures in which an artist is seen sketching the mellow landscapes around him; this elegant intimation of the figure's connoisseurship is exercised now in practice where once (Hogarth's *The Fontaine Family*, for instance) it would have been more likely to take the form of studying finished views of gardens and pastoral scenes. In *The Family Group* the man might well be drafting a study for exactly the same group of figures (his own family) that Wheatley shows us from his perspective; in *An Artist and a Lady in a Landscape* [plate 63] it is the dog that seems alert to our presence, while the lady shares the pleasure of comparing their sight of the landscape with what is already fully captured on the man's sketching block. These images convey something of the range not only of physical and mental relationship between artists and scenery but of our involvements. To be watched or ignored by figures in the painted landscape appreciably determines our response; if we lean over Wilson's sketcher through our surrogate, the peasant, we are yet keenly aware, I imagine, of our superior taste which adjudges the finished canvas; we seek to disentangle Beaumont and Farington from the scenery in which they are

203   THE LANDSCAPE OF SENSIBILITY

PLATE 64
Francis Towne, *Tivoli*.
Ink and wash drawing (1781).

engrossed, or we admire the refined accomplishments of sketching among redolent English vistas; we note, too, the adjudication between borrowed painterly idioms and what Farington called Wilson's "own genuine impressions".

Not only do we learn to read artists' relationships to landscape in space, but in time also. Beaumont and Farington are sketching in oils, a most unusual activity in the late eighteenth century; like Wilson's artist at Tivoli, they are presumably recording memoranda on the spot from which later to construct finished studio pictures. But other sketches from nature, notably Wright of Derby's records of Roman fireworks or the eruption of Vesuvius, seem to have authority not only as memoranda but as important visual experiences in their own right. Especially oil sketches, local notes in the medium of permanent statements, were evidence of the instinct to combine art as process and art as product. But when paintings were created later from sketches and studies, the artist's memory plays its part in the final version: that is the means by which historical and literary associations become part of landscape subjects, as Roman or British ruins, for example, provide foci for recollections and mood at the same time as they are themselves images won from an artist's remembered experience on the spot.

PLATE 65   Francis Towne, *Haldon Hall, near Exeter.*
Oil painting (1780).

This 'emotional alembic of recollection' plays its part in final versions of landscape together with any number of formal manoeuvres, which are themselves eloquent of the relationship of artist to scenery. Alexander Cozens, for example, would sometimes reduce his impressions to simple forms and patterns, flat schemes of dark and light, which particularly honoured and called attention to the medium in which he worked. Francis Towne employed flat planes of tinted colour, specific shapes fluently outlined and sharply juxtaposed: his pen and wash drawing of Tivoli [plate 64] represents his most remarkable style and serves to isolate this formal strategy in face of nature by contrast, say, with Wilson's view of Tivoli. But Towne was typical of his generation in wishing to make his name only with finished landscapes ('I never in my life exhibited a *Drawing*'), and these, like his *Haldon Hall, near Exeter,* [plate 65] betray a more conventional faith in finished prospects. The most fascinating example of formal response to scenery, Gainsborough's, will be discussed later.

The articulation of emotional and mental experience is often at odds with formal interests in painting, though most landscapists managed to combine them. The earliest account of foreign landscape painters in English made clear the associative force of painted scenes treated with a concern for related ideas:

of all the Landskip-Painters *Claude Lorrain* has the most Beautiful, and Pleasing Ideas; the most Rural, and of our own Times. *Titian* has a Style more Noble. So has *Nicolas Poussin*, and the Lanskips of the Latter are usually Antique, and [sic] is seen by the Buildings, and Figures. *Gaspar's* Figures are Such, otherwise he has a Mixture of *Nicholas* and *Claude*. *Salvator Rosa* has generally chosen to represent a sort of wild, and savage Nature; his Style is Great, and Noble; *Rubens* is pleasant, and loves to enrich his Landskip with certain Accidents of Nature.

The Richardsons mention, of course, the major figures who provided conventions for many later English painters. The *ideas* of a landscape involve our responding to visual objects by articulating their associations. Even Turner, who was to develop the formal excitements of landscape pictures beyond any eighteenth-century practice, would attach poetry to his pictures for this purpose: *Dolbadern Castle* was exhibited in 1800 with lines specially composed by the painter:

How awful is the silence of the waste,
Where nature lifts her mountains to the sky.
Majestic solitude, behold the tower
Where hopeless OWEN, long imprison'd, pin'd,
And wrung his hands for liberty, in vain.

Another picture of *Caernarvon Castle* elicits our recollections of Gray's bard with its accompanying verses. Such landscapes with English subjects became an established form by the end of the century for uniting visual and verbal responses, just as Italian scenes had been somewhat earlier. In 1799 Girtin and a group of associates founded a club 'for the purpose of establishing a school of Historic Landscape, the subjects being original designs from poetick passages'.

We connect literary or verbal experience with our sight of such landscapes primarily, I suspect, through responding to the figures in them. As early as 1700 Roger de Piles had discussed how figures, not engaged in any action in a picture, may still be 'made to appear inwardly active'. Thus in Turner's *Dolbadern Castle*, as in Wilson's versions before him, the figures by the water are foci for our thoughts, as we project upon them our 'inward action' or at least compare their liberty with that denied to Owen, as we seek ways in which the literary and visual experiences that Turner offers may be combined. Two versions by Wilson of this same landscape, one in Melbourne, one now in Exeter, make this particularly vivid: the version in Australia shows two youths engaged in fishing, the Exeter picture only one solitary angler. The difference in mood between the scenes, though the topography is identical, is substantially dependent upon our projecting into the minds of Wilson's figures a version of the social or private emotions which Burke contrasted.

Our recognition of emotions in figures represented in pictured landscapes draws us into the experience of scenery which the painter records. Nobody in the eighteenth century was

PLATE 66   Joseph Wright of Derby, *The Earthstopper on the Banks of the Derwent.* Oil painting (1773).

more attentive to psychological landscape that Joseph Wright of Derby. In such paintings (not landscapes, of course) as *A Philosopher Giving a Lecture on the Orrery* or *An Experiment on a Bird in the Air Pump* he depicts various emotions in the participants —wonder, fascination, fear, suspense, patience, even boredom —which a viewer of the picture first identifies in Wright's characters and then, all together perhaps, in himself. Wright extends this process from the magic of science into genre scenes like *The Blacksmith's Shop* and out into landscapes in the *Hermit Studying Anatomy* or *The Earthstopper on the Banks of the Derwent,* [plate 66].

Before his visit to Italy Wright was associated with John Mortimer, whose fondness for Rosa-like scenes of horror doubtless confirmed Wright's interest in similar dramatic scenes. But he has a finer skill than Mortimer, and it consists in providing more opportunity for a spectator's involvement in his pictures. We become intimate at once with Brooke Boothby, reading his mind and sharing his tastes. The hermit who studies anatomy and the approaching strangers (our surrogates?) behind him all announce varying emotions that we, by identifying, come to share. The earthstopper, blocking foxes' holes before the morning's hunt, partakes both of the wildness of the scene—broken trees, moon behind cloud and foliage—and the methodical calm of his patient horse and his own steady labour: it is in this conjunction of rival moods of excitement and repose that we make contact with the painting. Even in landscapes with little or no dominance of human figures—*Rocks with Waterfall* or the *Grotto in the Gulf of Salerno*—his skill with focusing human reaction to landscape is maintained in the affective treatment of the scenery. He achieves this in the first by brushing aside what Benedict Nicolson calls the 'decorum of contemporary art . . . in order to preserve the wildness' in an unmediated, directed response. The series of Vesuvius pictures articulates a whole spectrum of nervous reaction without the presence of figures in the landscape at all: this is often achieved by his own physical proximity or distance from the eruption and by a constant dedication to capturing or (later) recapturing 'the fever of the mountain . . . upon him'. His attention at its best to the emotional power of landscape may be seen if his image of Arkwright's mills in the early 1780's is contrasted with the same scene, painted about 1790: in the first a strong bond is organized between the spectator, the foreground figure with a cart, and the unseen workers behind the lighted windows of the mill; in the second drama has become merely picturesque, it is a deflection and a defection into a 'convention of elegance'.

Though Wright can be discussed in terms of his visual syntax and techniques, it is the 'poetry' and 'sentiment' that the pictures release with which we must finally come to terms. Benedict Nicolson laments a decline in his later career, when he relied only upon generalizations and the invocation of conventional sublimity as the backdrop for scenes of wild distress. What is lost, in fact, is an uncanny ability to link psychological event with the facts of nature. Even a scene like *Chee Tor* of the late 1780's, devoid of human presence, is able to focus Wright's response to the sublime interplay of dark moor and white cliff in a scene of distinct naturalism. By comparison, the Lake District works of the 1790's are merely charming, placid notations of scenery without drama, and *River in a Rocky Gorge* (1787) an easy melodrama in which minuscule but sharply defined figures gesture in a wild landscape of generalized forms.

It seems to me no accident that Wright was diverted in later years into themes from Beattie, Milton, Percy, Langhorne, or Sterne; for his art was distinctly superior when it explored the sort of human experience which literature is more capable of defining. The picture of *The Lady in Milton's "Comus"* [plate 67] uses his careful regard of gesture and the excitements of sharply concentrated light to allow immediate access to Milton's

PLATE 67   Joseph Wright of Derby, *The Lady in Milton's 'Comus'*.
Oil painting (1784).

masque with its 'sequence of glimpses into the nature of grace';
we appreciate in Wright's image the excitements and debates of
Milton's ideological drama translated into his own resonant
idiom. Maybe because the literary energies of Beattie's *The
Minstrel* are inferior to Milton's, Wright's *Edwin* [plate 68] is far
less satisfying. Yet Walpole thought the boy's head was 'finely
expressive of passion and enthusiasm', which suggests that for
one contemporary at least Wright did capture the bardic tones.
There is perhaps for us today too much in *Edwin* of the 'gentler
genius of the plain'—dreamy, melancholy (note the iconography
of the hand supporting the head); yet the landscape, partly
detailed beneath his feet, partly misty and vague beyond,
provides something of the appropriate scenery. So that,
whether we assent with Walpole to the aptness of Wright's
understanding of Beattie's minstrel or are forced to acknowledge a different interpretation, it is still a painting where we
must respond to more than visual texture.

Wright seems to have appealed strongly to poets: he is
apostrophized in Erasmus Darwin's *The Botanical Garden* and
William Hayley's "Essay on Painting in Two Epistles to Mr
Romney", and their passages of natural description often seem

209   THE LANDSCAPE OF SENSIBILITY

THE FIGURE IN THE LANDSCAPE

the result of attending closely to Wright's work, perhaps
inevitable in their tight community. And Thomas Gisborne, a
friend of Wright's from 1777, is able to echo in the verses of
Walks in a Forest the same combinations of sharply seen and
deeply felt scenery that Wright provided:

Soon o'er the hill the yellow-tinctured moon
Rose through the twilight, and with slanting ray
Gilded the topmost boughs; while all the vale
And all its sloping boundaries lay wrapt
In shade unvaried

PLATE 68   Joseph Wright of Derby, *Edwin, from Dr. Beattie's Minstrel.*
Oil painting (1777–78).

PLATE 69   Francis Wheatley, *St Preux and Julia.*
Pen and wash drawing (1785).

PLATE 70   Maria Catharina Prestel, *The Country Churchyard*. Aquatint after Gainsborough (1790).

With Gisborne the visual and pictorial dominates, as the feeling with Wright.

Literary subjects for paintings were a well-established practice by the 1780's. Precisely because such pictures carried references beyond their own structure, they were especially susceptible to becoming the vehicles of emotion and sentiment. Wright at his best focuses and releases the emotions associated with the Burkean sublime, as presumably did Alexander Runciman's paintings in the Hall of Ossian at Penicuik House. An artist like Francis Wheatley is more capable of the social emotions of beauty, not to say the pretty. Indeed, Wheatley can effectively reduce sublimity to a Boucher-like rococo. The subject of his *St Preux and Julia* [plate 69] is taken from *La Nouvelle Héloïse*, where Rousseau's sublime sentiment is linked with a rejection of the trivial design and unnatural *assemblage* of gardens like Stowe. Though Wheatley's repertoire of crags, broken trees, foaming torrents, and distant precipices is properly sublime, his handling of their texture is rather too elegant; the relationship of the lovers to the scenery seems to serve as decorative addition rather than any dramatic involvement. This withdrawal from psychological turmoil is matched by Wheatley's distancing himself from the scenery he paints. *Landscape with Figures near a River* or *Lake Scene with Ferry* remove us effectively from any but a mildly generalized rapport with mountains and crags; the figures in those landscapes are, like us, uninvolved in anything but their marvellously gentle submission to the role of picturesque ornament. There is more mastery but no less strenuous involvement in Gainsborough's *The Cottage Door*. So that when George Crabbe came in 1783 to argue for his own emphasis in *The Village*, it seems no accident that he wrote 'I *paint* the Cot, / As Truth will *paint* it, and as Bards will not'. For painters like Wheatley had indeed concentrated upon the 'charms' and 'pleasing scenes' of rural idyls.

Very few artists seemed to have shared Gainsborough's dislike of figures in a landscape: 'do you really think that a regular Composition in the Landskip way should ever be fill'd with History, or any figures but such as fill a place (I won't say stop a Gap) or to create a little business for the Eye to be drawn from the Trees in order to return to them with more glee'. One suspects that historical or sentimental narrative—reading what the figures are doing—merely distracted from Gainsborough's preoccupation with the two-dimensional space (the places and gaps of the canvas) and with the undisturbed glee of the eyes' business. Yet this often quoted declaration cannot be the full account, if only because figures still occupy landscapes to which we know he gave his complete attention; and Constable was perfectly correct in observing that Gainsborough's 'object was to deliver a fine sentiment'. His handling of human involvement with scenery represents the most radical *painterly* attitude of this period, and accordingly will serve to conclude this section.

The literary content of landscape pictures examined so far evidently bored Gainsborough, and attempts to associate his statements of rural calm and simplicity with Gray's or Goldsmith's seem wide of the mark. He did actually paint *The Country Churchyard*, exhibited at the Royal Academy in 1780, but now surviving in a fragment and an aquatint by M. C. Prestel [plate 70], in which two peasants study a tombstone in a decaying cemetery. Yet the artist's known dislike of literary men and their works (he thought Gray and Dr. John Brown on the Lake District were 'tawdry fan-Painters') should make us hesitate before seeing *The Country Churchyard* as illustration or deliberate invocation of Gray's nonpictorial ideas. His refusal to paint a topographical view for Lord Hardwicke was made in terms of preferring something 'of his own Brain'. And his own brain, as Ronald Paulson has demonstrated, worked in ways which first display his absorption with formal pictorial effects and then his consideration of human relationships to landscapes. And I believe that his variations on this latter theme involve seeing figures, as it were, from the landscape's, not the human's, viewpoint. We know from William Jackson that Gainsborough was 'fond of referring everything to nature.'

First we should notice Gainsborough's refusal to employ conventionally readable meanings. He shared the objections to academicism of the St. Martin's Lane group ('You know my cunning way of avoiding great subjects'), and he shunned any devices that would provide, iconographically or otherwise, information and morality. His *Haymaker and Sleeping Girl*, for which the nineteenth century tried to discover or invent a story, is derived from Renaissance paintings where a Priapus or satyr comes upon a nymph or Venus asleep in the countryside. But mythological images and meanings are declined in favour of certain preoccupations with linear tensions (the various angles of arms, fencing poles, dog's nose, branches, boy's stick) and with a sentiment that is strongly grounded in those formal delights. It recalls his remark about *Two Shepherd Boys with Dogs Fighting* that next time 'I shall make the boys fighting and the dogs looking on'—as if the events in such a fancy piece were less important than the relationship of their visual ingredients. In some of the late landscape drawings especially we feel the distinct *absence* of figures: compared with Wheatley's *Salmon Leap at Leixlip with Nymphs Bathing* or Boucher's *Diana*, Gainsborough's determination to work via landscape forms alone is clear. This intention and success are made all the more obvious by the rare occasion that he did execute a *Diana and Actaeon* or *Hagar and Ishmael*, for those mythical or biblical figures are metamorphosed into peasants totally at one with the rough landscape forms.

Secondly, we know how strongly Gainsborough felt about the spectator's physical relationship to his works. He resigned from the Royal Academy because they would not hang his pictures where the 'likenesses and Work of the Picture' will be seen: he told David Garrick that his portrait 'was calculated for breast high and will never have its Effect or likeness otherwise'. These scruples, together with Reynolds's remarks in the fourteenth *Discourse* on the readability of Gainsborough's shapes and colours—close up they were merely 'odd scratches and marks' but 'by a kind of magick, at a certain distance assume[d] form'—direct our critical attention to Gainsborough's major invention. For what Reynolds called his 'peculiarity of manner, or style, or we may call it—the language in which he expressed his ideas' was designed to involve us and the figures within the landscapes by means of his formal presentation of them. The composition and the paintwork, not the myth or narrative, capture and disclose the sentiment that Constable remarked. *The Country Churchyard*, like other landscapes [plate 71] that Ronald Paulson has examined, seems to locate the peasants on a gradual but accelerating downward movement to the right:

foliage and tombstones, humans and undergrowth, ruined wall and stone fence all slip, merge, into some undifferentiated point, to which the brushstrokes also lead. This descent into some vague, even bottomless, pool or hollow of ground works, like Burke's sublime, to release our thoughts to fill the void. The merger of human and natural, so like Wordsworth's first sight of the leech-gatherer, 'unawares', as some huge stone upon an eminence, becomes for the painter an absorption by the land-scapes he loved ('how strong my inclination stood for Landskip'); in this he reverses the process both of Wordsworth's poem, by which the old man whose voice was 'like a stream' gives the poet 'human strength', and of other landscapists where figures emerge from their scenery to alert our attention.

In other ways Gainsborough's identification of human and natural forces the scene back upon the spectator who makes it his own. In landscapes the congruence of 'figure and ground becomes the scene in which trees bend down towards peasants and their wagons [or herds] passing beneath, and all three merge in a common substance'. The generalized shapes of animals and trees and people leave their discrete identities to be identified by the spectator, who thereby 'creates' the landscape in his fashion. Even portraits that Gainsborough was obliged to do for a living manage to examine the formal relationship between sitter and scenery: sometimes they share the same qualities of paint or brushwork or are seen as variations of some basic shape, entering as much as portraiture allows into each other's essence. Viewing them, when as Reynolds noticed we

PLATE 71   Thomas Gainsborough, *Wooded Landscape with Herdsman Driving Cattle Downhill.* Chalk, wash, and oil drawing (early 1770's).

THE FIGURE IN THE LANDSCAPE

make good their imprecisions with our imagination, draws us into their compositional meanings.

This involvement is formal with Gainsborough, dramatic only in his exploration of how humans and trees may gleefully aspire to each other's condition. We may see his peculiar talent more distinctly by comparing his work here with Loutherbourg. Gainsborough's peepshow landscapes invite our scrutiny of light, colour and shape, 'referring everything to nature'. But Loutherbourg's *Eidophusikon*, a miniature theatre complete with sound machinery, artificial lighting, and transparencies, first shown in 1781 (and from this Gainsborough certainly derived his peepshow), is designed to explore the dramatic encounter between, say, Satan and the raising of Pandemonium beside the Fiery Lake. Loutherbourg's other work, as 'impresario' or landscape painter, confirms these dramatic intentions. At Fonthill in 1781 he designed for William Beckforth a labyrinthine and 'negromantic' scenery in which guests acted their Christmas masquerades for three days and nights. This experimental drama of figures in changing landscape which led directly to his work with the *Eidophusikon* is equally consistent with much of his painting. *Avalanche or Ice-Fall in the Alps* depicts the horrific drama of humans destroyed by natural forces. It is similar to Fuseli's psychological explorations in pictures like *The Nightmare* (not a landscape, though significantly Erasmus Darwin's account of it turns it into one): in both exterior images press literally upon figures into whose 'inward action' we are accordingly propelled.

PLATE 72 Philip James de Loutherbourg, *Llanberis Lake.* Oil painting (1786).

The drama of Loutherbourg's *Llanberis Lake* [plate 72] is more subtle, but his fishermen are stilled and belittled by the massed forms of the surrounding mountains, their dark shapes emphasised against the light reflected in the water behind them. Similarly the figures of *Coalbrookdale by Night* not only have an explicable relationship with the scenery (they work there), but in their movement away from the reddish smoke and yellow glare of the iron works they suggest less simple motives: the leading horse seems to strain forward, the figure on the cart gestures in the same direction, away from the fires, and one figure behind rather defiantly confronts or maybe marvels (such is the dramatic ambiguity) at the sublime industrial vision.

Loutherbourg's interest in human drama—he painted *The Bard*, various historical and mythological events, as well as stage scenery—is remote from Gainsborough's world in its intentions as well as in subjects, despite their point of contact. Gainsborough's pictures do not identify what is seen in the real world —though he reveals careful observation of natural effects—but what has passed within *his* brain. His generalized forms are not those of Price, with whom he was friendly, or of Gilpin's picturesque, but the workings of his own subjective response and reorganization of landscape memories. We know that at night, after a day's work on portraits or other commissions with some reference to the objective world, he would play with endless sketches of landscape items in an effort to purge his mind of the ideas that had been teeming there all day. These forms, metamorphoses of visual encounters (sometimes only encounters with bits of coal, glass, vegetables), became the language of personal meaning. Like the American poet, William Carlos Williams, a hundred and fifty years later, 'whether it was a tree or a woman or a bird, mood had to be translated into form'. The subjects mattered less than what Jackson called the 'hasty loose handling' or than the composition (Gainsborough is on record about ill-composed landscapes where 'half a Tree was to meet half a Church to make a principal object'). The handling and the composition are the means of uniting in one common act of appreciation the artist, the spectator and the landscape.

Shape and soul were the two ingredients that Gainsborough knew he had to bring together to portray Shakespeare in his Garrick portrait: 'I intend . . . to take the form from his Pictures & statues just enough to preserve his likeness *past the doubt of all blockheads*, at first sight, and supply a soul from his Works'. A similar manoeuvre characterizes his landscapes. He was perhaps unique in his day for relying for the expression of sentiment and emotion in his landscapes, not upon literary event or allusion, but upon formal invention and a radical manipulation of his visual medium. In this he may be contrasted, for example, with Gilpin, who was already publishing his picturesque *Tours* when Gainsborough died in 1788. To one commentator Gilpin was the 'ne plus ultra of the pen and the pencil united'. But of course he relied upon a written commentary to express the 'solemnity' and 'awe' of a scene and upon sketches to convey its forms.

Like Gainsborough, 'Capability' Brown had no literary pretensions; his often cited remark to Hannah More (*'there* I make a comma, & there, where a more decided turn is proper, I make a colon') seems just a quick-witted analogy to impress a literary lady. Nor does Brown have Kent's visual sensibilities, though Joseph Warton thought of him as a great painter. If he is to be considered as one, it must be as the gardenist equivalent to Gainsborough—rejecting 'great subjects' and literary and myth-ological associations, invoking the forms and shapes of nature and adapting them to his own alert and special vision of what he called 'Place-making'.

With Brown the human figure in the landscape becomes less important than the landscape's absorption of them and all other items. Though he wrote to Thomas Dyer that gardening should 'supply all the elegance and all the comforts which Mankind wants in the Country and (I will add) if right, be exactly fit for the owner, the Poet and the Painter', his designs are dedicated completely to natural lines and rhythms—the curves of banks along water or the grass sweeping up to the very mansion. One has only to compare earlier views of Stowe or Woburn Farm with any sympathetic artist's view of one of his finished designs to realize how much in one of Brown's parks the figures are designed just 'to create a little business for the Eye to be drawn from the Trees in order to return to them with more glee' [see plate 73]. Some of his delight in this formal manipulation is apparent in the jokes he made about his control over nature ('Thames, Thames, you will never forgive me!'). And two poetic commentaries—by Cowper and William Whitehead, the poet laureate—both recognize his 'gleeful' commitment to visual formalism. Cowper's lines register it with some irony:

The omnipotent magician Brown appears!
Down falls the venerable pile, the abode
Of our forefathers

. . . .

Lo, he comes!
He speaks, the lake in front becomes a lawn;
Woods vanish, hills subside and valleys rise,
And streams, as if created for his use
Pursue the track of his directing wand.

'His use' is a penetrating comment. Whitehead, predictably, is less perceptive, but his lines on "The Late Improvements", in which Brown and 'Dame Nature' debate to which of them credit

PLATE 73   Joseph Constantine Stadler, Nuneham Courtenay.
Engraving after Joseph Farington, from Boydell's *The River Thames* (1794).

for Nuneham Courtenay should go, also stress Brown's fascination for 'flowing outline', 'elegant sweep' and 'undulations . . . That heave from the lawns' [plate 74].

Before Brown, landscape gardening had taken forms analogous to historical or mythological subjects and 'fancy pieces' in painting; after Brown, Humphry Repton manoeuvred the garden finally from associationist or formalist designs into an intimate, social, and 'gardenesque' mode.

The 'history' or 'fancy' garden (Walpole's 'Real prospects are little less than visions') was a structure to which eye and mind responded. A series of carefully prepared prospects, in which the eye was not allowed to encounter anything accidental or inessential, were discovered along a defined itinerary at Castle Howard, Stowe, Rousham, or Stourhead. The 'meaning' of each vista or landskip was available to all informed visitors—at Stowe, Benton Seeley's guidebooks, bought at the local inn, prompted the less informed; the mind, especially the literary and historical imagination, completed the visual structures. Whether as at Stourhead or in the Elysian Fields at Stowe, there was an a priori literary programme for the garden's iconography, as there presumably had been for many Italian Renaissance gardens, or whether it was created after the event by the alert and inventive visitor, like Walpole at Castle Howard or Rousham, it was an essential element in the experience of a garden. *And allusions to Roman pietas or civitas* (Studley Royal and Stowe), to Elysian Field or Garden of Eden, were instructive

219   THE LANDSCAPE OF SENSIBILITY

emblems, designed to shape and influence visitors; as Sir John Clerk of Penicuik neatly explained it in his poem on "The Country Seat" of 1731. 'This lovely Prospect may your busy mind / With usefull Speculations entertain'. It had been since Cicero traditional to find moral instruction in works of art, but it became something of a vogue in eighteenth-century England, and the garden was more affected than most: Aaron Hill's Moral Rock Garden, with a Kennel of Envy and Grotto of Independence, is an extreme example. Even William Blake, in retirement at Felpham ('a perfect model for cottages'), was still reading a landscape in this way, albeit after his visionary fashion:

Heaven opens on all sides her Golden Gates; her windows are not obstructed by vapours; voices of celestial inhabitants are more distinctly heard, and their forms are more distinctly seen, and my cottage is also a shadow of their houses.

But Brown, well before Blake was in Sussex, created gardens in which these mental or moral patterns were absent. His interest lay in the 'capabilities', while Pope's had focused upon the 'genius', of a place. This difference, between formal and readable structures, marks a decisive change in thinking about and in gardens.

The pre-Brownian, Augustan, garden made great use of inscriptions, and this verbal strategy, supplementing the visual, lingered on long after Brown had begun to make his mark. But it seems totally at odds with his imagination. Shenstone, for example, explained in verse and prose the function of inscriptions:

Here we ascend some airy seat,
Or little temple's close retreat,
Beneath a shady bow'r:
And oft some moral sentence find,
To please, or to instruct the mind,
And pass each tedious hour.

And in his *Unconnected Thoughts* he says that inscriptions 'somewhat strengthen' the effect of a particular part of the garden, 'supporting its title by suitable appendages——For instance, the lover's walk may have assignation seats, with proper mottoes——Urns to faithful lovers——Trophies, Garlands, Etc.' The collected works of innumerable poets besides Shenstone are full of their exercises in this genre, all seeking to provide a voice for the genius loci: there are Akenside's inscriptions "For a Statue of Chaucer at Woodstock"; Shenstone's inscriptions "On the back of a Gothic Seat", "On a Small Obelisk in Virgil's Grove"; Thomas Warton's "Inscription in a Hermitage" or "Inscription over a Calm and Clear Spring in Blenheim Gardens". This habit of verbalizing about a landscape's particular virtù was derived from the experience of exploring classical ruins—a *locus classicus* is Poussin's *Et In Arcadia Ego*—and extended beyond the garden into, most obviously, Gray's churchyard or Wordsworth's "Lines left upon a Seat in a Yew-tree". This 'call from a monument in the landscape or from the landscape itself, which deepens the consciousness of the poet and makes him feel he is on significant ground' also characterized Ossian's mountains: Blair talks of songs 'found engraven upon rocks in the old Runic character', and Wright of Derby similarly depicts some engraved verses on the rock behind Beattie's *Edwin*, 'supposing them to be his *own compositions*'.

Yet despite the absence of inscriptions there is still a strong sense of discovery in Brown's gardens. His successor, Repton, was insistent that a garden must appeal to the mind and understanding, but resisted any emblematic structures, about which he was even rather snide: when the owner of Langley Park wanted to retain an 'unsightly' house because his mother had liked it, Repton agreed to give it a Doric facade—'thus ornamented, may be considered as a temple to filial piety'. The discoveries which the sensibility is allowed to make in Brown's and, with some reservations, in Repton's parks are much freer than in earlier gardens. The mind is not attracted out to encounter and understand something specific beyond itself; but, undirected, expatiates in its own territory. The analogue—moments in poetry apart, which will be considered later—is *Tristram Shandy*, where we are rarely presented with the objects of discussions, but only minds' variations upon ungiven themes. Brown still directed the steps of his garden visitors, and he utilized from earlier designs like Woburn Farm the idea of a circuit of the garden, which he modified into a perimeter belt of trees with a path or drive within it. But this device has none of the intellectual force, as Pope described it:

But may not one say Homer is in this like a skilful Improver, who places a beautiful Statue in a well-disposed Garden so as to answer several Vistas, and by that Artifice one single Figure seems multiply'd into as many Objects as there are Openings whence it may be viewed.

Multiple views for Brown contrive only many variations upon some natural forms—notably, as in his Wimpole plans, a slowly changing prospect of the lake, bridge, and adjoining meadows, or, in the plan for the grounds at Heveningham, the circling drive, which brings the garden from *landskips* into *kinema* [plate 74]. It was one of the characteristics of the paintings that influenced early gardenists—and so of their gardens—that distant prospects were contained by side wings of trees and buildings, so that the eye was gradually pushed down the axis of vision. But both Brown and Repton opened out such vistas to allow continuous imagery, flowing like one unbroken serpentine line. At Blaise Castle, for instance, Repton redesigned the view of the River Severn ('like peeping thro' a long tube that is instantly snatched from the eye') to provide a sequence of open prospects across the valley.

Brown must have found associations hard to exclude at Alnwick, for instance, or in his unexecuted design for the Cambridge Backs. But his reliance upon a limited repertoire of selected shapes (clumps of trees) and lines (edges of water) within which to see buildings undoubtedly absorbed much of their most dominant ideas into the subtleties of formal pattern. This negligible intellectual content of a Brownian park was, in fact, sustained by much contemporary aesthetics and psychological theory. Hogarth in *The Analysis of Beauty* urged the spectator to forget what he's read in art treatises and to look for himself; Hume, though he was later to qualify this extreme position, located 'Beauty . . . merely in the mind which contemplates' objects rather than in the objects themselves; even Burke's discussion of Beauty, which Christopher Hussey has seen as an exact expression of the *feeling* of a Brown landscape, is offered in terms of a person's sensations ('the sense . . . of being swiftly drawn in an easy coach on a smooth turf') not ideas with an independent existence.

Brown's successor, Repton, concerns us very slightly. He worked mostly in parks where Brown had already improved and the gradual discovery of his own original contribution reached fruition only after the period covered by this book is over. But some aspects of his designs are relevant. Whereas the landscape

PLATE 74   Lancelot ('Capability') Brown, plan for Heveningham Hall grounds (1782).

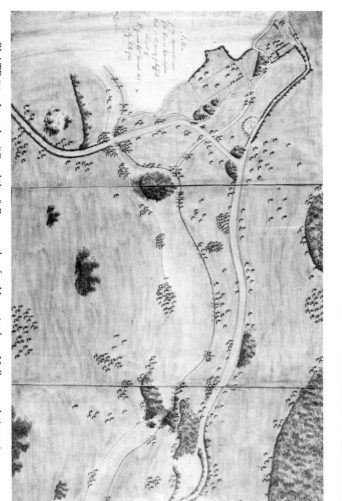

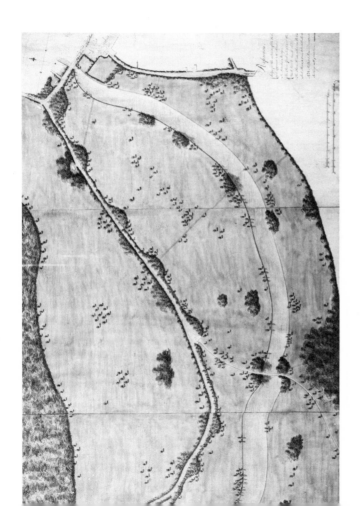

garden had formerly looked to painting and literature, Repton followed Brown in refusing the structures of either: though, as does Gilpin in his picturesque *Tours*, he relies in his Red Books upon the resources of both watercolours and prose to intimate the final experience of his designs. His quarrel with Price and Knight was mainly with their failure to attend to the *use* of landscapes by their owners and with their apparent determination to judge a garden by whether it was a 'fit object for the representation of the pencil' (L 101). Their picturesque associations—with 'scenes of horror, well calculated for the residence of Banditti' (L 101)—had little relevance to the needs and comforts of Repton's clients. Increasingly it became his concern to ensure the 'convenience of the mansion' (L 540). Unlike Brown, who seemed to use the house as a central point in a visual scene, to be viewed from outside while moving round the circling drives, Repton saw it as the centre of his design, from which, as in daily life there, clients began by looking and moving outwards. Accordingly he reintroduced terraces, raised flower-beds, conservatories, gravel walks: at Cobham he was particularly proud of 'a striking example of artificial arrangement for convenience, in the grounds immediately adjoining the house' (L 421).

It was as if Repton recognized that the garden under Brown had already lost its appeal for poets and painters and could resume some of its former artificiality. But this return to previous garden styles did not at all mean the revival of

PLATE 75 Nuneham Courtenay, Mason's flower garden. Engraving from Paul Sandby's *The Virtuosi's Museum* (1778).

previous garden ideologies. When he offered his clients a classical or a gothic architecture (L 57–58), it was not, as it had been at Stowe, to make some allusion to patterns of cultural heritage, but only to satisfy visual tastes. Yet what he did contribute—as William Chambers and William Mason [plate 75] had also done—was a fresh delight in 'close-up'; the flowers and architectural structures near a house allowed the eye to rest upon their more intricate shapes and colours as some relief from distant prospects. It was a gardenist development that had its analogues in literature—Erasmus Darwin's *The Botanical Garden*—as well as its consequences.

Prospects for Poetry

Landscape poetry is this period often seems distracted from its proper occupation by a nostalgia for painterly or gardenist modes of proceeding. When Addison prophetically urged the Imagination out of a garden's 'narrow compass' into the 'wide Fields of Nature [where] the sight wandered up and down without confinement', he begged a question—always difficult to answer even for later poets—as to what was the literary imagination's proper mode of seeing. Poets were especially perplexed, as the authors of *Clarissa* or *Tristram Shandy* were not, to discover ways of talking about 'what spontaneously arose in the author's mind' on some particular occasion and in some specific location. We can best observe this perplexity and its various elucidations by tracing the prospect poem from mid-century (though with some backward glances) until Wordsworth's "Lines Written … above Tintern Abbey", arguably the last and the best of its kind.

The painterly nostalgia of such poems is intelligently analysed by John Scott's biographer, writing of his *Amwell, a descriptive poem* (1776):

The face of the country here is very picturesque; but perhaps it will be found, that local description is far more adapted to the powers of the pencil than the pen. Those marking and peculiar features which the painter gives, with a few strokes, to the eye, will lose almost all their discrimination in the words of the poet; a hill, a vale, a forest, a rivulet, and a cataract, can be described only by general terms; the hill must swell, the vale sink, the rivulet murmur, and the cataract foam.

This worry, echoed later by Coleridge, is rarely so explicit in discussions of landscape description. At most it takes the form of empty hyperbole:

So *here*, where *nature* does her triumphs show,
And with majestic hand adorns a STOWE;
Descriptions fails—all fancy is too mean,
They only can conceive it—who have seen!

It took the romantic poets to register the cliché and alter their tactics radically as a result. But the prospect poem had in fact begun, as it was to end, with little inclination to ape the painters.

Pope's Windsor Forest, and before it Denham's *Cooper's Hill*, were concerned little with the visual or the topographical. The energies of Pope's poem are literary ('Non iniussa cano'), its metaphoric allusions to mythology, though they share the same iconography as Claude or an Italian Renaissance garden, are determinedly verbal, and the vision of Windsor is at some distinct remove from any sight or thought of its actual scenery ('I roam from Shade to Shade, / By God-like Poets Venerable made'). The poem may be the result of knowing Windsor (Pope, of course, did), but what it offered is neither an account of looking nor in any direct fashion a product of looking: the mental territory is the poet's landscape. The force of his images is general and abstract: the idea of 'waving Groves a chequer'd Scene display' is provided for its hint of *concordia discors* and a sense thereby of Pope's literary obligations to Denham, not for any allusion to some painted chiaroscuro of landscape. 'Fruitful Fields', 'tufted Trees' and 'teaming Grain' establish the scenery in literary memories of Milton and Virgil rather than 'out there' where Pope passed his childhood; nor do they signify the imitation of any garden structures, though Spence was right to note that 'Mr Pope's ideas of Windsor Forest in 1704 [were] like his ideas *afterwards* for gardening'. Significantly, the 'Groves of Eden . . . Live in Description, and look green in Song' is still a long way from 'Nature shall join you, Time shall make it grow / A work to wonder at, perhaps a Stow'.

Denham, less skillful than Pope, had equally little to do with visual gesture: when he points out Old St Paul's on the horizon, it is to recall Edmund Waller's 'Muse whose flight / Has bravely reach't and soar'd above thy height'. Neither Denham nor Pope give any indication that their poetry depends upon the habits of viewing and organizing topography that were displayed by Hollar, Dancherts, or Jan Vorsterman. Where painting does enter prospect poetry decisively is with John Dyer's *Grongar Hill* (1726).

Dyer had returned from two years in Rome studying to be a painter when he wrote *Grongar Hill*; its invocation of the visual arts—'Painting far the form of Things', 'Draw the Landskip bright and strong', the 'various Dies' of trees—has none of the force of similar phrases in *Windsor Forest*: Pope's metaphors ('My humble Muse . . . / Paints the Green Forests') insist only upon the mythopoeic vision of the celebrating poet, who would ensure a permanent idea of Windsor and accordingly invokes the arts that bestow permanence ('The Muse shall sing, and what she sings shall last'). Dyer, in contrast, is not bothered with this form of panegyric. His verses are best read as a vivid—note their present tense—account of a painter in the process of looking at a landscape: various possibilities of composition are suggested:

At the Fountain of a Rill,
Sate upon a flow'ry Bed,
With my Hand beneath my Head;
And stray'd my Eyes o'er Towy's Flood

and there is a quick attention to contrasts of 'long and level Lawn' bright against the 'dark hill', some reorganization of the topography to compose another *landskip*:

Deep are his Feet in Towy's Flood,
His Sides are cloath'd with waving Wood,
And antient Towers crown his Brow,
That cast an awful Look below.

His 'wand'ring Eye' is exercised in ways that suggest the aspiring painter: the topographical breadth of lines 105–13; the translation of items in the scenery into painterly techniques, such as the 'streaks of Meadow' in the distance or the sunlight catching 'broken Rocks'; the 'Vistoes shooting Beams of Day: / Wider and wider spreads the Vale', with its distinct associations of such Dutch landscape as Rembrandt's *The Three Trees*. And in his other poem of the same date, "A Country Walk", he displays an identical delight in colour ('yellow Barn'), form (the pyramid-shaped hill), and light. There is more identification of picture subjects—the wearied swain, an old man in his cottage garden, solitary angler—all dramatis personae from Italian and Dutch landscape paintings.

Probably no other prospect poem managed these painterly manoeuvres so adeptly, with so much skill in suggesting through words the visual associations that we should bring to meet them. But what is lost is any interesting sense of mental territory. For Dyer's inability to 'instruct our wand'ring Thought', though it proceeds in the same nimble octosyllabics, is quite mechanical. Little effort is made to unite the 'wand'ring Eye' with the 'wand'ring Thought' in *Grongar Hill*. The latter's activity is conventional:

A Sun-beam in a Winter's Day
Is all the Proud and Mighty have,
Between the Cradle and the Grave.

Its presentation is in the laziest of analogic syntax: the river runs through changing scenery, 'A various Journey to the Deep, / *Like* human life to endless Sleep!'; or light makes a far field seem strangely close, '*So* we mistake the Future's face.' In "A Country Walk" there is one fleeting register of some finer congruence of mind with landscape in the poet's sudden confrontation with the silence of the countryside:

Oh powerful *Silence*, how you reign
In the Poet's busy Brain!
His num'rous Thoughts obey the Calls
Of the tuneful Water-falls.

But the image is dissolved in whimsy. Otherwise the matching of introspection with its surrounding landscape is conveyed via the topoi of Narcissus and Echo, the latter named directly ('See her Woods where *Eccho* talks'), the former implicitly assumed as the poet's role when he bends over the water beside some oak. The popularity of this myth of introspection, self-knowledge and dialogue with nature—both Poussin and Claude painted it—allowed poets to allude to it as an easy image of meditation, promoted and answered or not by natural surroundings. When Thomson 'under closing shades' lies down beside a 'lowly brook' to whisper to his dreams (*Autumn*, ll. 1369–71), he is alluding covertly to the Narcissus story. Even those paintings which confront some anonymous figure in the landscape with a waterfall or precipice [see plate 24] are relying, I imagine, upon precisely the same mythic metaphor of the contemplatist finding his echo or mirror image in the natural world.

In the 1720's the landscaping taste had perhaps not much disturbed traditional garden design in South Wales: Dyer gazes down from the top of Grongar Hill onto his own home:

Her Gardens trim, her Terras Walks,
Her Wildernesses, fragrant Brakes,
Her gloomy Bowers, and shining Lakes,
Keep, ye Gods, this humble Seat,
For ever pleasant, private, neat.

When the landscape taste spread and 'neatness' surrendered gradually to more intricate organizations of space, poets—as we have seen already with Thomson—found that the experience of exploring a garden offered a rival structure to that of paintings by which to organize mental existence. Gray carried his garden-ist habits of looking and thinking with him when he explored the countryside of Scotland or Cumberland. Poetry that is organized after the pattern of landscape gardens is character-ized by its concern with movement through scenery, the 'kinema' not the prospect picture, the mysterious process of discovering what comes next to eye and mind rather than an apprehension of landscape at a distance which is surveyed rapidly by what Thomson called 'the raptured eye, / Exulting swift' (*Summer*, ll. 1409–10).

We can see this difference at work in several, very ordinary, poems during the middle years of the century. The painterly prospect eagerly announces its visual ambition:

The vale beneath a pleasing prospect yields
Of verdant meads and cultivated fields;
Through these a river rolls its winding flood,
Adorn'd with various tufts of rising wood;
Here, half conceal'd in trees a cottage stands,
A castle there the opening plain commands;
Beyond, a town with glittering spires is crown'd,
And distant hills the wide horizon bound.

But the same poet, Lyttelton, changes his tactics when he leaves the 'romantic mountain's airy head' for the grounds at Blenheim: here he roves 'Along the shady paths' and communicates their meditative potential, not in some wide-angle picture where all the items are quickly apprehended, but with yet another covert allusion to Echo and Narcissus:

            Amid the mazy gloom
Of this romantic wilderness once stood
The bower of Rosamonda, hapless fair,
Sacred to grief and love; the crystal fount
In which she used to bathe her beauteous limbs
Still warbling flows, pleas'd to reflect the face
Of Spencer, lovely maid, when tir'd she sits
Beside its flowery brink, and views those charms
Which only Rosamond could once excel.

Poems celebrating landscape gardens—Stephens on "Lord Ba-thurst's Park", Giles on "The Leasowes" or "Richmond

Gardens" in *The London Magazine*—seem aware of the tensions that gardens themselves contained between 'boundless prospect, fair' where 'thoughts expatiate free' and psychological 'kinema' ('Pursue her thro' each grot and grove').

At Cirencester Stephens begins by announcing the park's invitation to explore what a footnote glosses as 'a shady, serpentine walk, which runs from the house a mile and a half, and terminates at a building commonly known by the name of *Pope's Seat'*:

When first the beauteous EDEN we survey,
Unfolding shades a gravell'd walk display
Which leads meand'ring; onward we pursue
Our silent course

But the landscape design itself distracts our sense of 'course' with prearranged, static, and 'vary'd prospects'; these Stephens itemizes like any picture, adding rather lamely before he concludes that we register these 'along the Terras, as we move'. Poetry's narrative form can best express movement and the sense of exploration and discovery ('Surrounding paths our wand'ring feet invite'). But the psychological excitements of landscape disclosing itself through 'yon parting woods' vie with the picturesque temptations, when it seems that poetry sets itself to mimic visual accounts of country seats:

But see, that nobler Visto tempts our stay,
And leads the eye delighted far away.

When the feet can follow the eye ('Hence guide me, Muses, thro' th' imbowering groves'), the verse takes on an excitement that is denied the very limited structure of surveying a prospect from some fixed station. Compare Stephens, first, with a section from the *Richmond-Gardens* poem:

For prospect built, a beauteous Temple there
Swells in proportion elegantly-fair;
To diff'rent views remoter buildings stand,
Neat these, and those in Gothic order grand.
The prospects, blending with surprising grace,
Adorn, correctly-rude, the blissful place.
The chearful greens of various shades arise,
And, sweetly mingling, recreate the eyes.

The final verb, not only signifies the eye's pastime, but implies its reassembling of the already carefully picturesque objects (a rather mechanical recreation). And though Stephens elsewhere hints at more intricate mental pleasures ('sweet delusion') and concludes with an unctuous passage on how the landscape alters as Lord and Lady Bathurst move through it—a poor example of a crucial notion that each garden visitor is creator of its immediate meaning—he can nowhere match the poet of Richmond in giving an impressionistic experience of a garden.

The Richmond poem begins with the customary homage to painting and 'Prospects [that charm] my sight'. There is much that suggests irony and satire, not least the bathetic expression of disappointment that an exploration of the garden produces. With distinct echoes of Pope's dunces, the poet, released momentarily from the obligations of the immediate scenery, confesses an ambition to celebrate Heaven's landscape:

Wrapt in a world unknown beyond the skies,
Where all the saints immortal treasure lies;
I'd paint the matchless pomp that world contains,
Her beauteous landskips, and extended plains.

Succeeding instalments of the poem betray some flagging invention; the second seems to mock the analogic reading of landscape, even while offering no alternative: 'The lively impress of creating power; / Some useful lesson let the trees convey'; the third combines a playful account of the *beatus ille* theme with a mockery of picturesque requirements in a landscape:

Blest with a comely, but a modest wife.
My humble cot shou'd stand serenely, still,
Just on the verge of some declining hill. —
Edg'g with young trees: the solemn shade should skreen
Her scarce perspective roof, and just between
The op'ning boughs, the sun's mild rays shou'd pierce.

From these uncertainties of attitude and tone we return to the early passage with some respect for its parody and ambiguous celebration of the mind's involvement in a garden's structure:

Forward advancing, but by slow degrees,
Straight I'm convey'd between the thick'ning trees.
Encompass'd round, I dart my eyes on high,
But scarce can trace a passage to the sky.
The sylvan scene with more than nature drest,
Involves the thoughts of her admiring guest.
In ranks confus'd, yet rang'd in order too,
Ten thousand towering floriars greet my view.
The winding circles of the mystic maze
Wrap me in wonder, while intent I gaze.
The treach'rous paths in cross confusion stray,
In little couples steer th'elaborate way;
Uncircumscrib'd they aim at distant space,
But faithless wander to their destin'd place,
Attract the labouring eye, a giddy round,
Then wind their courses to the center'd ground,
Roving at random in one circle meet,
And disappoint the curious wand'rer's feet.

The landscape seems to take possession of him, its maze provokes amazement; but its excitements prove empty trickery and the serpentine paths fail to yield what they had promised. Read ironically, it provides an intelligent appraisal of the artful devices of modish landscape designs.

Published a few years before Warton's rejection of Stowe, *Richmond-Gardens* at least suggests the negative possibilities of a mind's meeting with scenery. Compared with other effusions on Richmond, Stephen Duck's or Joseph Giles's, its scepticism is refreshing. Giles provides exactly the conventional claims for the psychology of a landscape garden that the *London Magazine* poet parodies. In the 'delightful labyrinth's winding way' at Kew, we are told, 'The muses happy thoughts, may smoothly stray': but the empty gestures are neither arresting nor at all convincingly related to the actual landscape. It could be anywhere or nowhere that inspires 'the mind with peace', floats it 'in seas of intellectual joys' or allows 'Philosophy . . . [to] here extend her wings'. If Kew allows the mind liberty, it is a freedom wasted. Earlier Giles had used yet again the image of Narcissus's reflection to imply that thought is linked to images of landscape 'improved' on the surface of the Thames:

Like pleasing views, thy floating mirror shows
Each lovely scene, that on thy margin grows.
Gay mansions, woods and groves, with gardens lie
In miniature exprest, beneath the sky:
The lucid stream each object so improves,
A new creation in its bosom moves!
Narcissus may admire the pleasing scene,
Smit with himself, might fondly gaze again

But the poet himself is too engrossed in contemplating the repetitions of well-established generalities.

Several problems can be identified as facing poets of landscape. They too often display only a modish social impulse, sharing their special sensibilities, like Addison's 'man of a Polite Imagination [who] finds a greater Satisfaction in the Prospects of Fields and Meadows than another does' (*Spectator* 411), by manipulating accessible generalities. Thus Giles finds more pleasure in contemplating Narcissus's solitary meditation as a 'secret Refreshment in a Description' (Addison) than exploring its private resonance. What Roger de Piles called 'inward action' of figures in a landscape painting needs in its poetic counterpart to be located in minds that exercise their own function over what the eye informs them and in minds that have some confidence in their special powers: for as Wordsworth remarked later, 'Minds that have nothing to confer / Find little to perceive'. At best the poet hesitates between the external world and his mind's art, like the *Richmond-Gardens* writer, sceptically poised between 'knowledge and power'.

Mark Akenside makes the best of both worlds, separately: he looks well at scenery and he attends feelingly to his mind's functions, but he rarely achieves much union between the impulses. *The Pleasures of Imagination* was first published in 1744, deriving its inspiration essentially from Addison's *Spectator* essays on the same theme; but Akenside started republishing the poem in 1757, having revised it in the light of Burke's *Inquiry*. In 1744 Akenside simply equates accurate knowledge of the world outside the mind with the mind's power itself.

> so haply where the powers
> Of fancy neither lessen nor enlarge
> The images of things, but paint in all
> Their genuine hues, the features which they wore
> In nature; there opinion will be true,
> And action right

[3:18–23]

Although later sections of that third book attend to the excitement of that 'lessening' and 'enlarging' of exterior images in the imagination, they are still dominated by the knowledge of the eyes' treaty with the world.

The long 'prospect' in Book Three, beginning at line 285, is introduced with the recognition of how the 'sense of man' beholds 'in lifeless things, / The inexpressive semblance of himself'. The landscape description that follows, however, inspires too general a response ('religious awe') and its 'inexpressive' mirror-image of the poet is provided with an easy, painterly vocabulary of some Claudean or Poussinesque scene:

> as if the reverend form
> Of Minos or of Numa should forsake
> The Elysian seats, and down the embowering glade
> Move to your pausing eye.

The gesture, then, towards the outward scenery ('Behold the expanse / Of yon gay landscape') is only precariously kept within verbal scope: the sun is 'doubtful' and the expressive potential of the ambiguous weather is elicited by the reader, who is asked to

> say, within your cheerful breast
> Plays not the lively sense of winning mirth
> With clouds and sun-shine chequer'd.

Akenside then launches into an extended exposition of the associationist experience (ll. 312–436). He communicates something of the mysterious and exciting process of what he calls the 'memory', as it works on stored images of landscape; yet the very effort of the verse to *explain* only serves to emphasise the basically mechanical nature of the psychological theory:

> the secret union, when we feel
> A song, a flower, a name, at once restore
> Those long-connected scenes where first they mov'd

The attention: backward through her mazy walks
Guiding the wanton fancy to her scope,
To temples, courts, or fields

Despite the garden rather than pictorial imagery, the explication fails to match the mental process it attempts to elucidate.
The uneasy presence of these structures from painting and
landscaping ('the sister powers of art') constantly deprives
Akenside of a chance to focus upon the imagination's verbal
activity. 'Colours mingle, features join, and lines converge'
echoes with the instructions of the sketching lesson and the
gardening manual. Momentary perceptions of rival processes
are hedged with anxieties about their precision:

    From them he oft resolves

To frame he knows not what excelling things;
And win he knows not what sublime reward
Of praise and wonder.

The 'plastic powers' of the mind resume their sway and the
ensuing analysis of its selective habits (ll. 391–95) anticipates
Gilpin's picturesque reorganizations of remembered landscapes.
Yet Akenside still gropes towards what one feels is for him the
essential encounter between mind and nature, the 'object ascer-
tain'd':

The various organs of his mimic skill,
The consonance of sounds, the featur'd rock,
The shadowy picture and impassion'd verse,
Beyond their proper powers attract the soul
By that expressive semblance, while in sight
Of nature's great original we scan
The lively child of art; while line by line,
And feature after feature we refer
To that sublime exemplar whence it stole
Those animating charms.

The 1757 version of the poem neglects almost entirely these
accounts of the eye's contribution: indeed, the 'mind / For its
own eye doth objects nobler still / Prepare' is how Book One
begins. Burke's sublime and beautiful are rehearsed now instead
of Addison's preoccupation with the sight. Burke's preference
for poetry over painting as the most suitable medium for the
expression of emotion is undoubtedly influential in curbing
Akenside's merely pictorial energies. The urge to inquire and
explain the mind's workings, present in 1744, increases in
fascination, and we learn how to conduct

From sense, the portal turbulent and loud,
Into the mind's wide palace one by one
The frequent, pressing, fluctuating forms,
And question and compare them.

                                                    [2:56–59]

Sometimes the habits of generalization that dogged the earlier versions are recognized; yet the 'various bias' of the 'multitude of minds' promises, but does not deliver immediately, some more personal exemplum. Instead Akenside seems to concentrate upon those special souls whose affective sensibility allow them to appreciate the ideas divinely ordained and impressed upon nature, once generally accessible to the alert enquirer:

What wonderous things had to their favor'd eyes
And ears on cloudy mountain been reveal'd,
Or in deep cave by nymph or power divine,
Portentous oft and wild.

The allusions—to Moses, Numa or Egeria—are still general; but Akenside is equally alert to the prestige of the bardic sublime—the premium upon the mind's reception of vast sensations which enlarge its sense of power, derived from Burke, colour the whole of Akenside's new section on Solon in Book Three. It is only in the final, fragmentary book, where the celebration of poets over other artists seems to come to a climax, that Akenside produces the telling sequence about his own Northumberland childhood:

O ye Northumbrian shades, which overlook
The rocky pavement and the mossy falls
Of solitary Wensbeck's limpid stream;
How gladly I recall your well-known seats
Belov'd of old, and that delighted time
When all alone, for many a summer's day,
I wander'd through your calm recesses, led
In silence by some powerful hand unseen.

[4:38–45]

Memory, urgent enough now and certainly personal, combines with an apprehension of mystery ('powerful hand unseen'). The mechanical, too, is lost in that succeeding confession of possession: 'Those studies which possess'd me in the dawn / Of life, and fix'd the colour of my mind'. Yet it is not sustained. Indecisions about poetry's own voice and themes probably contributed to Akenside's leaving his second version incomplete.

These indecisions and revisions can be seen by looking briefly at a sequence of prospect poems, from Akenside himself, through Thomas Warton, Richard Jago, John Scott, to Bowles and Coleridge. The least successful of these, it will be seen, still cling to what Akenside's *Pleasures* had hailed as 'general habits' and the 'arts which grow / Spontaneous in the minds of all mankind' (4:59–60). These may involve either the social impulse of Scott's 'Descriptive Muse':

ye, whoe'er in these delightful fields
Consumed with me the social hour, while I
Your walk conducted o'er their loveliest spots

[p. 22]

or, more strenuously, the attempt to create a common, undifferentiated bond between the poet and his (presumably) many readers. The most obvious means of effecting this was to invoke the long-familiar machinery of nymphs and dryads, a poetic language that might be made to talk of the spirit of place without undue or original effort on either the writer's side or his readers'. Yet this increasingly failed to serve the poet's purposes: Akenside's "Ode" on Goulder Hill shifts uneasily from that tired machinery to his own inward invention. Another tenacious means of 'socializing' poetry, and one which was ultimately more crippling of poetic invention, was to rehearse contemporary aesthetics, theology, or psychology. Whereas the poet had once, as E. R. Wasserman saw, thought analogically he now consciously thinks 'about thinking analogically'. The poetry of process becomes enmeshed in telling us what it is doing rather than doing it: and when poets are 'forever interrupting their scene-painting to find its moral or emotional analogue', they lose the urgency of incorporating into a scene the very personal act of interpreting it; they miss, to paraphrase Whitehead, energizing with value the essence of matter of fact.

Akenside's "Ode" (1758) finds it particularly difficult to connect his inward and his outward experience. The genre of hill-poem ('Thy verdant scenes, O Goulder's hill, / Once more I seek') and the ostensible occasion of the ode ("On Recoverong from a Fit of Sickness") are but casually combined. What does stir one in reading the poem is the tension between his present languid state and his memories of earlier, happier, and more energetic visits, which locates the action within his mind. And the return of his imaginative with his physical and psychological strength also centres the poetic action within. But the consequences of this escape from dejection ('My Dorian harp shall now') merely disappoint expectations. For the vocabulary that comes readily to his revived muse is that of the genii loci:

Now, ere the morning walk is done,
The distant voice of Health I hear
Welcome as beauty's to the lover's ear.
'Droop not, nor doubt of my return,' she cries

The 'nymphs and zephyrs' who escort his returning muse even lose their connection with Goulder, which becomes finally a fanciful combination of the Athenian Academy and Cicero's Tusculum.

In contrast, *Edge-Hill* (1767) is stolidly located in the 'ridge of hills, which is the boundary between the counties of Oxford and Warwick'. The motto from Addison ('Our Sight is the most perfect, and most delightful') and the claims of his preface that each section forms 'an entire picture' in which 'general reflections . . . naturally' arise from the subject, clearly defines the thoroughly derivative scope of Jago's endless poem. Reading it is an instructive experience, however, on two counts: firstly, the paralysing hold of the analogic mind over landscape poetry is nowhere more amply illustrated—after describing a Browni-an garden at Packington, Jago shifts into moral gear (though with a sudden flash of self-criticism):

Say, now my dear companions! for enough
Of leisure to descriptive song is giv'n;
Say, shall we, ere we part, with moral eye,
The scene review

[p. 121]

More seriously, *Edge-Hill* suggests that this dedication to reading 'Nature's moral plan' actually precludes an imaginative role for the poet. Book Three ponderously disposes of what Boswell, in another more readable context, described as 'Bishop Berkeley's ingenious sophistry to prove the non-existence of matter, and that everything in the universe is merely ideal'. But the terms of Jago's dismissal curiously contrive to remind us of exactly those areas of fantasy and imagination which he fears and which, as we have already seen, have begun to appeal to poets:

Shall we, because we strive in vain to tell
How Matter acts on incorporeal Mind,
Or how, when sleep has locked ev'ry sense,
Or fevers rage, Imagination paints
Unreal scenes, reject what sober sense,
And calmest thought attest? Shall we confound
States wholly diff'rent? Sleep with wakeful life?
Disease with health? This were to quit the day,
And seek our path at midnight. To renounce
Man's surest evidence, and idolize
Imagination. Hence then banish we
These metaphysic subtleties, and mark
The curious structure of these visual orbs,
The windows of the mind . . . .

　　　　　　through which the soul,

As thro a glass, all outward things surveys.

[p. 77]

The soul and mind become merely passive registers of this 'outward form of things', and the poet's task, Jago's delusive ambitions notwithstanding, is reduced to explaining the 'corres-pondence with external things' of our sensory experience.

Scott's *Amwell* (pub. 1776, but written in part by 1761) rescues little for the imagination from similar explorations of the natural world; but it does hint at the break-up of those traditions of prospect poetry which were no longer able to contain and shape meditation. Scott moves rapidly from pros-pect to prospect, lamenting finally that he has not the skills of Claude, Rubens, or Smith of Chichester. But that confession of inadequacy (in itself a standard one) is sometimes beside the point: for the drive of much of the poem seems to be to force his readers to visualize images rather than imitate them himself. Consider this passage:

How picturesque the view! where up the side
Of that steep bank, her roofs of russet thatch
Rise mix'd with trees, above whose swelling tops
Ascends the tall church tower, and loftier still
The hill's extended ridge. How picturesque!
Where slow beneath that bank the silver stream
Glides by the flowery isle, and willow groves
Wave on its northern verge, with trembling tufts
Of osier intermix'd. How picturesque
The slender group of airy elm, the clump
Of pollard oak, or ash, with ivy brown
Entwined

[pp. 31–32]

The refrain ('How picturesque') seems an invitation to review the scenery in our own minds with our own available visualiz-ing habits: the very generalized trees at the end of the passage, for example, may suggest something like Gainsborough's *Beech Trees at Foxley*, one of his more modish picturesque views. There are also moments (provoked in the first place by the thought of Goldsmith's *Deserted Village*) when Scott identifies 'the cottage sire' or 'the cottage maid'

o'er the stile
Leaning with downcast look, the artless tale
Of evening courtship hears.

[p. 33]

But it is the reader who involves himself by filling out these brief résumés of narrative, synopses for some 'Fancy Piece' by Gainsborough or Wheatley where we are also involved in proposing some sentimental incident to fit the picture's facts: indeed, Scott later says that the 'Muse / Bids Fancy's pencil paint the scene' (p. 26). Because this device allows each reader to bring his own visual experience (different for each reader presumably) to bear upon the lines, Scott's social muse ensures both a wider participation and a curiously creative involvement of each reader. There are other places where he seems to want the readers to complete the meaning, to fill the 'moment's pause of solemn thought' or to imagine for themselves the 'deep sequester'd vale' at Langley—a lengthy footnote actually sug-gests the pattern by which the scene may be 'adapted to contemplation'. Yet for equal parts of *Amwell* Scott provides conventional prospects ('Obvious to Fancy's eye') and 'full image[s]' where the reader is nothing except passive spectator. This passivity is even required at one point, when an 'airy prospect yields' a 'pleasant interchange' of plain, woods, winding rivers, rural towns; the sublime is deliberately refused—'Not vast and awful, but confined and fair;/ Not the black mountain and the foamy main'—'because it is not the reader who must be 'animated' but the 'whole' prospect which is kept at a safe painterly distance (p. 22).

Scott appeals there to our acquiescence in certain habits of seeing and knowing; he is scornful, for example, of those who do not know the Roman Campagna or who have not read Wotton on Fanshaw's garden. Thomas Warton also trades in the traditional and familiar. He peoples his lines on "The First of April" (pub. 1777) with dei ex machina; young Zephyr, Flora, and Ceres are, in fact, trivial in intention as well as in effect. The delightful force of the poem lies in its record of how slowly spring arrives in the landscape;

Reluctant comes the timid Spring.
Scarce a bee, with airy ring,
Murmurs the blossom'd boughs around,
That clothe the garden's southern bound:
Scarce a sickly straggling flower
Decks the rough castle's rifted tower:
Scarce the hardy primrose peeps
From the dark dell's entangled steeps.

[p. 178]

'Reluctant' is the restrained affective response to this detailed scene, and it is the cautious welcome for the discrete, sharply registered particulars of nature that is so quietly moving:

Scant along the ridgy land
The beans their newborn ranks expand:
The fresh-turn'd soil with tender blades
Thinly the sprouting barley shades.

[p. 179]

A picturesque prospect ('the landscape' typically signals it) intrudes, but its scope is not solely visual and the lark's song is mingled with the effects of light. At this point, had the poem ended, it would have survived as a distinct and strangely personal utterance. But Warton suddenly shifts his perspective, and a poem with no separation of figure and landscape—the account of the latter *being* the former's presence—changes into an account of that activity:

Musing through the lawny park,
The lonely poet loves to mark
How various greens in faint degrees
Tinge the tall groups of various trees

[p. 183]

The focus is changed so radically into a picture of distanced, generalized activity that it never recovers its sharply particularized vision. Though 'the poet' appears only that once, the language of the remaining third of the poem seems to observe the decorum of his appearance—it stays imprecise ('The field, the forest, green and gay'), and the return of Juno and Ceres is inevitable.

Joseph Warton, Thomas's brother, taught W. L. Bowles at Winchester and, according to Coleridge, the master's influence was vital in Bowles's 'gay prime'. The generalized limpidity of Bowles's verse maintains a careful balance between exterior image and interior reflection, as his lines composed "On the Front of a Hermitage" clearly convey:

To mark life's few and fleeting hours
I placed the dial 'midst the flowers,
Which one by one came forth and died,
Still withering by its ancient side.
Mortals, let the sight impart
Its pensive moral to thy heart!

[2:330]

Yet in his resistance to the pictorial in sonnets like "At Tynemouth Priory" or "On a Beautiful Landscape" he is moving landscape inward ('much musing'). Sounds of nature begin to impress the poet as much as its sights (this had been true, too, of *Amwell*). Stillness, the absence of sound, allows the sonnets to expand their modest reflections into that vacuum 'beyond all speech'. Though the sonnet "On a Beautiful Landscape" protests its visual mode—'I could look on thee / For hours' (1:27)—it nevertheless locates its sentiment in the freedom from looking that an intensely visual scenery may promote. His sonnets *Written Chiefly on Picturesque Spots* (1789) often neglect what would have attracted Gilpin and instead attend to the influence of sounds—at Ostend the bells

with lessening cadence now they fall
And now, along the white and level tide,
They fling their melancholy music wide.

[1:13]

What Coleridge admired in Bowles at first was 'Imagery' prompted, but not synonymous with, 'surrounding Scenery'; later he came to miss in the sonnets a 'Passion' by which inner and outer worlds could be fused in 'meditative observation'.

Coleridge and Wordsworth, though that is another story, also draw upon the starts and hesitations of late eighteenth-century landscape poetry for their youthful work. What they eventually win from imitation is an isolation of some successful stratagems, employed but rarely sustained by previous poets. The role of memory is one, and in "Sonnet to the River Otter" (c. 1793) we may see the pressures of recollected childhood requiring Coleridge to turn a very visual poem into one where images are 'deep imprest' behind shut eyelids. Mental visitations of landscape are helped in Coleridge's "To an Evening Star" (c. 1790) by his 'pure joy and calm Delight' in reflected light. He may practise the banishment of 'natural form[s]' and a concentration instead upon the 'Invisible' in rather extreme ways—his "Hymn Before Sunrise in the Vale of Chamouni" was composed without ever going to the place. But his frequently musical, not pictorial, metaphors are a more profitable way of intimating the relationship of figures to landscape. His "Lines Composed While Climbing . . . Brockley Coombe" (1795) seem to provide as thorough a prospect as Thomson or Scott; yet his attention to 'sweet songsters' and the reorganization of the natural imagery to suggest the gradual progress towards the emotional climax keep it from the merely visual.

Wordsworth, too, hears before he sees at Tintern Abbey; when he does 'behold', it is a scenery where cliffs

on a wild secluded scene impress
Thoughts of more deep seclusion; and connect
The landscape with the quiet of the sky.

The language itself announces a landscape already linked in memory to the poet's inward life, for which the poem and not the landscape speaks. Much later in his career Wordsworth saw the 'outward forms' of ruined towers dissolved in the music of thought:

Truth fails not; but her outward forms that bear
The longest date do melt like frosty rime,
That in the morning whitened hill and plain
And is no more; drop like the tower sublime
Of yesterday, which royally did wear
His crown of weeds, but could not even sustain
Some casual shout that broke the silent air,
Or the unimaginable touch of Time.

This fine vision, from *Ecclesiastical Sonnets* 34 (1822), may require our fleeting contribution of visual experience; but its confidence is solely verbal, announcing the poet's moral ear for what in the previous century had often been just a visible emblem of time's touch.

This survey of prospect poems has so far neglected two extensive and, by comparison, accomplished examples: Goldsmith's *The Deserted Village* (London, 1770) and Cowper's *The Task* (London, 1785). They are prime examples of descriptive poetry in the age of sensibility and with their very different attention to figures in a landscape this study must close.

The traditions of prospect poem and country house panegyric are renewed and revised in Goldsmith's meditation, while the arts of painting and gardening contribute their special habits of seeing without frustrating the poetic. The opening lines may seem to follow the standard description of a landscape from some hilltop (ll. 1–34). But it is the poet's memory that provides the eminence from which the recollected scenery is reviewed. And by the time we come to passages that in fact establish the poet's actual presence in the landscape ('Near yonder copse') we are so subtly planted in the poet's mind that these visual gestures and similar phrases ('as pondering here I stand') seem as eloquent of the pressures of the poet's nostalgia as of any topographical stance. The poem's firm location in the mind also eases those transformations from what in Jago, for instance, were 'delineation' to 'moralizing'. A highly personal and reflective tone is spread throughout *The Deserted Village* in a fashion that subsumes into the same style and mood of consciousness both

> thy tangling walks and ruined grounds
> Where once the cottage stood, the hawthorn grew

and

> Ill fares the land, to hastening ills a prey
> Where wealth accumulates and men decay

Part of this combination of eye and imagination derives simply from the fact that wherever Goldsmith's memory takes him there is *nothing to describe* of the former village; then the poem is forced backwards into its own imaginative territory where seen and felt are one. And it is perhaps the one landscape poem of the century in which we encounter the formal skills of public utterance joined to a highly personal response (for which letters—Pope's or Gray's—have been the more usual medium).

In two original ways, I think, Goldsmith adapts what his fellow-poets merely use. There is much in the poem that might be compared with Gainsborough's 'Fancy Pieces'—the themes are compactly rehearsed in one passage:

> The swain responsive as the milkmaid sung,
> The sober herd that lowed to meet their young;
> The noisy geese that gabbled o'er the pool,
> The playful children just let loose from school

But Goldsmith eschews the visual. The opportunities for genre pictures—the schoolmaster or the parson—are transformed into recollected narrative, where poetry can employ its structure of process or stream of consciousness, reliving the past with the ever-present tension of knowing it is no more. There are moments when the poet seems to play with language of picturesque description:

> No more thy glassy brook reflects the day,
> But, choked with sedges, works its weedy way.
> Along the glades, a solitary guest,
> The hollow-sounding bittern guards its nest;
> Amidst thy desert walks the lapwing flies,
> And tires their echoes with unvaried cries.

But the images seem to work against conventional meanings —there is no mirror for Narcissus, all echoes are exhausted —and it is the song of solitary birds that seems to speak for the figure in the landscape.

Associationist habits are, of course, the basis of Goldsmith's poem:

Where once the cottage stood, the hawthorn grew,
Remembrance wakes with all her busy train,
Swells at my breast and turns the past to pain.

'Train' is the technical language of eighteenth-century associationist psychology. But unlike many of his contemporaries who waver between rival theories, Goldsmith manages a fine and imaginative accommodation of them. What was basically at issue throughout the latter part of the century was whether the aesthetic and emotional experience could be located in objects outside the mind (Price and Gilpin provide versions of that) or whether (Knight and Alison are the chief spokesmen here) it was not the property of the thing itself but a way of looking, a habit of the subjective mind. We have seen these hesitations in the poetry of landscape. They may also be followed in the history of gardening; for places like Stowe, which provided structures of carefully composed visual and verbal items, directed the mind from without; but Brownian parks returned the initiative to the mind, which seemed to read its own meanings and moods into less specific scenery. Goldsmith's deserted village is a landscape where these awkward irresolutions are avoided: objects are scanty enough to allow the mind full scope ('Imagination fondly stoops to trace'), yet sufficiently present to authorize the fond imagination.

It is perhaps no accident that the subject of Goldsmith's poem has recently been shown to be the removal of the village of Nuneham Courtenay, near Oxford, to make way for a landscape garden. For the fashion in which Goldsmith revisits the remembered village scenes is exactly the progress around and through a landscape garden. This explains the associationist experience, as well as, in part, the absence of prospect passages. The language, too, acquires additional ironies: 'lawn' or 'bowers' are both the vocabulary of garden design and traditional, perhaps even moribund, poetic diction. So the words themselves are eloquent of a landscape that in the poet's mind is indeed both 'a garden and a grave'.

Cowper, too, seems to mistrust the landscape garden. His encomium on Brown, as we have seen, mixes irony with some appreciation. And The Task rarely visits such Brownian landscapes: its sense of a garden is that of the dedicated amateur gardener ('Who loves a garden, loves a greenhouse too'), and when Cowper's poetry tackles larger landscapes they are outside the park. He oscillates, in fact, between the detailed 'closeups' of Book Three, that anticipate Erasmus Darwin, and the large prospect pictures which were an inevitable constituent of descriptive poetry. But what still fascinates about *The Task* is the sense it gives of a lively and playful mind, sharply alert to natural phenomena, but not always able to sustain a poetry in which one is matched with the other.

The Task differs, of course, from *The Deserted Village* both in its lack of a specific subject (sofas apart) and in its length. It is a poem of mental process which facetiously seeks epic form and language; when Cowper's Advertisement spoke of 'pursuing the train of thought to which his situation and turn of mind led him', it seems to propose as a subject what is only a method. Book Two can describe the excitements of the latter:

> The shifts and turns,
> Th'expedients and inventions, multiform,
> To which the mind resorts, in chase of terms
> Though apt, yet coy, and difficult to win—
> T'arrest the fleeting images that fill
> The mirror of the mind, and hold them fast,
> And force them sit till he has pencill'd off
> A faithful likeness of the forms he views.
>
> [ll. 286–93]

The painterly joke maintains the scepticism he has already expressed about Italian landscape pictures, but it also betrays a lingering habit of proceeding pictorially in a poem even when least apt ('lost in his own musings, happy man' 2: 301).

His prospect passages ('My relish of fair prospect', 1:141) announce above all his 'admiration feeding at the eye' (1:157). Unlike Thomson, he does not read prospects as if they were pictures to be scanned with a rapid eye, but as if he were composing one:

> Now roves the eye,
> And posted on this speculative height
> Exults in its command. The sheepfold here
> Pours out its fleecy tenants o'er the glebe.
> At first, progressive as a stream, they seek
> The middle field; but scatter'd by degrees,
> Each to his choice, soon whiten all the land.
>
> [1:288–94]

The delight is in aesthetic effects taking shape, the progressive achieving completion. Yet if Cowper is therefore in some sense outside his landscapes, he still conveys the strength of his pleasure in them: 'And still unsated, dwelt upon the scene' (1:158). Especially when he attends, not to sights, but to sounds, he seems possessed by them, as they 'fill the mind':

> There is in souls a sympathy with sounds;
> And, as the mind is pitch'd, the ear is pleased
> With melting airs, or martial, brisk, or grave.

Some chord in unison with what we hear
Is touch'd within us, and the heart replies.
How soft the music of those village bells,
Falling at intervals upon the ear
In cadence sweet, now dying all away,
Now pealing loud again and louder still,
Clear and sonorous as the gale comes on!
With easy force it opens all the cells
Where memory slept.

[6:1-12]

That is a moment to be treasured in *The Task*. Cowper's release from visual obligations can come, as there, through sounds or through situations when he feels that his mind is not required to be simply a mirror. Similarly, when in Book Six he hears the 'wintry music' (l. 143) of the wind through barren branches, or when he celebrates the dazzling pageant of smell and colour in springtime (ll. 149-76), the poetry admits us readily into a mental world at once agile and original. Particularly when he can escape from such natural scenes to the 'glowing hearth', for instance, he is capable, like Coleridge in "Frost At Midnight", of suggesting the excitements of a creative interiority:

Me oft has fancy, ludicrous and wild,
Soothed with a waking dream of houses, towers,
Trees, churches, and strange visages express'd
In the red cinders, while with poring eye
I gazed, myself creating what I saw.

[4:286-90]

But he is mistrustful of the 'ludicrous' fancy and recoils from what the eye does not sufficiently authorize.

Yet he can, in fact, create what he sees, his eye and imagination concurring in wonder, in passages where he explores the detailed permutations of frost along the frozen riverside or, more playfully, the grotesque shadows thrown by the oblique winter sun:

And see where it has hung th'embroider'd banks
With forms so various, that no powers of art,
The pencil or the pen, may trace the scene!
Here glitt'ring turrets rise, upbearing high
(Fantastic misarrangement!) on the roof
Large growth of what may seem the sparkling trees
And shrubs of fairy land. The crystal drops
That trickle down the branches, fast congeal'd,
Shoot into pillars of pellucid length,
And prop the pile they but adorn'd before.
Here grotto within grotto safe defies
The sunbeam: there emboss'd and fretted wild,
The growing wonder takes a thousand shapes
Capricious, in which fancy seeks in vain
The likeness of some object seen before.
Thus nature works as if to mock at art

[5:107-22]

And there surely he reveals himself.

The careful eye for natural effects draws the marvelling mind towards them. He seems to see in the capricious forms of frost a miniature landscape which is beyond the pen or pencil because it is, he feels, authentically natural. So he declares that nature mocks at art. But the perception of that detailed winter scene is every bit as creative as a garden, a painted prospect, the naiads of Book One, or the iconographical figure of winter in Book Four. The mind there *is* its own artist; but the predisposition of the poet is to acclaim the reality and not, what a recent critic has called, his 'incipient inwardness of perception'. Cowper lacks the confidence which a later figure in the landscape possesses, a confidence in the ultimate mystery of the mind's encounter with natural phenomena: 'Thought and reality are, as it were, two distinct corresponding sounds, of which no man can say positively which is the voice and which the echo'.

Postscript

When Walpole spoke of poetry, painting, and gardening as the three new Graces, he was primarily concerned with the third. This newest and latest sister was hailed throughout the eighteenth century as an original British contribution to the arts. Variously known through Europe as *le jardin anglais, il giardino inglese* or *der englische Garten*, in its country of origin the landscape garden provided a wholly new artistic form in which to record and represent man's relationship with nature. Though with hindsight we may see that the English landscape garden did not spring fully armed from the head of, say, Addison or Pope, the contemporary pride in its *invention* by the British was pervasive. Thus Smollett in his *Travels through France and Italy* is particularly scornful of Italian villas which 'destroy that effect of rural simplicity, which our gardens are designed to produce';

In a fine extensive garden or park, an Englishman expects to see a number of groves and glades, intermixed with an agreeable negligence, which seems to be the effect of nature and accident. He looks for shady walks encrusted with gravel; for open lawns covered with verdure as smooth as velvet, but much more lively and agreeable; for ponds, canals, basins, cascades and running streams of water; for clumps of trees, woods and wildernesses, cut into delightful alleys, perfumed with honey-suckle and sweet-briar, and resounding with the mingled melody of all the singing birds of heaven: he looks for plots of flowers in different parts to refresh the sense, and please the fancy; for arbours, grottos, hermitages, temples, and alcoves, to shelter him from the sun, and afford him means of contemplation and repose; and he expects to find the hedges, groves, and walks, and lawns kept with the utmost order and propriety. He who loves the beauties of simple nature, and the charms of neatness, will seek for them in vain amidst the groves of Italy.

Smollett offers a curious mid-century compendium of gardenist ideas. The evidence of art's geometric order coexists for him with scenes in a 'wilder' taste. His anthology of new and old designs, however, is a reminder that in 1766, when he published his *Travels*, the English landscape garden was still having to accommodate itself within older and more traditional designs. Those with either abundant funds or a quick appreciation of fashion may have made a clean sweep of their boundary walls, straight avenues, and octagonal ponds: we may see this 'instant' realization of the idea of an English landscape garden offered in some of Brown's designs or recorded in Wilson's paintings. But more frequently the introduction of the new taste either was achieved piecemeal or was in fact delayed until long after the ideas had established themselves. While Mr. Darcy's park at Pemberley was 'neither formal, nor falsely adorned' in *Pride and Prejudice* (ch. 43), Mr. Rushton in *Mansfield Park* had still to eliminate what was virtually a late seventeenth-century layout at Sotherton.

Just as the implementation of new designs proceeded in fits and starts, so did the development of garden imagery and the history of its influence upon visitors' minds. Generally, the process during the century was from emblematic to expressive forms of imagery. But a garden's use of emblems, a traditional vocabulary for ideas, survived into the new style of gardening; visitors had still to 'read' a various iconography of statue, temple, or inscription among glades and a natural scenery that began to exert a less intellectual, more affective, influence upon their imaginations and feelings. Yet when a garden's spaces came to be less regarded for specifically intellectual messages and emblematic declarations, their effect upon the sensibilities was still appreciated as one which the landscape itself had organized. Gardenist art like Brown's continued or, at least, appeared to continue to influence by design.

Writers played a crucial role in promoting the English landscape garden. Literature's involvement with this new art may have contributed to its literary qualities, the 'readable' structures invoked by the new garden designs. But this involvement also ensured that writers derived fresh energies and strategies from garden art. Experience gained in exploring a garden, as was seen in the case of James Thomson, conditioned habits of visiting scenery outside; much later in the 1820's William Cobbett invokes the ha-ha to explain his experience of the Wiltshire downland. Above all, poetry learnt the delights and possibilities of *moving through* scenery instead of merely recording it as if it were some painted prospect. Whether this movement encountered an emblematic repertory or a more expressive scenery was less relevant at first than that the poet learnt to register the succession of images and the resulting process of his own reactions to them. This response by the senses to a richly varied landscape is conveyed vividly by Gilbert White's "The Naturalist's Summer-Evening Walk":

To hear the drowsy dor come brushing by
With buzzing wing, or the shrill cricket cry;
To see the feeding bat glance through the wood;
To catch the distant falling of the flood;
While o'er the cliff th'awaken'd churn-owl hung
Through the still gloom protracts his chattering song;
While high in air, and pois'd upon his wings,
Unseen, the soft enamour'd woodlark sings:
These, *Nature's* works, the curious mind employ

The mind's employment among that natural scenery became increasingly the poet's concern.

The dangers and uncertainties for the poet in developing this new affective poetry were many. He could be too pictorial: as J. S. Mill wrote in his *Autobiography*,

Wordsworth would never have had any great effect on me, if he had merely placed before me beautiful pictures of natural scenery. Scott does this still better than Wordsworth, and a very second-rate landscape [i.e., landscape painting] does it more effectually than any poet.

The landscape garden, by offering different modes of seeing and thinking from those encouraged by pictures, could certainly divert poetry from too pictorial ambitions. But there still remained to adjudicate between recording the outward world and articulating the inward; as late as the 1820's Keats found that in a poem like Clare's "Solitude" the 'Description too much prevailed over the Sentiment'; contrariwise, Clare considered that Keats's poetry 'often described nature as she appeared to his fancies & not as he would have described her had he witnessed the thing he describes'. This late debate focuses the difficulties that were encountered by much poetry of what may be called the landscape of introspection in the late eighteenth century. The solutions attempted or achieved by the poets were analogous to the movement from emblem to expression in the gardenist and painterly arts.

The visual arts, however, realized these solutions more easily than poetry. This is perhaps evident if Akenside's "Hymn to the Naiads" and Erasmus Darwin's *The Botanical Garden* are compared with paintings by Francis Wheatley and Turner. The poets invoked allegorical machinery to explain phosphorescence and the interaction of sunshine and running water; in Akenside's case, these devices, needed to relate the 'natural' to the 'moral' world, impress us rather by their own energy than by their success as a language of connection between the poet and his landscapes. Moreover, they exclude opportunities for direct observation of scenery by the poet. In Wheatley's *Salmon Leap at Leixlip with Nymphs Bathing* and Turner's watercolour of 1802, *The Fall of the Clyde*, which alludes directly to Akenside's "Hymn" in its subtitle, the naiads also appear prominently; yet their presence does not prevent some affecting attention to the real as opposed to the allegorical images of nature. While by the 1830's, when Turner paints *The Fall of the Clyde* again, this time in oils, the nymphs become a much muted, almost indistinct item in the artist's vision of light and water.

Poetry experimented much with similarly disappearing naiads. Akenside himself writes "To the Honourable Charles Townshend; from the Country" and relates his loss of 'the rural gods':

But ah! in vain my restless feet
Traced every silent shady seat
  Which knew their forms of old:
Nor Naiad by her fountain laid,
Nor Wood-nymph tripping through her glade,
  Did now their rites unfold.

Though Akenside clears the landscape of these figures, it is only to announce his sadness; they will be restored and 'Receive me in their genial train', once his friend joins him in the country. Yet the frequency with which poets record the (even temporary) disappearance of the traditional emblems of animated nature ('the Genii of the woods and streams') suggests that they were concerned to explore landscapes without those conventional images of meaning. The alternative to naiads is a machinery of description, which is not a verbal mimicry of pictorial description, but one whereby the natural scenery becomes animated by, and consequently eloquent of, the perceiving imagination of the poet.

The garden provided an exciting territory in which the poet could discover and practise his poetry of introspection. At first this meant rehearsing the ideas suggested by an apparatus of emblems: Robert Morris's *Lectures on Architecture*, delivered in the 1730's, justify the 'little *Fabricks* erected in the Gardens of some NOBLE *Patron* of Arts' by showing how they promote a 'Chain of Thought' and open 'to the Mind a vast Field to entertain the Tongue or Pen of a Philosopher'. As such emblems gave way to landscape of 'natural' forms, the poet endeavoured to respond without the aid of an answering emblematic vocabulary. This new gardenist experience is discussed in Shenstone's *Unconnected Thoughts on Gardening* of 1764; thirty years later Knight's *The Landscape* was still describing the calculated effects of

nature's common works, by genius dress'd,
With art selected, and with taste express'd;
Where sympathy with terror is combined,
To move, to melt, and elevate the mind.

Such a taste for the sublime lured poets outside the garden, where all was unordered and unselected and certainly devoid of emblems; yet the imagination trained within landscape gardens soon formed and explained its experience of natural scenery in terms first learnt and tested among the landscapes of such places as Stowe, Stourhead, or The Leasowes. It became possible for poets not only to describe the essential forms of a landscape but to involve their readers in the experience of seeing them. Thus in 1783 William Blake's pastoral song welcomes the stranger into a spot where 'the trees do laugh with our merry wit, / And the green hill laughs with the noise of it'.

Notes

These notes contain all the references and documentation as well as the acknowledgment of many debts incurred in the writing of these interdisciplinary essays. But it seemed best not to burden the text with a heavy ballast of footnotes; instead, they are recorded here, linked to the chapters by section and by key phrases. Apart from customary abbreviations, the following will be used for works frequently cited in the notes:

Anderson: *The Works of the British Poets, with Prefaces, Biographical and Critical by Robert Anderson*, 13 vols. (London and Edinburgh, 1792–95).

British Poets: *The British Poets*, 100 vols. (Chiswick: C. Whittingham, 1822).

Hunt and Willis: *The Genius of the Place: The English Landscape Garden, 1620–1820*, ed. and introduced by John Dixon Hunt and Peter Willis (London, 1975). This is an anthology of major texts on the landscape garden and of contemporary illustrations.

Peake: *Poetry of the Landscape and the Night*, ed. Charles Peake (London, 1967).

Preface

Shebbeare: *Letters on the English Nation*, 2nd rev. ed. (London, 1756), 2: 266; also reprinted in Hunt and Willis.

Landscape Gardening Histories: See H. F. Clark, *The English Landscape Garden* (London, 1964); Christopher Hussey, *English Gardens and Landscapes, 1700–1750* (London, 1967); Miles Hadfield, *Gardening in Britain*, rev. ed. (London, 1969). See also the bibliography in Hunt and Willis, pp. 381–82.

Walpole and Horace: Respectively, *Satirical Poems by William Mason with Notes by Horace Walpole*, ed. Paget Toynbee (Oxford, 1926), p. 43, and *Carmina* III: xxi.

Gardenist: Isabel W. U. Chase, *Horace Walpole: Gardenist* (Princeton, N.J., 1943), p. 184.

Wordsworth on gardening: *The Early Letters of William and Dorothy Wordsworth (1787–1805)*, ed. E. de Selincourt (Oxford, 1935), p. 527.

Chapter One

Hermits in Their Landscapes

Hermitages: See Barbara Jones, *Follies and Grottoes*, revised and enlarged ed. (London, 1974) and Osvald Siren, *China and the Gardens of Europe of the Eighteenth Century* (New York, 1950).

Thebaid: See Ellen Callmann, "A Quattrocento Jigsaw Puzzle", *The Burlington Magazine* (May 1957), pp. 149–55.

Parnell: Text of *The Hermit* is in Anderson, 7: 19–20.

Britannia Illustrata: This was first published London, 1708; there were other editions between 1720 and 1729.

Stukeley: See *Itinerarium Curiosum* (London, 1724), pp. 50–52 and plates 13 and 14; see also Stuart Piggott, *William Stukeley: An Eighteenth-Century Antiquarian* (Oxford, 1950).

Johnson: *Prose and Poetry*, selected by Mona Wilson (London, 1950), p. 429. Johnson has another joke against hermits in his "Parody of Thomas Warton", *The Poems*, ed. D. Nichol Smith and E. L. McAdam (Oxford, 1941), p. 181.

Richmond: See B. Sprague Allen, *Tides in English Taste* (Cambridge, Mass., 1937; reprinted, New York, 1969), 2: 135–38.

Druids: See A. L. Owen, *The Famous Druids: A Survey of Three Centuries of English Literature on the Druids* (Oxford, 1962), where the supposed shape of Druid huts may be seen in the frontispiece. See also below, ch. Four.

Stowe Hermitage: Gilbert West, *Stowe: A Poem* (London, 1732), p. 7, also in Hunt and Willis. Kent's illustrations to *The Faerie Queene* appeared in the edition of 1751. On Kent as illustrator see Jeffrey P. Eichholz, "William Kent's Career as Literary Illustrator", *Bulletin of the New York Public Library* 70 (1966): 620–46. Gilpin's remarks are from his *Dialogue upon the Gardens . . . at Stowe* (London, 1748), p. 6, a work which I have edited, with an introduction, for the Augustan Reprint Society, no. 176 (1976).

Ruined classical hermitage: Illustrated in Alistair Rowan, *Garden Buildings* (London, 1968), plate 33.

Aubrey: Quoted Barbara Jones, *Follies and Grottoes*, p. 17.

Cunningham: Anderson 10: 710–11.

Traditions of melancholy, etc.: See A. Bartlett Giamatti, *The Earthly Paradise and the Renaissance Epic* (Princeton, 1966); Maren-Sofie Røstvig, *The Happy Man: Studies in the Metamorphosis of a Classical Ideal*, 2nd ed., 2 vols. (Oslo and New York, 1962, 1971); B. G. Lyons, *Voices of Melancholy* (London, 1971); André Chastel, "Melancholia in the sonnets of Lorenzo de' Medici", *JWCI* 8 (1945): 61–67; R. Klibansky, F. Saxl & E. Panofsky, *Saturn and Melancholy* (London, 1964).

Pye: *Poems*, 2nd ed. (London, 1772), p. 43.

Warton: *British Poets*, 68: 56–65.

Churchyards: The quotation is from an anonymous poem, *Contemplation* (1756), British Library shelf mark 11630 c 6(5). On this topic generally, see Amy Reed, *The Background of Gray's 'Elegy': A Study in the Taste for Melancholy Poetry, 1700–51* (London, 1924; reprinted New York, 1962).

Dyer: Peake, p. 88.

Spit in: Richard Graves, *Euphrosyne* (London, 1776), p. 262.

Hamilton: For this and other hermit stories I am indebted to Edith Sitwell, *English Eccentrics* (Penguin Books, 1971), ch. 2, to which Douglas Chambers originally drew my attention, as well as to Jones, *Follies and Grottoes*.

The Prelude: Lines 19–115 of the first book (1805 text).

The Old Hieroglyphic Landscape

Rochester: *The Complete Poems*, ed. David M. Vieth (New Haven, 1968), p. 97.

Cowley: *Essays and Plays*, ed. A. R. Waller (Cambridge, 1906), p. 394. All further references in this chapter are to this text.

Vaughan: *Poetry and Selected Prose*, ed. L. C. Martin (London, 1963), p. 236. All further references are to this text. On Vaughan's attitudes to nature see his own translation of Antonio de Guevara's *The Praise and Happiness of the Countrie Life* (1651); also F. E. Hutchinson, *Henry Vaughan: A Life and Interpretation* (Oxford, 1947), chs. 2, 7, and 13; James D. Simmonds, *Form and Theme in the Poetry of Henry Vaughan* (Pittsburgh, 1972); the quotations from Vaughan's letter to Aubrey are on p. 147 of Simmonds.

Hawkins: *Parthenia Sacra* was published in Rouen in 1633; the quotation is taken from a modern edition, with an introduction by Iain Fletcher (Aldington, Kent, 1950), p. 11.

New model: John Rea, *Flora*, 3rd ed. (London, 1702), p. 2.

The New Empirical Landscape

New tastes in landscape: For a survey of garden history see, among others, Derek Clifford, *A History of Garden Design*, 2nd ed., (London, 1966), and the list of further reading in Hunt and Willis. For an account of seventeenth-century taste in landscape painting see H. V. S. and M. S. Ogden, *English Taste in Landscape in the Seventeenth Century* (Ann Arbor, Mich., 1955).

Denham: Peake, pp. 24–37. See also Brenden O'Hehir, *Expans'd Hieroglyphicks: A Critical Edition of Sir John Denham's "Cooper's Hill"* (Berkeley and Los Angeles, 1969), and Earl R. Wasserman, *The Subtler Language* (Baltimore, 1959).

Hieroglyphicks: Thomas Browne, *The Works*, ed. Geoffrey Keynes, 4 vols. (new ed., 1964), 1: 25; later quotations (on 'mystical mathematics') are from 4: 226 and (on his garden) 1: 175; on 'Hieroglyphicks', Quarles, quoted O'Hehir, *Expans'd Hieroglyphicks*, p. 19.

Cowley: See Arthur H. Nethercot, *Abraham Cowley* (Oxford, 1931), chs. 14–17 for Cowley's retirement; R. B. Hinman, *Abraham Cowley's World of Order* (Cambridge, Mass., 1960), where the Sprat remark is quoted, p. 268; the quotation from *Plantarum* is from *Works* (1668), pp. 74–75; Stukeley's pilgrimage to Cowley's former garden is cited in Nethercot, p. 253.

Gombrich: *Art and Illusion* (New York, 1960), passim. See also his essay, "The Renaissance Theory of Art and the Rise of Landscape", *Norm and Form* (London, 1966).

Marvell's Gardens

Among the many books to consult here, three are perhaps most relevant: Rosalie L. Colie, *'My Ecchoing Song': Andrew Marvell's Poetry of Criticism* (Princeton, 1970), Donald M. Friedman, *Marvell's Pastoral Art* (London, 1970), and J. B. Leishman, *The Art of Marvell's Poetry* (London, 1966). The text used is that in *The Poems and Letters*, ed. H. M. Margoliouth, 3rd ed., rev. P. Legouis and E. E. Duncan-Jones, 2 vols. (Oxford, 1971).

Legouis: *Andrew Marvell* (Oxford, 1965), p. 45. The Danckerts painting—in the Victoria and Albert Museum—is illustrated in Hunt and Willis.

Montague: Quoted Røstvig, *The Happy Man* 1: 81.

Allen: *Image and Meaning* (Baltimore, 1968), p. 180.

Metamorphosis: See M. C. Bradbrook and M. G. Lloyd Thomas, "Marvell and the Concept of Metamorphosis", *The Criterion*, 18 (1938): 236–54.

Colie: *'My Ecchoing Song'*, p. 184 and, for the following quotation, p. 185. My own emphasis on Marvell's attention to changes in landscape design would be to unite *within the poem* the various and distinct visual traditions invoked by Colie—Dutch landscapists on the one hand (see pp. 192–96) and emblems on the other (pp. 196–201).

Italian gardens: On the iconographical images of Italian gardens see *The Italian Garden*, ed. David R. Coffin (Washington, D.C., 1972), and David R. Coffin, *The Villa D'Este at Tivoli* (Princeton, 1960). Even if Marvell did not reach Italy, he would have perhaps encountered descriptions of gardens there (accounts congenial to his own imaginative habits) in such works as John Raymond, *Il Mercurio Italico* (London, 1648), especially pp. 10–12 (gardens at Genoa), pp. 117–19 (at Frascati), or pp. 167–72 (on the Villa D'Este).

Hortus conclusus: On the relation of this traditional image to Marvell's poetry see Stanley Stewart, *The Enclosed Garden: The Tradition and the Image in Seventeenth-Century Poetry* (Madison, Wis., 1966).

Masque: On masque imagery in Marvell's poem see Louis L. Martz, *The Wit of Love* (Notre Dame, Ind., 1969), pp. 182 et seq. On the relation of gardens to theatrical art little work has yet been done, but see Hunt and Willis, pp. 36–37.

Wallace: *Destiny His Choice* (Cambridge, 1968), p. 233.

Wotton: *Elements of Architecture* (London, 1624), pp. 109–10.

Norgate: Cited Colie, *'My Ecchoing Song'*, p. 194.

Gardens of a New Model

Evelyn: *The Works of Browne*, 4: 275; the reference to the 'land of spectres' is from the dedication of Evelyn's *Acetaria* (1699).

Charles Evelyn: *The Lady's Recreation or the Art of Gardening*, 2nd ed. (London, 1718), pp. 11–12 and 10. Wren's design for the Hampton Court wilderness is illustrated in *The Wren Society*, 4 (1927): plate 2.

Evelyn to Browne: In Browne, *The Works*, 4: 274–75. On Evelyn as a gardenist see W. G. Hiscock, *John Evelyn and His Family Circle* (1955), especially ch. 2. On Sayes Court see also *Directions for the Gardiner at Says-Court*, ed. Geoffrey Keynes (London, 1932). *Plan of a Royal Garden* is reprinted in Hunt and Willis. On Evelyn generally, see Geoffrey Keynes, *John Evelyn: A Study in Bibliophily* (Oxford, 1968).

Mack: *The Garden and the City* (Toronto, 1969), p. 8. It is Mack who quotes Thomas Fuller's adage ('As is the Gardener . . .') on p. 4.

Switzer: *Ichnographia Rustica* (London, 1718), 2: 197.

Rawlet: *Poetick Miscellanies* (London, 1687), pp. 96–99; quoted, Røstvig, 1: 373–74.

French gardens: See *The French Formal Garden*, ed. Elizabeth B. MacDougall and F. Hamilton Hazlehurst (Washington, D.C., 1974).

Lawrence: *The Clergy-Man's Recreation*, Preface, A₃ recto.

Woolridge: Pp. v, 1–2; on Versailles, p. 4.

Aubrey: See Anthony Powell, *John Aubrey and his Friends* (London, 1948) for other sketches of his garden. On Danvers' gardens, see *Aubrey's Natural History of Wiltshire*, ed. John Britton (Newton Abbot, 1969), p. 93.

Royal Society and poetry: See Thomas Sprat, *History of the Royal Society*, 2nd ed. (London, 1702), pp. 111 et seq.

Landships . . . & Such Wilde Workes

London and Wise: See David Green, *Gardener to Queen Anne: Henry Wise (1653–1738) and the Formal Garden* (London, 1956). For more literature on this theme see the first part of Hunt and Willis.

Wotton: Elements of Architecture, pp. 99–100; Rea, Flora, p. 9; Nourse, p. 310. Pearce: These are illustrated in E. Croft-Murray, Decorative Painting in England, 1537–1837 (London, 1962), 1: figs. 79–82.

The Man of Mode: Act III, scene i.

Essay: Quoted by the Ogdens, English Taste in Landscape, p. 122. For Place, see the catalogue, Francis Place 1647–1728, of the exhibition held at York and Kenwood in 1971.

Sculptura: Published 1662; edited C. F. Bell (1906), pp. 100–101.

Blome: (1686), p. 226.

History of Landscape Painting: Ogdens, English Taste in Landscape, p. 163.

Dutch Art: Besides the Ogdens' book, see W. Stechow, Dutch Landscape of the Seventeenth Century (London, 1968) and, for the Dutch artists working in early English landscape painting, M. H. Grant, The Old English Landscape Painters, 3 vols. (London, 1926–47).

Italy: The main items to consult on Claude are Marcel Rothlisberger, Claude Lorrain: The Paintings, 2 vols. (New Haven, 1961) and Claude Lorrain: The Drawings, 2 vols. (Berkeley, 1968); also the catalogue for the London exhibition of 1969, The Art of Claude Lorrain. On Poussin, see Anthony Blunt, Nicholas Poussin, 2 vols. (London, 1967). On Rosa, material is more scattered, but see the catalogue for the Rosa exhibition in London, 1973; two articles by Richard W. Wallace in The Art Bulletin 47 (1965): 471–80 and 50 (1968): 21–32; Helen Langdon, "Salvator Rosa and Claude", The Burlington Magazine 115 (1973): 779–85; and John Sunderland, "The Legend and Influence of Salvator Rosa in England in the Eighteenth Century", ibid., 785–89. On Dughet, see Denys Sutton, "Gaspard Dughet: Some Aspects of His Art", Gazette des Beaux-Arts 60 (1962): 269–312, and Malcolm R. Waddingham, "The Dughet Problem", Paragone 161 (1963): 37–54. A general discussion of this Italian art in England is E. W. Manwaring, Italian Landscape in Eighteenth-Century England (New York, 1925; reprinted 1965).

Vanbrugh: See Hunt and Willis, pp. 13–14 and note 14.

Mason: Book I, ll. 64–71 in the York edition of 1783, with commentary by W. Burgh.

Norgate: The MS version is printed by the Ogdens, English Taste in Landscape, pp. 171–72. The printed version has been edited by Martin Hardie (Oxford, 1919), where the reference is to p. 51.

Burnet: The Sacred Theory appeared first in Latin in 1681 and in an enlarged English version of 1684; further additions in both Latin and English were made between 1689 and 1691. On Burnet see Majorie Hope Nicolson, Mountain Gloom and Mountain Glory (Cornell, 1959), ch. 5. The passage quoted from Burnet is from 4th ed., 2 vols. (1719), 1: 192.

Shaftesbury: Characteristics, ed. John M. Robertson (New York, 1964), 2: 123. This includes his Miscellaneous Reflections.

Alberti: De Re Aedificatoria, trans. G. Leoni, ed. J. Rykwert (1955), 9: iv.

Brooke Boothby: In another portrait by Wright of Derby, as Claire Pace has kindly pointed out to me, the subject is reading from Thomson's The Seasons; see B. Nicolson, Joseph Wright of Derby (London, 1968), plate 67.

Dryden's Virgil: Anderson, 12: 372.

Akenside's Ode: Anderson, 9: 789.

Horace: The quotations here are taken from the Loeb text of Satires, Epistles and Ars Poetica, ed. H. R. Fairclough (London, 1966), pp. 152, 210, 250, and 194 respectively. Poussin's version of the Vejanius lines is the painting illustrated as plate 211 and discussed in a note to p. 292 in Blunt, Poussin.

Dryden's Virgil: Anderson, 12: 372.

Nourse: See pp. 302–3 and 314–22.

Lovejoy: Arthur O. Lovejoy and George Boas, Primitivism and Related Ideas in Antiquity (Baltimore, 1935), pp. 9–11 and passim.

Dryden: Of Dramatic Poesy and Other Critical Essays, ed. George Watson, 2 vols. (London, 1962), 2: 220; The State of Innocence, Act II, scene ii.

Shirley: "The Garden", in Poems (London, 1646).

Cotton: 2nd ed. (London, 1683), pp. 76–77; also in Hunt and Willis.

Shaftesbury: Characteristics, 2: 125, 270.

Tomorrow to Fresh Fields

Montague: Quoted Røstvig, The Happy Man, 1: 233.

Gray: *The Correspondence*, ed. Paget Toynbee and Leonard Whibley, 3 vols. (Oxford, 1935), 1: 215.

Burton: *The Anatomy of Melancholy*, pt. 2, section 2, mem. 4.

Gainsborough: Illustrated as *The Mall* in Ellis Waterhouse, *Gainsborough* (London, 1958), plate 243.

Bolingbroke: "Of the True Use of Retirement and Study", *Letters on the Study and Use of History*, 2 vols. (Dublin, 1752), 2: 85.

Pope: *Poems*, 4: 211; for details of edition cited see headnote to ch. 2.

Chapter Two

An earlier version of this chapter appeared, with the same title, in *The Art Quarterly* 37 (Spring 1974): 1–30. All quotations from Pope's poetry in this chapter are taken from the Twickenham Edition of the poems (general editor, John Butt; London and New Haven, 1939 et seq.) and from his letters, from *The Correspondence of Alexander Pope*, ed. George Sherburn (Oxford, 1956), referred to respectively as *Poems* and *Correspondence*.

Scenes for Contemplation

Bolingbroke: *Study and Use of History*, 2: 83.

Pope's painting: See W. K. Wimsatt, *The Portraits of Alexander Pope* (New Haven and London, 1965), Appendix 3, item 2, where this oil painting is discussed; see also *Poems*, 3/i: xc.

Atterbury: *Correspondence*, 1: 454, my italics.

Another Correspondent: Ibid., 2:302; perhaps a reference here to his own translations of Homer.

My garden: Ibid., 4: 40.

Grotto: Ibid., 4: 279,262.

Artful Wildness to Perplex

Auden: From "In Praise of Limestone", *Nones* (London, 1952), p. 11.

Mack: *The Garden and the City*, p. 60.

Grotto's Workings: *Correspondence*, 4: 228.

Tickell: *Kensington Garden* (1722), in Anderson, 8: 434, my italics. Design for gravel-pit is reproduced in Hunt and Willis.

Liberty: See Rudolf Wittkower, *Palladio and English Palladianism* (London, 1974), ch. 12; for Thomson, see Anderson, 9: 267.

Pope: *An Essay on Criticism*, *Poems*, 1: 323, l. 715.

Locke: *The Conduct of the Understanding*, in *The Philosophical Works*, ed. J. A. St. John, 2 vols. (London, 1916), 1: 109.

Roger de Coverly: *Spectator* 110.

Imagination: These papers on "The Pleasures of the Imagination" constitute *Spectator* 411–21.

Moving pictures: See *Spectator* 414 in the edition by D. F. Bond, 5 vols. (Oxford, 1965), 3: 550n.

Landscape-painting: Joseph Spence, *Observations, Anecdotes and Characters of Books and Men*, ed. James M. Osborn, 2 vols. (Oxford, 1966), 1: 252.

Addison: On continental gardens see *Spectator* 414. On Italian examples of this mixture of garden and park see Elisabeth MacDougall, "*Ars Hortulorum*: Sixteenth Century Garden Iconography and Literary Theory in Italy", in *The Italian Garden*, ed. Coffin pp. 42–44.

Pindarick Gardener: *Spectator* 477.

Literary talents: *Spectator* 160.

My Structures Rise, My Gardens Grow

Structures rise: The title of this section is taken from Pope's *Poems*, 6: 225.

Windsor Forest: On similarities between this poem's view of landscape and Pope's later ideas on landscape design see Spence, *Observations*, 1: 251.

Kneller: See W. K. Wimsatt, *The Portraits of Alexander Pope* (New Haven, 1965).

Whately: *Observations on Modern Gardening* 5th ed. (London, 1793), pp. 154–55. See above pp. 189–90.

Evelyn: *Elysium Britannicum*, ms. 45 in Christ Church Library, Oxford; quoted by Hiscock, *John Evelyn*, p. 25.

Walpole: *Horace Walpole's Correspondence*, Yale edition, ed. W. S. Lewis et al. (New Haven, 1937 et seq.), 10: 314 (Walpole writing to Montagu in July 1770).

Dodsley: In *The Works in Verse and Prose of William Shenstone*, 2 vols. (London, 1764), 2: 381.

Vision: *Correspondence*, 2: 202.

To Digby: Ibid, 2: 115.

To Caryll: Ibid., 1: 163.

Horace: See G. K. Hunter, "The 'Romanticism' of Pope's Horace", in *Essential Articles for the Study of Alexander Pope*, ed. Maynard Mack (Hamden, Conn., 1968).

Mirror of Retreat: *Poems*, 4: 317.

Independence: Quotations from Pope in this paragraph are, respectively, from *Poems*, 4: 96, 173, 211, and 259.

Philosopher-King: See Mack, *The Garden and the City*, pp. 70–71.

Addison ms: See *The Spectator*, ed. Bond, 3: 550n.

Chief point of friendship: This and the succeeding quotations in the paragraph come, respectively, from *Correspondence*, 1: 74, 2: 44, 4: 260; Bolingbroke to Pope is in *The Works* (London, 1754), 3: 318.

Multiplied Scenes

Garden and grotto: Besides Mack, see Frederick Bracher, "Pope's Grotto: The Maze of Fancy", *The Huntington Library Quarterly* 12 (1949): 114–62, and A. Lynn Altenbernd, "On Pope's Horticultural Romanticisms", *JEGP* 54 (1954): 470–77.

Space: On the spaces of architecture, and so of landscape architecture, I have found much to interest me in Geoffrey Scott, *The Architecture of Humanism*, 2nd ed. (London, 1924).

Ha-ha: Chase, *Horace Walpole*, p. 25.

I am busy: *Correspondence*, 2: 328.

Camera Obscura: Ibid., 2: 296.

1748 visitor: The important account of Pope's garden and grotto by this visitor is reprinted from the *Newcastle General Magazine*, where it first appeared, in both Mack, *The Garden and the City*, and in Hunt and Willis. Cf Spence, *Observations*, 1: 254 (item 613).

Contrasts: Spence, *Observations*, 1: 254.

To Spence: Ibid., 1: 253.

Whimsical: Such a judgement is cited by H. F. Clark, in "Lord Burlington's Bijou, or Sharawaggi at Chiswick", *The Architectural Review* (May 1944), p. 127.

Lady Mary: *Correspondence*, 2: 82.

Walpole: Chase, *Horace Walpole*, pp. 28–29.

Atterbury: *Correspondence*, 2: 85.

Johnson: *The Works of the English Poets*, ed. A. Chalmers, 21 vols. (London, 1810), 12: 74.

Spence: *Observations*, 1: 257; this is discussed by Mack, *The Garden and the City*, pp. 37–40.

Serle: *Plan of Mr. Pope's Garden* (London, 1745).

Whately: *Observations on Modern Gardening*, 5th ed. (London, 1793), pp. 63–64.

Camera Obscura: *Correspondence*, 2: 296.

Switzer: This distinction is to be found in *Ichnographia Rustica*, 3 vols. (London, 1718), 3: 36 and *Nobleman's Recreation* (London, 1715), pp. xiii, xxviii.

Walpole: In Chase, *Horace Walpole*, p. 25.

To Bathurst: *Correspondence*, 2: 14.

Sherbourne: Ibid., 2: 236–40.

Cleland to Gay: In Pope's *Correspondence*, 3: 255.

Ornaments: Ibid., 4: 13. The following reference to Dr. Clarke is from *Epistle to Burlington*, 1. 78. There was nothing unusual in commemorating Clarke—his was a standard bust for libraries as well as hermitages, produced by the commercial sculptor, John Cheere—but Pope is indulging a personal dislike of the theologian, probably learnt from Bolingbroke, who disapproved of Clarke's insistence that the moral attributes of God could be known (cf. *An Essay on Man*).

Statuary at Stowe: See George Clarke, "Grecian Taste and Gothic Virtue", *Apollo* 97 (June 1973): 566–71.

Public and Private Virtues

God's own work: *Correspondence*, 2: 264.

Modern editor: F. W. Bateson in *Poems*, 3/ii, pp. xxiv and note.

Opus Magnum: *Correspondence*, 3: 401, 81.

Cobham's Dismissal: *The Gentleman's Magazine* notes among the promotions for June 1733 that of Henry E. of Pembroke, appointed to the Command of his

Majesty's own Royal Regiment of Horse in the Room of Ld Cobham who was removed' (p. 328). For this and the succeeding references I am greatly indebted to George Clarke of Stowe, as for his generosity in sharing his researches on Cobham and Cobham's gardens.

Montaigne: See *Poems*, 3/ii, pp. 16n, 27n.

La Bruyere: Cited *Poems*, 3/ii, p. 50n. Pope must have been particularly alert to these difficulties, being himself so frequently and so variously painted: see Wimsatt, *The Portraits of Alexander Pope*. For some discussion of this problem in portraiture and for some relevant contemporary comments, notably by Roger de Piles, see Gombrich's essay in E. H. Gombrich, Julian Hochberg, and Max Black, *Art, Perception and Reality* (Baltimore, 1972).

Inchoate structure: Bateson's judgement is that "*To Burlington* turned out to be something of a hotch-potch, one third philosophy, one third gardening, and one third architectural compliment"; *Poems*, 3/ii, p. xxvi.

Permanence of arts: On the Muse, *Poems*, 1: 166, and on Jervas, ibid., 6: 157.

'Better gardiner': *Correspondence*, 4: 6.

Stowe: Ibid., 3: 217.

Burlington: See Fiske Kimball, "Romantic Classicism in Architecture", *Gazette des Beaux-Arts* 25 (1944): 95–112; Wittkower, *Palladio and Palladianism*, passim; *Apollo of the Arts: Lord Burlington and His Circle*, a catalogue for the exhibition at the Nottingham University Art Gallery in 1973; also Clark, "Lord Burlington's Bijou'.

To Bathurst: *Correspondence*, 4: 25; see ibid., 170 and 178 for Pope's acquisition of urns to terminate points in his garden.

Wittkower: *Palladio and Palladianism*, p. 131.

Walpole: Cited by Mack, *The Garden and the City*, p. 13. Mack also stresses the georgic element in much contemporary thinking, pp. 19–20.

Ornithon: See the illustrations of this building in Castell, facing p. 70.

Professors of Gardening

Professors of gardening: Letter to the Earl of Stratford, *Correspondence*, 2: 309.

Hacks: Ibid. 2: 522.

To Swift: Ibid., 4: 5.

Old Montaigne: Poems, 4: 9.

Gardening more antique: *Correspondence*, 2: 264.

First man: Ibid., 4: 31.

To Bathurst: Ibid., 2: 13, where may also be found the note on Yocktan, from which I quote.

To Swift: Ibid., 3: 151.

Grotto: Respectively Ibid., 4: 228, 229 (but see also 4: 246, 261), and 4: 397.

Plato: Ibid., 4: 262.

Nature and State of Man: From Argument of *An Essay on Man* 2; my italics.

Building and planting: *Correspondence*, 2: 23.

To Bathurst: See Earl R. Wasserman, *Pope's Epistle to Bathurst: A Critical Reading* (Baltimore, 1960).

Chapter Three

All quotations from Thomson, unless otherwise stated, are taken from *The Seasons and The Castle of Indolence*, ed. James Sambrook (Oxford, 1972). I have also consulted *Thomson's Seasons, Critical Edition*, ed. Otto Zippel (Berlin, 1908); *The Castle of Indolence and Other Poems*, ed. A. D. McKillop (Lawrence, Kansas, 1961), and *James Thomson (1700–1748): Letters and Documents*, ed. A. D. McKillop (Lawrence, Kansas, 1958). Four works on Thomson are especially useful: A. D. McKillop, *The Background of Thomson's 'Seasons'* (Minneapolis, 1942); P. M. Spacks, *The Varied God: A Critical Study of Thomson's The Seasons* (Berkeley and Los Angeles, 1959); Ralph Cohen, *The Art of Discrimination: Thomson's The Seasons and the Language of Criticism* (London, 1964) and *The Unfolding of The Seasons* (London, 1970).

The Varied God and Man's Continual Changes

Kent's illustrations: See J. D. Masheck, "The First Plates for Thomson's *Seasons*", master's Thesis, Columbia University, 1966.

Constable: C. R. Leslie, *Memoirs of the Life of John Constable* (London, 1951), p. 328.

Iconography: See especially Mario Praz, *Studies in Seventeenth Century Imagery* (London, 1939); Jean Seznec, *The Survival of the Pagan Gods* (New York, 1953), and Erwin Panofsky, *Studies in Iconology* (Oxford, 1939).

Reni: See *The Seasons*, ed. Sambrook, p. 219, and Jean H. Hagstrum, *The Sister Arts: The Tradition of Literary Pictorialism and English Poetry from Dryden to Gray* (Chicago, 1958), p. 260.

Roman villa decoration: See Isa Belli Barsali, *Le Ville di Roma (Lazio I)* (Milan, 1970).

Johnson: *The Works of the English Poets* (London, 1810), 12: 406.

Lovers: On the way in which a lover's ideas colour his observation of landscape, see the later poem by George Crabbe, "The Lover's Journey", in *Tales* (1812).

Johnson: *Works of the English Poets*, 12: 411.

The Finished Garden

Rousham: See Peter Willis, *Charles Bridgeman and the English Landscape Garden* (in press) and Kenneth Woodbridge, "William Kent's Gardening: The Rousham Letters", *Apollo* 100 (October 1974): 282–91.

Pope and Bolingbroke: See above, pp. 64, 78.

Grammar of . . . structures: The phrase is from John Barrell, *The Idea of Landscape and the Sense of Place (1730–1840)* (Cambridge, 1972), p. 7; Barrell also offers an interesting discussion of this same passage, pp. 12–27. For the Kitson quotation, see Barrell, p. 10.

Heely: His *Letters* were published in two volumes, London, 1777; the section on Hagley is in 1: 119 ff. The title for this chapter is taken from 1: 222. An illustration of the landscape at Hagley is in Hunt and Willis.

Pope and variety: See Spence, *Observations*, 1: 151.

Canvas landscape: Heely does not always observe his own distinction—see, for example, pp. 68, 120.

Thomson's visit to Leasowes: In Hunt and Willis, as is an illustration of Shenstone's landscape.

Thy Villas Shine

Petersham: On this very early landscape garden see the letter by Samuel Molyneux in Hunt and Willis.

Elysian Fields: For an analysis of this section of the gardens at Stowe, see my essay "Emblem and Expressionism in the Eighteenth-Century Landscape Garden", *Eighteenth-Century Studies* 4 (1971): 296–304.

Temple of Friendship: Sambrook in his note on this line suggests (*The Seasons*, p. 232), I think wrongly, that this must be the Temple of Ancient Virtue; admittedly Thomson's own note, quoted by Sambrook, is misleading.

The Mind's Creative Eye

Ut pictura poesis: On this topic see Rensselaer W. Lee, *Ut Pictura Poesis: The Humanistic Theory of Painting* (New York, 1967), and Hagstrum, *The Sister Arts*.

Memory: On this element in Wordsworth's poetry, see Christopher Salvesen, *The Landscape of Memory* (London, 1965).

Pope: *Poems*, VIII: 261 note. Cf. E. R. Wasserman's remark that 'the eighteenth-century poet is forever interrupting his scene-painting to find its moral or emotional analogue', "The English Romantics: The Grounds of Knowledge", *Studies in Romanticism* 4 (1964): 20.

Narcissus: See on this theme Louis Vinge, *The Narcissus Theme in Western European Literature up to the Early 19th Century* (Lund, 1967).

Genius loci: For a brilliant exploration of this theme, see Geoffrey H. Hartman, *Beyond Formalism: Literary Essays 1958–70* (New Haven, 1970), pp. 311–36, to which I am much indebted.

The More Enduring Song

Shaftesbury: *Characteristics*, 2: 270–71n.

Cohen: *The Unfolding of "The Seasons"*, p. 17, and see index under 'Spatial Movement'.

Shaftesbury: *Characteristics*, 2: 125.

Hartman: *Beyond Formalism*, p. 126.

Chapter Four

All quotations from Gray and Collins are, unless otherwise stated, taken from *The Poems of Thomas Gray, William Collins and Oliver Goldsmith*, ed. Roger Lonsdale (Longmans' Annotated English Poets, 1969), to which I am also indebted for commentary on the poems. Quotations from Gray's letters are taken from *The Correspondence of Thomas Gray*, ed. Paget Toynbee and Leonard Whibley, 3 vols.

(Oxford, 1935). For further information and discussion of picturesque travel, see Christopher Hussey, *The Picturesque* (London, 1928), E. W. Manwaring, *Italian Landscape in Eighteenth-Century England* (New York, 1925), and Esher Moir, *The Discovery of Britain: The English Tourists, 1540–1840* (London, 1964), especially chs. 10 and 11. On 'graveyard literature' see especially Amy Reed, *The Background of Gray's Elegy: A Study in the Taste for Melancholy Poetry, 1700–51* (New York, 1924), and E. M. Sickels, *The Gloomy Egoist: Moods and Themes of Melancholy from Gray to Keats* (New York, 1932).

Wild and British

Warton: *An Essay on the Genius and Writings of Pope*, 2 vols. (London, 1782), 2: 411.

Walpole to Bentley: *Horace Walpole's Correspondence*, Yale Edition, 35: 251–52. On illustrations to Gray's ode see F. I. McCarthy, "The Bard of Thomas Gray: Its Composition and Its Use by Painters", *The National Library of Wales Journal* 14 (1965): 105–12 and figs. 4–11.

Jones: "Memoirs," *Journal of the Walpole Society*, 32 (1951): iv–v and (on Stonehenge) p. 21.

Parry: See Gray's *Correspondence*, 2: 501–2. A portrait of Parry is reproduced in John Steegman, *A Survey of Portraits in Welsh Houses*: 1: N. Wales (Cardiff, 1957).

British Ode and Sandby: *Correspondence*, 2: 475, 705, 706.

Wordsworth: *Poetical Works*, ed. E. de Selincourt and H. Darbishire, (Oxford, 1967) pp. 270–83.

Furnishing the Mind's Apartments

Reynolds: *Discourses on Art*, ed. S. O. Mitchell (New York, 1965), pp. 208–23.

Berkeley: *A New Theory of Vision* (Everyman's Library, 1963), pp. 30–31.

Woburn and Esher: Walpole's remarks on these gardens are quoted in notes to Gray's *Correspondence*, 1: 404, notes 8, 9. On Langley's gardening see Hunt and Willis.

Wordsworth: *Guide to the Lakes*, ed. Ernest de Selincourt (Oxford, 1970), p. 1.

Gray and Macpherson: For Gray's attitudes towards *Ossian* see his *Correspondence*, vol. 3, appendix L.

The Gentler Genius of the Plain

"The Fatal Sisters": Blake's illustrations to this poem aptly demonstrate his own conviction that 'mental deities' could not be abstracted from their objects (see *Marriage of Heaven and Hell*) and he accordingly makes the sisters and their weather virtually indistinguishable. See Irene Tayler, *Blake's Illustrations to the Poems of Gray* (Princeton, 1971).

Progress of poetry: *Poems*, pp. 171 and 161–62. On this theme in eighteenth-century poetics ('making the history of poetry itself their central myth') see Lawrence Lipking, *The Ordering of the Arts in Eighteenth-Century England* (Princeton, 1970).

Hartman: *Beyond Formalism*, p. 316.

Alternative habits of the imagination: Arthur Johnston argues in a recent essay, "Thomas Gray: Our Daring Bard", of which he was kind enough to show me a copy, that Gray's concept of the poet 'grows' between 1752 and 1761.

Descriptive and Allegoric

Grainger: Quoted by Lonsdale, *Poems*, p. 367.

Collins and painting: See J. Hagstrum, *The Sister Arts*, and Kenneth Clark, *Landscape into Art* (Boston, Mass., 1961), p. 70, for the comparison of Collins and Wilson that is quoted later. Collins's apostrophe to Rosa and Claude is fairly routine, but his invocation of Ruisdael is more interesting, for Ruisdael, together with Meindert Hobbema, van Goyen, and others, begins to make his appearance in English sale rooms at the time Collins is writing. More generally on Collins, see two essays by A. S. P. Woodhouse, "The Poetry of Collins Reconsidered", *From Sensibility to Romanticism*, ed. F. W. Hilles and H. Bloom (New York, 1965), pp. 93–137, and "Collins and the Creative Imagination", *Studies in English by Members of University College, Toronto* (Toronto, 1931), pp. 59–130.

Wild nature: I continue to be indebted in these discussions of the genius loci to Hartman's essay on the subject in *Beyond Formalism*.

Shenstone: *Letters*, ed. Marjorie Williams (Oxford, 1939), p. 552.

Rymer: Quoted Lonsdale, *Poems*, p. 368.

Syntactical ambiguities of "Ode to Evening": The various debates are summarised by Lonsdale, *Poems*, p. 465n.

The Idiom of the Soil

Burke: All references are to *A Philosophical Enquiry into Our Ideas of the Sublime and Beautiful*, ed. J. T. Boulton (Notre Dame, Ind., 1968), hereafter referred to as Burke/Boulton. For larger discussions of the sublime see Nicolson, *Mountain Gloom and Mountain Glory*, and Samuel H. Monk, *The Sublime* (Ann Arbor, 1960).

Ossian: Burke/Boulton, pp. cxiii, xxvi.

Verbal description: Ibid., pp. 175–76.

Warton: *Essay . . . on Pope*, 2: 165.

Expression: Burke/Boulton, p. 175.

Blair: Quoted ibid., p. lxxxviii. On Blair and Beattie see Boulton's introduction, pp. lxxxvi et seq.

Beattie: All quotations are taken from the Aldine edition of *The Poetical Works* and—unless otherwise stated—from the first book of *The Minstrel*.

Social and private: Burke/Boulton, p. 43.

Sublime obscurity: Ibid., p. 59.

MacPherson: The text used here, which includes, as well as the 'translations', Macpherson's and Blair's essays, is that of *The Poems of Ossian*, 3 vols. (London, 1812).

Warton on Macpherson: A ms. quoted by Joan Pittock, *The Ascendancy of Taste: The Achievement of Joseph and Thomas Warton* (London, 1973), p. 206, and his *History of English Poetry*, also quoted ibid., p. 199.

Percy: Beattie cites Percy's collections in a note to l. 519.

Unawares: *The Poetical Works of Wordsworth* (London, 1964), p. 415, from the fragment, "There was a Boy . . . ."

Druids: On their connections with bards see A. L. Owen, *The Famous Druids* (Oxford, 1962) and Macpherson, *Ossian*, p. 17. Blair defines the relationship as 'The Druids were their philosophers and priests; the Bards, their poets and recorders of heroic actions' (*Ossian*, p. 105).

Triumph of melancholy: *The Poetical Works*, p. 138.

Teneriff: *The Poetical Works of Thomas Warton*, 2 vols. (Oxford, 1802), 1: 68. Or in *British Poets*, 68: 56.

Coleridge: From "To the Author of Poems (Joseph Cottle)", *The Poems* (World's Classics, London, 1951), p. 76.

Keats: "Ode on Melancholy", *The Poems*, ed. Miriam Allott (London, 1970), p. 541.

Night Thoughts

Blackening the landscape: Warton, *Poetical Works*, 1: 80.

Stowe engravings: See Peter Willis, "Jacques Rigaud's Drawings of Stowe in the Metropolitan Museum of Art", *Eighteenth-Century Studies* 6 (1972/3): 85–98.

Wasserman: *The Subtler Language*, p. 169.

Parnell: Text in Peake, pp. 81–85.

Akenside: *The Pleasures of Imagination* (1744 version) 3: 284–86.

Pope and Young: The lines of Pope are from *The Dunciad*, in *Poems*, 5: 339–40, 409, those of Young from *Night Thoughts*, ed. G. Gilfillan (Edinburgh, 1853), 9: 20–21, 1: 92–98, 9: 2414–17. On Pope's visionary moments see above, pp. 73–75.

Illustrious objects: Warton, *Poetical Works*, 1: 89.

Haply: Ibid., 1: 84.

The moon: Cunningham, "The Contemplatist", in Anderson, 10: 710.

Solemn glooms: T. Warton, in *British Poets*, 68: 57.

Johnson: *Prose and Poetry*, selected Mona Wilson (London, 1950), p. 820; from Johnson's *Life of John Denham*.

Naming: See T. Warton in *British Poets*, 68: 58.

Akenside: Anderson, 9: 784.

Wordsworth: *The Recluse*, pt. I, bk. I, ll. 567–79.

Pencil's mimic skill: Cunningham, in Peake, p. 138. For a survey of poetry's use of 'idealized' landscapes see Jeffry B. Spencer, *Heroic Nature: Ideal Landscape in English Poetry from Marvell to Thomson* (Evanston, Ill., 1973).

Blake on eidetic imagery: See Morton D. Paley, *Energy and Imagination: A Study of the Development of Blake's Thought* (Oxford, 1970), pp. 201 et seq.

Warton: In *British Poets*, 68: 90, 91–92. Cf. Langhorne's specific invocation of Armida's vanishing garden in *The Visions of Fancy*, Anderson, 11: 223.

Blair: In Anderson, 8: 857.

Darkness has more Divinity: Young, *Night Thoughts*, 5: 128 et seq. 'half create . . .' from ibid., 6: 425 et seq. Cf. Wordsworth's "Tintern Abbey", ll. 106–8, and the poet's note.

George Eliot: Quoted Henry Pettit, "The English Rejection of Young's *Night Thoughts*," *University of Colorado Studies in Language and Literature* 6 (1957): 37.

Conjectures: (London, 1759), pp. 55, 37.

Walpole: Quoted Pittock, *Ascendancy of Taste*, pp. 67–68.

Can Stow Such Raptures Raise?

The Italian: Ed. Frederick Garber (Oxford, 1971). p. 412.

Warton: *British Poets*, 68: 256.

Walpole: *Horace Walpole's Correspondence*, Yale ed., 30: 257.

Druids' temple: For further information about such 'gothick' items in garden ornament see Jones, *Follies and Grottoes* and the forthcoming study on *Sanderson Miller of Radway* by Anthony C. Wood and William Hawkes. There are some interesting passages on the contribution of archaeological research to the Gothic Revival in Kenneth Clark, *The Gothic Revival* (London, 1928) and in the third part of Kenneth Woodbridge, *Landscape and Antiquity: Aspects of English Culture at Stourhead 1718 to 1838* (Oxford, 1970).

Gilpin: His account of St Augustine's Cave, the Temple of Sleep, and the Witch House are in his *Dialogue*, pp. 17–19; other quotations are from p. 58 and (third edition) pp. 2–3.

Brown: Some of the best commentary on Brown's garden designs is in Clifford, *Garden Design*.

Reynolds: *Discourses*, p. 203.

Chambers: *Dissertation on Oriental Gardening* (London, 1772), p. v. It was perhaps those who had grown bored with the garden that could best appreciate this aspect of Brown's work: see Gray's assessment of Chatsworth in *Correspondence*, 2: 785–86.

Rise and progress: (Leeds, 1767), pp. 10, 29.

Whately: *Observations*, pp. 154–55.

Warton: *Observations on the Fairy Queen of Spenser*, 2nd ed., 2 vols. (London, 1762), 1: 15–16; Pittock, *Ascendancy of Taste*, p. 95, writes of how Spenser and Milton offered Warton 'structures or fictions through which the evocation of different and highly personal feelings might affect the reader to an intimate emotional response'.

Gothic machinery: T. Richards, *An Essay on the Characteristic Differences Between Ancient and Modern Poetry* (London, 1789), p. 23.

Associationism: Both the theory and practice of this psychology became less rigid as the century advanced: compare, for example, Gilbert West's vision of the 'emblematic pile' (like Stowe's Temple of British Worthies) in his *Education: a poem* (in Anderson, 9: 493) with Boswell's reactions to *The Beggar's Opera* (in *Life of Johnson* [London, 1953], p. 874): West's mind is 'purged' of all unworthiness before the building and his education precisely advanced by an attentive reading of it; by contrast, Boswell only records how the musical airs 'never fail to render me gay, because they are associated with the warm sensations and high spirits of London'—a far vaguer impulse.

The Leasowes: On Walpole's comment that they mirrored Shenstone's mind see Hunt and Willis, p. 30.

Hogarth: *The Analysis of Beauty*, ed. Joseph Burke (Oxford, 1955), p. 42.

West: Thomas West, *A Guide to the Lakes* (London, 1778), pp. 193, 100.

Gray on Shenstone: *Correspondence*, 2: 566.

Chambers: *Dissertation*, pp. 35–41. He invented much of this version of Chinese gardening; see Burke/Boulton, p. 104, n. 99.

Knight: 2nd ed. (London, 1795), p. 51; later quotations are from pp. 38–39, 40. For other attacks on Chambers' Chinese exoticism, see Hunt and Willis.

Wordsworth: *The Prelude* (1805), 8: 120–70.

Strong imagination: *Designs of Chinese Buildings, etc.* (London, 1757), p. 19.

Repton on Downton: In *The Landscape Gardening of Humphry Repton*, ed. J. C. Loudon (London, 1840; reprinted 1969), pp. 102–3.

Price: *Essays on the Picturesque*, 3 vols. (London, 1794), 1: 337.

Frye: "Towards Defining an Age of Sensibility," *ELH* 23 (1956): 144–52.
Paideumatic: My coinage, with apologies to Ezra Pound's *Guide to Kulchur* (London, 1938): 'the tangle or complex of the inrooted ideas of any period . . . The Paideuma is not the Zeitgeist. . . . At any rate for my own use. . . . I shall use Paideuma for the gristly roots of ideas that are in action' (pp. 57–58).

Ibbetson: On its label see *Landscape in Britain c. 1750–1850*, catalogue of the exhibition at the Tate Gallery in 1973, p. 68. To this catalogue I am much indebted in the following discussions, as to Luke Herrmann, *British Landscape Painting of the Eighteenth Century* (London, 1973).

Repton on Movement: See *The Landscape Gardening*, pp. 81, 96, 105n; also the Blaise Castle Red Book, reprinted by Hunt and Willis, where the spectator's movement through a landscape is insisted upon.

Walpole: Chase, *Horace Walpole*, p. 37.

Gilpin: *Dialogue*, pp. 11–12.

Whately: *Observations*, pp. 154–55.

Smart: *Jubilate Agno*, ed. W. H. Bond (London, 1954), p. 98.

Landscape Business

Cowper: *The Task*, 1, ll. 422–30; the text used throughout this chapter is that of *The Poetical Works of William Cowper*, ed. H. S. Milford, 4th ed. (London, 1959).

Jones: "Memoirs", *Journal of the Walpole Society* 32: 19–20.

Fantasy: A term which covers, of course, a wide range of pictures—André Félibien, for instance, in his life of Poussin in *Entretiens Sur les vies et sur les ouvrages des plus excellens Peintres anciens et modernes*, 5 vols. (Paris, 1666–88), talks of the *Landscape with a Man Killed by a Snake*, in which we observe 'different degrees of fear and surprise', as a 'piece of fantasy'.

Farington on Wilson: Quoted Herrmann, *British Landscape Painting*, p. 53.

Emotional Alembic: *Landscape in Britain*, p. 25.

Towne: His remark is quoted in ibid., p. 57; he did in fact exhibit watercolours in 1805.

Richardsons: Jonathan Richardson, father and son, *An Account of the . . . Pictures in Italy, France, etc.* (London, 1722), pp. 186–87.

Dolbadern Castle: The verses for this picture are in *The Sunset Ship: The Poems of J. M. W. Turner*, with a commentary by Jack Lindsay (London, 1966), p. 77. For other discussions of these manoeuvres to capture poetry, see John Gage, *Colour in Turner: Poetry and Truth* (London, 1969); J. R. Watson, *Turner and the Romantic Poets*", *Encounters: Essays on Literature and the Visual Arts*, ed. J. D. Hunt (London, 1971), pp. 96–123; Adele M. Holcomb, "The Bridge in the Middle Distance: Symbolic Elements in Romantic Landscape", *The Art Quarterly* 37 (1974): 31–58.

Girtin: See "Girtin's Sketching Club", *Connoisseur* 63 (1922): 190.

Roger de Piles: *The Principles of Painting* (London, 1743), p. 140.

Wright of Derby: For my discussion of this painter I am indebted to Nicolson, *Joseph Wright*; subsequent references are to 1: 75, 77, 91.

Comus: Wright's painting is discussed more fully in my essay on "Milton's Illustrators", *John Milton, Introductions*, ed. John Broadbent (Cambridge, 1973), 208–24. The remark about 'grace' is from Philip Brockbank, "The Measure of *Comus*", *Essays and Studies* 22 (1968): 54.

Walpole on Edwin: Quoted Nicolson, *Joseph Wright*, 1: 63.

Darwin: *The Botanical Garden*, quoted ibid., 1: 131–32.

Hayley: *Poems and Plays*, 6 vols. (London, 1788), 1: 37 *inter alia*.

Gisborne: *Walks in a Forest*, 7th ed. (London, 1808), p. 44.

Runciman: See *Ossian*, the catalogue of an exhibition held at the Grand Palais, Paris, in 1974, and Henry Okun, "Ossian in Painting", *JWCI* 30 (1967): 327–56.

Wheatley: See Mary Webster, *Francis Wheatley* (London, 1970).

Rousseau and Stowe: See Peter Willis, "Rousseau, Stowe and *Le jardin anglais*: Speculations on Visual Sources for La Nouvelle Héloïse", *Studies on Voltaire and the Eighteenth Century* 90 (1972): 1791–98.

Crabbe: *Tales, 1812 and Other Selected Poems*, ed. Howard L. Mills (Cambridge, 1967), p. 2; my italics.

Gainsborough: *The Letters of Thomas Gainsborough*, ed. Mary Woodall (Greenwich, Conn., 1963), p. 99; all quotations, unless otherwise stated, are from this edition, hereafter cited as *Letters*.

Constable: *The Correspondence*, ed. R. B. Beckett, 6 vols. (London, 1962 et seq.), 3: 116.

Gray, Goldsmith, and Gainsborough: See John Hayes, *The Drawings of Thomas Gainsborough*, 2 vols. (London, 1970), text volume, pp. 16, 19. On the Country Churchyard picture see John Hayes, "Gainsborough's Later Landscapes", *Apollo* 80 (1964): 21–22, and *Landscape in Britain*, item 61.

Dislike of Literature: *Letters*, pp. 11, 125.

To Hardwicke: Ibid., p. 91.

Paulson: "Gainsborough's Landscape Drawings", *Eighteenth-Century Studies* 6 (1972): 106–17; to this and to the author's larger analysis of Gainsborough in *Emblem and Expression: Meaning in English Art of the Eighteenth Century* (London, 1975) I am much indebted in this discussion.

Jackson: *The Four Ages* (London, 1798), p. 167.

Great subjects: *Letters*, p. 43.

Boys fighting: Ibid., p. 43.

RA resignation: Ibid., p. 29; for Garrick portrait, ibid., p. 77.

Reynolds: *Discourses*, p. 220 and, for next quotation, p. 219.

Leech gatherer: *Poetical Works*, ed. E. de Selincourt and H. Darbishire (Oxford, 1940 et seq.) 2: 237.

Inclination for landskip: *Letters*, pp. 35, 167.

Common substance: Paulson, "Gainsborough's Landscape Drawings", p. 113.

Loutherbourg: See the catalogue for the Loutherbourg exhibition held at Kenwood in 1973; also Francis D. Klingender, *Art and the Industrial Revolution* (Paladin paperback, London, 1972), pp. 85–90, and Michael Clarke, "Gainsborough and Loutherbourg at York", *Preview* (City of York Art Gallery Quarterly) 104 (October 1973).

Darwin on "The Nightmare": See *Romantic Art in Britain: Paintings and Drawings 1760–1860*, catalogue for the exhibition in Detroit and Philadelphia in 1968 (Philadelphia, 1968), p. 124.

Gainsborough at Night: Described in the Farington ms. Diary, cited Hayes, *The Drawings*, text volume, p. 16. For the Williams quotation see the *John Marin Memorial Exhibition* catalogue (Los Angeles, 1955).

Loose handling: *The Four Ages*, p. 157.

Half a tree: *Letters*, p. 101.

On Shakespeare: Ibid., p. 67.

Ne plus ultra: Quoted William D. Templeman, *The Life and Works of William Gilpin (1724–1804)*, Illinois Studies In Language and Literature, 24, 3–4 (Urbana, Ill., 1939), p. 228. More recently on Gilpin, see Carl Paul Barbier, *William Gilpin: His Drawings, Teaching and Theory of the Picturesque* (Oxford, 1963). Gilpin's remarks on 'solemnity' were in fact made about Rosa's *Democritus*, then at Foots Cray Place, Kent (See *Southern Tour* [London, 1804], pp. 122–23).

Place-making

Hannah More: Quoted Dorothy Stroud, *Capability Brown*, revised ed. (London, 1957) p. 198.

Warton on Brown: Quoted Hussey, *The Picturesque*, p. 138.

Place-making: See Stroud, *Brown*, p. 217.

Thames: Thames: Cited Hussey, in introduction to ibid., p. 18.

Cowper: *The Task*, 3: 765–68, 773–76.

Whitehead: In "The Late Improvements", *Annual Register* for 1787.

Walpole on 'real prospects': *Horace Walpole's Correspondence*, Yale ed., 10: 314.

Seeley: These guides were issued from 1744 onwards.

Clerk of Penicuik: Text in Hunt and Willis.

Moral instruction: See, for example, Jonathan Richardson, *An Essay on the Theory of Painting* (London, 1725), p. 11; see David Watkin, *Thomas Hope and the Neo-Classical Idea* (London, 1968), pp. 148–51, for a full discussion and diagram of Aaron Hill's garden.

Blake: *Complete Writings*, ed. Geoffrey Keynes (Oxford, 1971), p. 802.

Shenstone: For *Unconnected Thoughts* see Hunt and Willis; the stanza on inscriptions is from Joseph Giles, *Miscellaneous Poems* (London, 1771), p. 4.

Call from a monument: From another perceptive essay, "Wordsworth, Inscriptions, and Romantic Nature Poetry", by Geoffrey H. Hartman, *Beyond Formalism*, p. 211.

Blair: *The Poems of Ossian*, 1: 87.

Wright: Nicolson, *Joseph Wright*, 1: 152.

Repton: See *The Landscape Gardening*, p. 120; on Langley, p. 262, and against statues and other emblems, p. 259. Further references to Repton's writing will be to this volume, indicated thus: L 259. For a fuller discussion of these aspects of Repton's gardens see my "Sense and Sensibility in the Landscape Designs of Humphry Repton", to be published.

Pope: "Essay on Homer's Battles", preface to *Iliad*, vol. 2 (London, 1716).

Blaise Castle: Quotation from 'Red Book', reprinted in Hunt and Willis.

Hogarth & Hume: Both cited by Ronald Paulson, "The Pictorial Circuit and Related Structures in 18th-Century England", *The Varied Pattern: Studies in the 18th Century*, ed. Peter Hughes and David Williams (Toronto, 1971), pp. 179, 181.

Burke: Quoted Hussey, introduction to Stroud, *Brown*, p. 16.

Banditti: A similar scepticism is expressed about the seat of Sir Rowland Hill by Dr Johnson in his *Journal* for 25 July, 1774, in *The Works* (Yale, 1958), 1: 174-75.

Terraces: Brown, in fact, retained at least one terrace at Chilham.

Chambers & Mason: Derek Clifford makes this point about Chambers in *Garden Design*, pp. 162-63; for the passage on Mason's flower garden see Hunt and Willis.

Prospects for Poetry

Addison: *Spectator* 412.

Spontaneously: From Young's preface to *Night Thoughts*.

Scott: Quoted Anderson, 11: 725. Coleridge similarly objected to poetry that mimicked the details of Dutch pictures, see *Shakespearean Criticism*, ed. T. M. Raysor (London, 1960), 2: 134.

Stowe: Samuel Boyse, "The Triumphs of Nature", *Gentleman's Magazine* 11 (1742): 436.

Non iniussa cano: Part of the motto to *Windsor Forest*, taken from Virgil's sixth eclogue; see Pope's *Poems*, 1: 145.

Spence: *Observations*, 1: 251, item 605. For Pope quotations see *Poems*, 1: 148-49, 3/ii: 143.

Denham: Peake, p. 24 and note for Waller allusion.

Dyer: Text in Peake, as is that of "A Country Walk", discussed later.

Lyttelton: Anderson, 10: 251 and (for "Blenheim") 10: 253.

Garden poems: Those referred to in the following discussion are Edward Stephens, "On Lord Bathurst's Park and Wood", *Miscellaneous Poems* (London, 1747), pp. 51-56; Joseph Giles, "The Leasowes", *Miscellaneous Poems* (London, 1771), pp. 1-13; anon., "Richmond-Gardens: a poem", *London Magazine* 7 (1738): 38-39, 91-92, 147-48; Stephen Duck, "On Richmond Park, and Royal Gardens", *Poems on Several Occasions* (London, 1738), pp. 51-61. For other examples of garden poems (themselves a sub-genre of prospect poems) see R. A. Aubin, *Topographical Poetry in xviii-Century England* (New York, 1936).

Wordsworth: *Poetical Works*, ed. de Selincourt and Darbishire, 2: 25.

Piles: See above, p. 265.

Knowledge and power: Martin Price, "The Picturesque Moment", *From Sensibility to Romanticism*, p. 271. Price's ingenious and perceptive argument that picturesque taste was a revision and extension of earlier habits of wit does not perhaps sufficiently take account of the *private energies and motivation* of this later poetry.

Akenside: Both versions of his poem are to be found in Anderson, 9: 733-73.

Prestige of the bardic: Bishop Percy discusses this prestige and its historical manifestations in his "Essay on the Ancient Minstrels in England", prefixed to his *Reliques*.

Prospect poems: A comprehensive list of these may be found in Aubin, *Topographical Poetry*; see also R. D. Havens, *The Influence of Milton on English Poetry* (New York, 1922), especially ch. 12, and M. A. Goldberg, "The Language of Art and Reality: A Study of 18th-Century Hill Poems", *Boston University Studies in English* 3 (1959): 65-76. The poems that are discussed in the following pages are: Akenside, "On Recovering from a Fit of Sickness", *Odes*, 2: 12, in Anderson, 9; Scott's *Amwell*, in British Poets, 70; Jago's *Edge-Hill; or the Rural Prospect Delineated and Moralized* (London, 1767); Thomas Warton's

"The First of April", in Peake; Bowles's sonnets in *Poetical Works*, 2 vols. (Edinburgh, 1855); poems by Coleridge, *The Poems* (World's Classics, London 1951); those by Wordsworth, *Poetical Works*, ed. de Selincourt and Darbishire, vols. 2 and 3.

Wasserman: "Nature Moralized", *ELH* 20 (1953): 71. For the second quotation about 'scene-painting' see Wasserman, "The English Romantics," p. 20.

Whitehead: So paraphrased by D. Wesling, *Wordsworth and the Adequacy of Landscape* (London, 1970), p. 9.

Boswell: *Life of Johnson*, p. 333. Johnson's refutation of Berkeley has the merit of economy over Jago's; he struck 'his foot with mighty force against a large stone, till he rebounded from it'.

Coleridge and Bowles: Coleridge's *Collected Letters*, ed. E. L. Griggs (Oxford, 1956 et seq.), 1: 139 and 2: 864. On Coleridge's landscape poetry there is a short but admirably perceptive analysis in R. Watters, *Coleridge* (London, 1971), pp. 22–60; see also J. R. Watson, *Picturesque Landscape and English Romantic Poetry* (London, 1970), especially ch. 6.

Removal of Village: This aspect of Goldsmith's poem has been elucidated by Mavis Batey, "Nuneham Courtenay: An Oxfordshire 18th-Century Deserted Village", *Oxoniensia* 33 (1968): 108–24. Yet it is awkward to *confine* Goldsmith's poem to this motif, which is touched upon specifically at lines 275 ff.; Goldsmith enlarges the scope of the poem, as I have shown, from its original inspiration.

Aesthetic effects: This aspect of Cowper is discussed in P. M. Spacks, *The Poetry of Vision* (Cambridge, Mass., 1967), pp. 1–12.

Cowper's recent critic: Vincent Newey, "Cowper and the Description of Nature", *Essays on Criticism* 23 (1973): 102–8.

Thought and reality: This perception is Coleridge's in *Anima Poetae*, ed. E. H. Coleridge (London, 1895), p. 143; the text is slightly altered in *The Notebooks*, ed. K. Coburn (London, 1962), vol. 2, item 2557.

Postscript Smollett: *Travels through France and Italy*, letter 31 (World's Classics edition, 1907), pp. 261–62.

Cobbett: *Rural Rides* (Penguin Books, 1967), p. 304.

Emblem and expression: See Ronald Paulson, *Emblem and Expression: Meaning in English Art of the Eighteenth Century* (London, 1975).

White: For this text, as for those quoted later by Akenside and Blake, see *The Penguin Book of English Pastoral Verse*, ed. John Barrell and John Bull (London, 1974), pp. 372, 357, 450, respectively. A 'dor' in the Gilbert White passage means a 'dung-beetle' that flies by night.

Mill: *Autobiography* (New York, 1960), p. 104.

Keats and Clare: Cited John Barrell, *The Idea of Landscape and the Sense of Place* (Cambridge, 1972), pp. 129, 146.

Naiads: The text of Akenside's "Hymn" is in Anderson, 9: 797–99. For a discussion of the various paintings and their relationship to the literary texts see the catalogues of *Landscape in Britain*, entry for item 218, and of the 1975 *Turner* exhibition at the Royal Academy, entries for items 482 and 621.

Morris: For Morris and Shenstone see Hunt and Willis.

Knight: *The Landscape* 2nd ed. (London, 1795), pp. 38–39 (bk 2, ll. 160–63).

265 NOTES TO PAGES 235–49

Index

The John Hopkins University Press

This book was composed in PTS Andover text and display type by Jones Composition
Company from a design by Susan Bishop. It was printed on 60-lb. Old Style Wove
paper and bound in Roxite linen cloth by The Maple Press Company.

Library of Congress Cataloging in Publication Data

Hunt, John Dixon.
    The figure in the landscape.
    Includes index.
    1. English poetry–18th century–History and criticism.
    2. Aesthetics, Modern–18th century. 3. Gardens, English.
I. Title.
PR555.A34H8   821'.6'09   76-17227
ISBN 0-8018-1795-1